From Irv Yalom, MD:

This is quite a wonderful and original book. The stories are compelling and the writer's observations on the stories are wise and compassionate. Congratulations on this superb work.

From Dean Delis, PhD:

Our Emotional Footprint is a rare treasure that reminds us of the often nightmarish traumas of everyday life and the inspirational triumphs that "common" people have achieved over the harsh hands that have been dealt to them. Some childhood traumas – neglect, abuse, belittlement, parental substance abuse, poverty, injury and death to loved ones – occur so commonly behind closed doors that we grow numb to the painful toll they take on the individual. Dr. Levine, one of the most gifted and respected psychiatrists and psychotherapists in the country, has written a masterful book that invites us to appreciate and praise the silent heroism that everyday people show in refusing to let their lives be defined by their past traumas. The book resonates with deep compassion and rare wisdom, and leaves us feeling proud of the triumphs that we have all achieved over our own inescapable setbacks and tragedies. In writing this book, Dr. Levine also teaches us to open our hearts and minds to the strangers sitting down the aisle from us, to learn of their hidden hardships and horrors, and to celebrate with them in the heroism of everyday life.

From E. Fuller Torrey, MD:

Our Emotional Footprint reflects the author's lifetime of psychiatric experience in a variety of settings. Although we tend to be obsessed with the private lives of the rich and famous, Dr. Levine demonstrates that the private lives of all of us are equally as interesting. In analyzing the lives of ten individuals, Dr. Levine helps us to analyze our own 'life tapestry' and to assess the 'emotional footprint' that will be our heritage. The book is well written and leaves the reader with important questions to ponder. Strongly recommended.

Saul Levine has written and published five
previous books for the general public:

Radical Departures: Desperate Detours to Growing Up, Harcourt Brace
Jovanovich

*Dear Doctor: Sensitive, Sensible Answers to Teenagers' Most Troubling
Questions* with Kathy Wilcox, MD. Lothrop, Lee and Shepard Books

Tell Me It's Only a Phase! A Guide for Parents of Teenagers, Prentice Hall

Phoenix From the Ashes: Rebuilding Shattered Lives, Key Porter Books

Against Terrible Odds: Lessons in Resilience From Our Children, with
Heather Wood Ion. Bull Publishing Company

OUR
EMOTIONAL
FOOTPRINT

OUR EMOTIONAL FOOTPRINT

ORDINARY PEOPLE and THEIR EXTRA-ORDINARY LIVES

Saul Levine, MD

OUR EMOTIONAL FOOTPRINT
ORDINARY PEOPLE AND THEIR EXTRA-ORDINARY LIVES

The life histories depicted in this book are fictionalized amalgams of many individuals, and are not meant to be representations of any specific persons, alive or dead

iUniverse books may be ordered through booksellers or by contacting:

iUniverse
1663 Liberty Drive
Bloomington, IN 47403
www.iuniverse.com
1-800-Authors (1-800-288-4677)

ISBN: 978-1-4917-4608-0 (sc)
ISBN: 978-1-4917-4609-7 (e)

Library of Congress Control Number: 2014920638

Print information available on the last page.

iUniverse rev. date: 4/29/2015

To My:

Beloved wife, Ann, and darling daughter, HannaMei;
Dear sons, Jaime, Mischa, and Zachary, and their wonderful families;
Dad Mike, avatar of a positive emotional footprint;
Mom Bess, fighter for social justice.

Contents

Author's Note

Our *Emotional Footprint* is about all of us, our journeys and inevitable intense experiences—and how we handle them, how we evaluate our progress, and how we affect each other. We share common joys and challenges over the course of our lives, but we are all "originals," individuals with our own hopes, successes, and disappointments. Our paths may differ, but we are all on important odysseys, quests to find love, achievements, and meaning in our lives.

In the course of our lifelong journeys, we inevitably affect other people, our families, friends, colleagues, to be sure, but also people in our neighborhood shops and streets, and over time we leave impressions on others, for better or for worse.

In a climate of increasing incivility in the media, politics, on the internet, and in everyday discourse, we are bombarded by tones and messages of disrespect and aggression. Just as we are correctly being urged to pay attention to our carbon footprint, it is equally important to consider Our Emotional Footprint while we are on the planet, and as our legacies when we depart.

My subtitle, *"Ordinary People and Their Extra-Ordinary Lives,"* is in part inspired by composer Aaron Copland's, "Fanfare for the Common Man," the stirring music he dedicated to ordinary citizens during World War II. Copland's music evokes the colorful rhythms and souls of ordinary people who he felt deserve profound respect and honor, and should be celebrated for their unassuming uniqueness.

A major inspiration for this book was my late father, who was born in a *shtetl* (like the mythical *Anatevka* in *Fiddler On The Roof*) in Lithuania. He lived with his parents and nine brothers and sisters in a one-room clapboard-walled house with a grass-thatched roof, an earthen floor, and a single potbellied stove for heat. (I am in awe that I live in such relative comfort.) He suffered through bitter poverty, persecution, and pogroms, and Nazis and other Jew haters killed many of his family members.

My dad came to the New World as a teenager; he spoke no English and had little education and no money. He worked at menial jobs, learned some manual trades, fell in love, and married my mother, with whom he raised three children. Over the course of his long adult life (he died at age ninety-one), he had his share of heartening experiences, and he endured setbacks, including illnesses, losses, an autistic child, business failure, and romantic convolutions, to name a few.

My father could easily have been an embittered man, but instead, he was appreciative and kind, interested in others, and generative. He affected the people around him with his warmth, compassion, and gratitude. This unassuming "ordinary man" led an *Extra*-ordinary life, and he left his family, friends, and community with a wonderful legacy, or Emotional Footprint—memories of him as a loving human being whose life positively touched those around him.

You know (or are) individuals like my father—people whose lives are complex and difficult at times and fulfilling and rewarding at others, yet who grace the world with their warm presence.

Nevertheless, many people are more fascinated by following the lives of others, especially celebrities, fawning over their style, fretting at their stumbles, marveling at their luxuries, and criticizing their foibles. Instead of appreciating and drawing meaning from their own lives, they look to reality television or to celebrities' lifestyles as sources of envy or emulation. The truth is that the lives of these "others"—the stars, celebrities, those fallen from pedestals—are not nearly as fascinating as they seem, nor are their lives as interesting, dramatic or fulfilling as those we all lead.

Our own lives are rich tapestries colored by stories of love and loss, elation and sadness. They are full of joy and sorrow, serenity and conflict. We've been happy and known despair; we've been generous and acted selfishly; we've been courageous yet tasted fear; and we've had successes and failures.

What counts most, however, is how we have dealt with our remarkable journeys through life, how we handled successes, came back from setbacks, and how we treated others. When we appreciate the fullness of our personal journeys and the positive impact we've had on others, our lives are profoundly enhanced.

We are unique, not ordinary, but we do have in common life's unpredictability and changes. We are the actors in our own unique dramas. Twists and turns are not exceptions in our paths; they are the rule. We all experience, exult, and endure over the course of our lives.

This book celebrates ordinary people, the women and men who are a great majority, but who are anything but ordinary, in the sense of mundane. We are in fact *Extra*-ordinary, remarkably unique, and all our lives are full of intense dramas and complex relationships, frequent changes and unexpected events.

I've also borrowed from Alfred Hitchcock whose classic movie thriller *Strangers on a Train* prompted my use of a similar literary construction in this book: Picture ten disparate strangers in a single passenger train car, traveling alone yet together, each with a dramatic story to tell. You happen to be in that railcar as well, and you observe each of them and wonder about these people and what their lives are all about.

As the train rattles on, their stories unfold, and you realize that your own life story could easily be included here. These individual stories offer a glimpse at life's unique pathways and complexities and how we deal with our hopes and expectations.

You will see that ordinary people do in fact lead *Extra*-ordinary lives.

Acknowledgments

I based this book, with gratitude, on the lives of people I've had the pleasure of knowing throughout my lifetime, including family, friends, classmates, colleagues, students, patients, readers, listeners, and others.

I am profoundly grateful for the privilege and honor of being allowed into the private lives of so many people who taught me about the remarkable fullness and complexity of each person's odyssey through life and the human condition. This is especially so for the many individuals on whom I loosely based this book's ten train passengers. Their stories represent the yin and yang of all our lives, filled with resilience and frailties, benevolence and selfishness, successes and failures, and loves and losses.

I extend a special appreciation to Jean Femia for her creativity, encouragement, and her friendship and that of her husband Joe during the infancy of this book, and deep gratitude to the late John DeMarco, passionate artist and friend, whose evocative painting *Crossroads* serves as the cover of this book.

I deeply appreciate my treasured stays at the Leighton Artists' Colony at the Banff Centre, which enabled me to write in an idyllic setting. I am grateful to the various editors and others at iUniverse who guided and helped bring this book to fruition.

To those dear friends who generously read excerpts and provided invaluable critical feedback or helped in other ways, I can only reiterate how much they mean to me. These include Johanna Jones, Aviva Layton, Natasha Josefowitz, Marie-Francoise Schulz-Aellen, Zac Rattner, Kathy Kim, Ken Sherman, Angie Angerstein, David Deitch, Keith Oatley, Morty Schiff, Sandy J. Brown, Haim Goldberg, David Lippman, Berl Schiff, Cambria DeMarco, James Jensen, Mili Smythe,

Zachary and Catherine, Mischa and Marcia, Jaime and Karin, and of course, Ann Garland and HannaMei Levine.

Ann and HannaMei have created a home environment that is warm, loving, and supportive, and somehow manage to keep me in line. These wonderful women are a testament to the best essences of humanity, including kindness, respect, tenderness, intelligence, and love.

Prologue

Life is never static. It's all about dynamic action: change, exploration, growth, and wonderment as we emerge from our childhoods into the realm of adulthood and make our way through the years and decades that comprise our lives. Through it all remains the constancy of change, the inevitable thrust of forces that move us about, in part due to our own choices and in part due to events we cannot control.

We all experience dramatic or unexpected events over the course of our lives, and the array of emotions that accompany them. Sudden or dramatic changes can spur us to make choices and create new paths that can enhance our lives. But they can also make us feel uncomfortable, even fearful. The negative ramifications that can arise from our resistance to change, as we shall see, can lead to negative views of our relationships and ourselves and even to destructive behaviors.

Years ago, I interviewed hundreds of older adolescents and young adults in widely diverse settings as part of studies I engaged in as a professional in the field of psychiatry. I found that when these people evaluated their lives and the choices they'd made, they most often brought up four recurrent themes. When I later interviewed many retired people who were looking back at their much longer journeys, they emphasized those same four areas. Their perception of the worth of their lives was not about how important or powerful they were or about the material possessions they'd accumulated. Instead, their focus was on issues that were far more meaningful to them. These interviews percolated in my mind for many years as I practiced and taught psychiatry in Canada and the United States over a fascinating and fulfilling career. Finally, my thoughts and realizations crystallized, and the result is the book you are reading now.

The four universal core concerns central to adults of all ages when they are assessing the quality of their lives can be broken down into what I call the four Bs:

1. **Being:** Whether they have been decent, caring, and estimable people
2. **Belonging:** Whether they were close to and cared for others and felt appreciated and liked in return
3. **Believing:** Whether they had meaningful values and ethical principles that governed their behavior
4. **Benevolence:** Whether they enhanced the lives of their families, friends, and communities

In addition to these four themes representing the foundation of this book, we will also explore the concepts of resilience, of being able to accept the inevitable challenges in life that we all face, and the emotional footprint, the intangible legacy we leave behind us. If we lead our lives in a caring and benevolent way, we'll create a positive emotional footprint. On the other hand, if we lead our lives in a disrespectful, selfish, or cruel manner, we'll leave a legacy of negativism. Either emotional footprint can impact our loved ones, friends, and community for years into the future.

Let's take a look in more detail at the *Four B's, Resilience, and Our Emotional Footprint*, as we shall soon use these *key themes* to examine each of the lives of our passengers, as well as our own life journeys.

Being

People with a sense of being have inner peace and self-acceptance. They feel proud of how they have usually behaved and what they've accomplished. They emanate a positive energy because they feel grounded, more at ease, and comfortable in their skin.

They are aware of their faults and limitations and have tried to improve themselves. They are not beset by guilt and self-recriminations. They don't have to prove their worth to themselves or others; they've shed vestiges of arrogance and are humbler and wiser. They are freer to be their own person, to pursue personal goals to the beat of their own drummer. They've finally achieved identity resolution, the answers to questions like "Who am I?" and "Where am I going?" There are more tolerant of themselves and others.

They have a realistic image of themselves and can look in a mirror (real or metaphorical) and appreciate the person staring back at them, in spite of imperfections. They made mistakes and might have behaved poorly at times, but they have redeemed themselves, hopefully.

Most of us eventually achieve a sense of being and come to appreciate our strengths and compensate for our frailties.

Belonging

A sense of belonging is an appreciation of being an integral member of one or more groups or communities important to us, where we share values and traditions with others who provide comfort, support, appreciation, and respect.

The groups can be large or small and can be in a variety of situations—for example, a family, clan, choir, club, company, union, church, team, sect, gang, troupe, party, or platoon. The relationships in the group reflect friendship or collegiality with bonds of closeness that are mutual, cherished, and secure.

Human beings are a social species who need connection with others. Sharing a joyful or sad occasion is a precious experience that validates us and fulfills our need to be cared for and to care for others. This need is as profound and compelling as the need for food and water.

Close friends are among the most meaningful and important relationships in our lives. They provide nurturance and stimulation, solace when necessary, and toughness when indicated. They enrich us psychologically, energize us, and enliven us. Those without close human bonds can feel as if they're living in a wasteland. Some people thrive with multitudes of friends, whereas others prefer just a select few or even one. It is not the number of friends that is critical—it is the quality of the feeling of connection.

True belonging is reciprocal. We yearn for and bask in meaningful, close relationships. Supporting and loving others is uplifting when we receive the same sentiments from others.

We experience the glow of belonging at our deepest visceral levels; it enhances our emotional and physical health and our quality of life.

Believing

A sense of believing is about having values and ethical principles guiding our lives. Many people wonder at times about meaning in their lives; they feel that there must be more to life than materialism and the proverbial rat race. We all sometimes feel over our heads in demands from family, career, work, bills, health, and other pressures. At those times, people often ask, "Is this what my life is all about?"

Millions of people venerate some kind of God, which gives them comfort and hope and provides answers to existential questions, such as where we come from, and a set of ethical rules for our conduct. Religious beliefs can be comforting and can serve as a moral compass for behaviors, but as many atheists will tell you, fervent belief in a God has precipitated and fueled terrible carnage as well—paradoxically and tragically, in the name of that very God!

Religious followers are no more humane, compassionate, and honest than agnostics and atheists. You don't need to believe in a traditional God to display faith, hope, and charity. Many find their beliefs elsewhere—within themselves, another community or ideology, or other deities or spiritual paths.

Some find their beliefs through science or nature. The recent startling photos from the Hubble telescope and other exploratory cameras have presented us with photos that inspire wonderment and awe. Our universe is vast beyond comprehension and might be only a tiny speck among millions of other universes, or a multiverse. We are infinitesimally tiny in the grand scheme of things, yet we are as large as life itself.

It is clear that humans have a need to believe, but this need goes beyond the worship of an all-powerful deity. Our beliefs enable us to pursue systems of values and principles guiding ethical behaviors and to contemplate explanations about our origins and place in the cosmos, with the possibility of other dimensions beyond our material existence.

Beliefs inspire traditions and rituals, which stay with us for life. A measure of our beliefs is that we wish to pass them on to our children. If we live by guiding values and principles that stand for civility (equal rights, tolerance, honesty, responsibility, trust), whether these are dictated by a God, an ideology, or from within, we and society will benefit.

When we search for meaning in our lives, we wonder about issues beyond materialism. We can remove ourselves from the frenzy and fray of everyday life and transport ourselves to a more spiritual realm. This can occur in the context of religious beliefs and practices, but people with secular values can have strong attachments to spiritual states of being.

Believing in core values and principles that guide our ethical behavior and finding meaning to our lives beyond the material in the wonderment of our existence (e.g., beauty in nature, the experience of love, and the awesome universe) enhance our lives.

Benevolence

A sense of benevolence refers to the positive effects we've had on others and how generous we have been. When we think of our personal legacies to our family and our community, we often concentrate on largesse (i.e., the "stuff" we will leave for others) and tend to forget about the importance of our acts of caring and kindness. The positive effects we have on people in our day-to-day lives, and those recalled and cherished when we are gone, are Our Emotional Footprints.

In spite of our history of aggression and violence, humans are actually predisposed to be helpful to others whom they perceive to be in need. (We observe such behavior in toddlers as young as eighteen months of age). We have also learned that benevolent motives such as tolerance and generosity, can be successfully inculcated in people. These attributes are as much a natural part of our genetic makeup as are our tendencies to be selfish and aggressive.

One's legacy is obviously an important issue for the elderly, but it's also a gauge for younger people, who see their contributions to others as a major reason for pursuing alternative routes. Idealism has always been a hallmark of youth, whether in revolutions throughout history or in social and educational programs dedicated to help others.

The United States has an enviable history of gift giving by foundations and wealthy individuals, but the fact is, hardworking middle-class citizens (our so-called common men and women) give more of a percentage of their wealth.

Many of us give of our time and talents as well. Volunteerism is now permeating all age groups, including people in their eighties and beyond. More people are joining volunteer programs because of their heightened awareness of deprivation in the world, and they want to make a difference.

Benevolence has to do with generosity of spirit—supporting, helping, and inspiring others. When we evaluate our lives, we think about whether we have enhanced the lives of our family, friends, and communities. The good we bestow on others is the essence of benevolence, but it also bestows on the giver an enhanced appreciation of one's worthiness.

All four Bs are necessary to give us a genuine appreciation of the quality of our lives. They interact and strengthen each other, and the absence of one part of the tetrad weakens the entire edifice.

Benevolence is the sum of our personal report card, and it is always in the context of having achieved the other three Bs as well. This is the ultimate measure of our worth as individuals: Our Emotional Footprint.

Resilience

Life is tough sometimes, and it's easy to feel down in those periods when life throws you a curveball and to fall into negative thinking and behavior. But you've come back from disappointments and despair before, and you've learned important lessons. I know this because all of us have experienced serious crises and losses in our lives, and we've managed to recover our health, equilibrium, and vitality.

We all have the capability to be resilient—to rebound from adversity and come back stronger after misfortune and setbacks. There is a natural process of recovery in the human body: *Homeostasis*, discovered by Claude Bernard, which refers to the tendency of human cells that are disturbed to return to a state of stable balance. This predisposition applies to setbacks and dire moods as well: people can and do recover, even after trauma and calamities.

Children who have suffered egregious early experiences find it harder to regain their sense of stability, and such experiences contribute to physical and emotional problems later in life. Studies have shown that many adults who suffer from chronic physical disorders (such as heart disease, diabetes, or obesity), substance abuse, or emotional disorders experienced traumatic events (ACE, or adverse childhood experiences) when they were children.

Child abuse is an inherently terrible experience both at the time of its perpetration and often for years thereafter. But let us not forget that for many victims, the permanent scarring predicted by many is not an inevitability. But by labeling children as "survivors," we lead to exprectations of inevitability, like a self-fulfilling prophecy.

When we study children prospectively, that is, follow their lives forward, we learn that many abused children manage to overcome their earlier calamitous experiences and go on to have fulfilling and generative lives. This is not said in any way to condone these abominable acts, but it is rather to point out the remarkable resilient capacity of human beings.

We all want healthy, safe, and nurturant environments for our children, adolescents, and families. However, children raised in difficult circumstances, sometimes called "orchid children," will bloom if they receive corrective "greenhouse care." The hurt individual begins to blossom; strength and confidence return; and he or she learns to cope with stress, feels new hope, and begins to plan for the future.

You will see in the stories below that resilience is a part of our inherent nature as human beings. If you are in despair and wonder what meaning there is in life, you can take solace in the fact that you are not alone, and especially that you will see better times ahead. Resilience, like homeostasis, is part of our protoplasm, an integral part of who we are.

Our Emotional Footprint

In its simplest form, our emotional footprint is based on our relationships and our impact on others. It can be either positive or negative, though in practice, it's usually somewhere in between. Nothing in life is pure black or white; everything is always a mixture of shades. How humans treat each other psychologically and socially and how we affect each other determines whether we will leave a positive or a negative emotional footprint.

We create a positive emotional footprint via the warm, respectful, tolerant, and caring vibes we give off to others, be they family, friends, colleagues, or everyday people we meet in the community.

We create a negative emotional footprint when we direct rudeness and aggression at one another. There has been a palpable increase in private and public displays of unpleasantness and anger, which negatively affects our individual moods and pollutes our ambient social atmosphere.

Many people are discourteous in their day-to-day relationships at home and in the community. Some feel entitled to be pushy and antagonistic, expressing opinions loudly and aggressively. Our airwaves, screens, Internet sites, and blogs are filled with angry rants, and the substance and tone of political discourse are often nasty.

Our children observe personal attacks in the private and public spheres, and they learn to emulate these behaviors.

Having different opinions is as natural a human activity as breathing, and in a democracy, society should cherish differing views. However, when people express their views using invective and derision, we enter into a dangerous social climate that can lead to aggression, hate, and violence.

Social Internet sites widely transmit verbal assaults, which have resulted in suffering and even suicide. Constantly spewed hostility affects us all, agitating personal moods, and can push deranged or malevolent individuals over an extremist edge, which we have all witnessed.

Rudeness is contagious. Pervasive nastiness and incivility do real damage to our psychological and social atmosphere and can be as dangerous and toxic as chemical and biological pollutants. A negative emotional footprint is a sad legacy to leave our children.

A positive emotional footprint is the greatest gift we can bestow on our loved ones and the world. Respect, tolerance, and generosity of spirit exemplify a positive emotional footprint. Positive sentiments are also contagious, enhancing the giver and the recipients.

We are a social species, with a strong need for affiliation with others. Bishop Desmond Tutu said the Bantu concept *ubuntu,* "the essence of being human," emphasizes that we are members of many different communities but especially of one common social network: the community of humanity.

Achieving a Positive Emotional Footprint indicates that we have succeeded in conveying and spreading to others "vibes" of respect, caring, civility and empathy. In cultures that espouse and value respect and cooperation and use them as models of behavior, the predominant moods are positive and generative, and antagonistic and aggressive behaviors diminish.

The Power of Stories: Strangers on a Train

Now that we have our key themes, we can use these as signposts in how we choose to lead our lives. But how do these concepts come into play in our day-to-day lives? What does it mean when we feel a sense of belonging or loneliness, when we feel a sense of being or confusion, or when we believe in something or feel lost?

The answers lie in one of the most common forms of communication known to humanity: Our life stories. Stories have captivated us for thousands of years; they teach us about our selves and our traditions; they entertain us, make us laugh or cry, and teach us important lessons.

With this in mind, I invite you to board our imaginary train on its way to a city somewhere in the United States in the middle of a weekday morning. The throngs of commuters have already arrived at work, so the train car is not crowded. Only ten other passengers accompany you. As you sit and pass the time until your next stop, imagine that you're unemployed and heading to a job interview. You've experienced trouble in your life, economic and emotional, and you're in a vulnerable frame of mind. You're anxious about your future. You question your place in the world.

In that context, the train becomes a metaphor for life itself and our universal struggle to find our place and our direction. As you read the stories of the ten other passengers, you'll imagine your own story and its complexity. As in real life, you'll know each person has a story. You'll wonder how the four Bs factor into the story of each person you see on the train. As you do, you'll find yourself lost in reveries, and those reveries illustrate the concepts we've been discussing here.

At the end of each story, we'll see how the Four B's apply to the lives of the characters, and we'll look at their Emotional Footprints and Resilience. As you read the stories, I'll offer occasional commentaries touching on key points from my personal and professional perspective. The passengers' stories are composites of many individuals I've known in a variety of contexts, and I hope they will immerse you in their lives, with me along as a "tour guide" of minds and emotions.

So all aboard—the train is about to depart!

1

Patricia Arbitson

The Observer

The bright sun shines through the dirty window next to you. The warmth of the rays comfort, though they are weak in intensity on this cold winter day. Outside the train is the typical industrial gray of factories, warehouses, and loading docks with tractor trailers backed up to load or offload cargo. The city is still far off, easily another hour, yet you see its sprawl everywhere you look. Stifling a yawn, you lean back in the seat with its worn, cheap upholstery, and you try not to think about the job interview you've got in a couple of hours. You need this job—really need it. The wolf is at the door, and you're not sure what you'll do if yet another interview doesn't pan out into a steady paycheck and some health care benefits.

To get your mind off your own troubles, you look around at the few people in the train car. You start counting passengers and find there are just ten. Several hours earlier in the morning would have seen the car packed, every seat taken, and all or most passengers engaged with their smartphones, iPods, or tablets. A few of the older riders would have had newspapers, but the readers of print are a dying breed, and you know it. Yes, the train would have been full of lucky people with jobs. You hope to join them soon.

Up the aisle to the right is an overweight lady in her early fifties staring out the window. She's alone. When you saw her board, you noticed she was wearing a diamond-studded crucifix, was nicely dressed, and carried a briefcase. As you survey her now, you see that she's rather plain looking, yet you sense something impressive about her. She gives off an air of dignity and self-confidence you instinctively admire. You close your eyes, wondering about her story and imagining all sorts of paths. Let's explore the twisting path her life has taken.

The Rider: Patricia

Patricia Arbitson was ten years old when her mother, Delores, suddenly left home, abandoning Patricia and her father, Alfred. The departure was a terrible blow to them, but in truth, it was not entirely unexpected.

Life with Delores had been a challenge, keeping everyone on edge. Her moods were unpredictable—gregarious and engaging one moment, irritable and angry the next. No matter which state her mother happened to be in, Patricia found her to be loud and annoying. In contrast, her father, Alfred, was serious and dour. He was a ship's steward who was away at sea for weeks at a time, and when home, he showed his wife and daughter no affection or interest. Delores and Alfred disagreed about almost everything, but they both felt that Patricia had to have a strict Catholic upbringing, as they had experienced. They pushed her to attend Mass and Sunday school, and years later, Patricia felt they wanted the Church to take over their child rearing. They never attended services themselves, which always struck Patricia as hypocritical.

Delores was twenty-two when she married the thirty-five-year-old Alfred, who was working on a passenger liner and impressed her with his worldliness. She'd long dreamed of a glamorous acting career, and she could now envision this as a real possibility, an exciting life for herself.

But alas for her, none of this came to be. Alfred didn't have the means, time, or desire to support Delores's "crazy dreams," as he called them. Delores resented his attitude, which fueled her dissatisfaction with her marriage and life. When she turned to their parish priest for guidance, he rebuked her for feeling sorry for herself and lectured her about a woman's place in the family. He prescribed Hail Marys and Rosaries, which infuriated her. She was certain of her destiny as a famous actress and resented the painful reality of being trapped with Philistines.

Delores's rants included calling Patricia plain, tall, and big boned (her euphemism for *fat*), and she cursed Alfred as boring. Delores felt stifled by her marriage. "This is not what I signed on for," she railed. She felt condemned to a life sentence.

Early on a cold winter morning, Delores disappeared. She'd placed a pink envelope tied with a red ribbon on the kitchen table, where her husband and daughter were sure to see it. It was Patricia who found the note. She came in from school after a long and frustrating day, and she was facing an equally long and lonely evening. Seeing the letter, she picked it up, her hands shaking as she tore open the envelope and began reading:

> My Dear Alfred and Patricia, You know how unhappy I have been here ... I just had to be free. I am going to the Continent [*sic*]. I have a wonderful opportunity to act in the theater. I know you'll understand, and you'll be fine.

That was it: no specifics, no apologies or pleas for forgiveness, and nothing about her love or keeping in touch or returning. "I know you will eventually understand," she added, which they found particularly cruel as well as dead wrong: they never did come to understand. Recalling the farewell note years later, Patricia described it as "typical, a lot of show, little substance, hurtful."

"Poof," Patricia said. "She was gone." She left no forwarding address or contact number. She left them with nothing except an abrupt absence, their pain, and an eerie quiet.

Trapped in a Marriage

Women and men who feel trapped in miserable marriages sometimes contemplate leaving, but few actually do so. The prospect of leaving can be daunting, and sometimes situations improve.

When major arguments occur in front of children, the children are often confused and frightened. Spouses use their friends or family as sounding boards or consult with religious guides, and many seek professional counseling. Others use destructive drinking, gambling, or love affairs as outlets for their misery.

But the frustration can grow into desperation when the pain becomes unbearable, and that individual breaks away. Few leave suddenly or irrevocably, and others often describe them as irresponsible, narcissistic, or crazy. However, when the marriage is visibly toxic, others sometimes credit the miserable spouse with being justified or courageous.

Either way, the effects on those left abandoned are hurtful. When a parent abandons the family, the children bear the brunt of the pain, feeling bereft and betrayed. A child feels sadness and self-blame. "What did I do to make her leave?" is a poignant feeling. The abandonment can cloud the lens through which they view themselves, their lives, and their world.

Patricia's mother, who was completely wrapped up in herself, abandoned her, and her father was emotionally and physically unavailable. She had to learn to compartmentalize (i.e., wall off emotional wounds from present realities) in order to compensate and grow.

(Delores might have suffered from a psychiatric disorder, such as bipolar or personality disorder, which, if treated, might have averted the painful desertion of her family.)

Patricia and Alfred had the awful feeling that Delores deserted them because neither of them was good enough for her. Delores would have agreed.

Alfred withdrew even more. When he noticed Patricia's school marks dipping and more weight gain, he was more annoyed than sympathetic. The term *depression* didn't enter his mind.

Four months after Delores's disappearance and just before a ship's tour, he decided that Patricia would go live with her grandmother Sonya, Delores's mother, who lived alone in a modest two-bedroom cottage on the other side of town. Alfred told Patricia disingenuously, "This is in your best interest." Sonya had little interest in taking her granddaughter in, but Alfred's financial offer convinced her.

Sonya had actually hoped that Delores might make it big in the theater. "She's so talented," she said to Patricia, who was aghast. Patricia's mother and father had already wounded her, and now her grandmother had too. She felt like a commodity, negotiated and bartered by those who supposedly loved her.

Sonya did provide a clean bedroom and wholesome food, but she imposed rules, duties (e.g., housework, chores, errands), and endless cautionary homilies.

Actually, there were similarities between Patricia and her grandmother. They were both heavy women, each with no social life. They gradually got to know each other, and after a year had passed, there was some ease and spontaneity, occasional humor, and some grudging affection. Patricia's mood and schoolwork improved.

When Alfred died suddenly a year later of a heart attack while aboard ship, Patricia felt no emotion. "When my mother left and then he sent me away, the family died," she said.

Patricia and Sonya soon came to realize their living arrangement was beneficial. Patricia was no longer living in a hostile home, and Sonya had a semblance of a family. Deserted by the same close person, they gave each other an emotional lift. Both alone and heavy, they'd each suffered slings and arrows from tormentors and the hurt of loneliness.

Sonya told Patricia that she'd also been painfully shy ("a shrinking violet"). She'd never married; her daughter, Delores, was the result of a painfully quick liaison with a proverbial drunken sailor on

Obesity

Overweight people face prejudice on a daily basis. Society treats them disrespectfully, and they often receive derisive looks and comments. They get fewer job opportunities and lower pay, and many people assume they have character flaws, a lack of will or self-control, or even moral failure.

Our culture worships the beautiful people prominently displayed in the media. Research has shown we are more likely to ascribe to attractive individuals positive characteristics, such as honesty, trustworthiness, and competence, but we draw opposite conclusions about those we consider unattractive, assuming negative traits, such as dishonesty, laziness, or irresponsibility.

Our society is rightly concerned about the prevalence of obesity and the potential effects on individuals' health, but adopting demeaning attitudes and approaches is even worse.

leave. Being Catholic, Sonya wouldn't consider an abortion, and giving up her infant for adoption was impossible: "I held Delores close to me, smelled her, felt her—she was mine."

Patricia described how homely and fat she felt. Children had ignored her and called her nasty names. "It was like I wasn't really there," Patricia told me. "Like that song 'Cellophane Man'" (from the musical *Chicago*).

The two women became friends, to their surprise and pleasure. They enjoyed Sundays sitting and reading in the same room, going to church together, or playing piano duets, listening to classical music, and occasionally going to concerts. Their protective shells melted away, especially when they'd sip wine or vodka in the evening and talk into the night.

They shared intimate thoughts and feelings and their common experiences with rejection and aloneness. This fifty-eight-year-old grandmother and her eighteen-year-old granddaughter revealed their desires for passionate sexual experiences. They talked about "hot passages" in literature, as they called them, and about their erotic fantasies. Patricia was a virgin, while Sonya had had that single roll in the hay when she was about her granddaughter's age.

They provided strong emotional support to each other, shared music and religious experiences, drank and talked, bemoaned and fantasized, and laughed. When they were somewhat inebriated, they joked, ruefully agreeing, "We're two lonely, horny, fat women." Having both known rejection, they'd often return to this theme with carnal allusions, double entendres, and ribald laughter, a mixture of pleasure and regret, both wondering, *Will I ever?*

Four Catholic colleges accepted Patricia, and she chose the one in town so that she could live with Sonya. When college rules dictated that freshmen had to live in dorms, Patricia took this requirement as a sign from above that she should strive for independence. With trepidation, she made a concerted effort, pushing herself to join the Young Republicans, the Classical Music and Chorale Societies, and the Campus Catholic Club. She attended meetings, volunteered, and participated actively, but no one invited her, few returned her calls, she made no friends, and she once again felt, as she put it, "on the outside looking in."

To complicate matters, Sonya became less available: she had met Peter, a sixty-nine-year-old retired labor lawyer, a widower who was totally smitten by her. In her exuberance, Sonya let Patricia know that their vivid fantasies about sexual delights were, if anything, underestimated. Patricia was happy for her soon-married grandmother, but she felt some jealousy and sadness, yet another reminder that there was a painful void in her life.

However, Patricia was resolute. If her lack of friends and lovers was to be her lot in life, she had to get her act together. She left the Young Republicans and the Classical Music and Chorale Societies, which had only reinforced her sense of rejection, and she remained a member of the Campus Catholic Club, which she found more comfortable and receptive. She felt drawn to the liturgy, rituals, and beliefs that were part of her upbringing. Patricia had a conflicted relationship with Catholicism, but the Church gave her a sense of "being home," as she put it.

In her senior year at college, Patricia worked part-time for the state attorney general's office, a job arranged by Sonya's husband. She enjoyed the work and showed such a knack that her boss gave her supervisory responsibilities. She graduated and earned a degree with majors in political science, theology, and music.

After graduation, Patricia spent a year in Europe, courtesy of a traveling fellowship and the modest inheritance Alfred had left ("My bounty," she commented). She wanted to see the Continent, the place that enthralled her mother. She had a vague sense of hope—and fear—that she might find Delores, who had left eleven years earlier. She'd heard not a word from her since. She contacted Interpol, but there was no trace of her mother. She was both disappointed and greatly relieved.

She spent much of that year soaking up concerts, museums, galleries, and churches. Rome entranced her, and shrines in other parts of Italy moved her, but it was in the Vatican that she found herself overcome with tears of joy, marveling at its architecture, art, solemnity, music, and grandeur.

Enthralled by the Mother Church, Patricia sought out sisters from various orders at St. Peter's Basilica, wanting to inquire about the possibility of becoming a nun. But when she pictured her life as committed to Christ and the Catholic Church, it bothered her that she wasn't inspired by them. The church hierarchy and male dominance, including papal infallibility, offended her. "All these men on power trips," she said. She decided against the sister route.

The months in Rome refreshed Patricia, who returned home energized and enthused, prepared for her new life. She felt more aware of herself and the world, feeling that she was a marketable commodity (as opposed to the commodity her father had "sold" to Sonya). She was confident she'd find a good career.

The men (largely) and women responsible for filling positions in the corporate and bureaucratic world were impressed by her résumé and invited her in for interviews, but their positive attitudes evaporated at the meetings, and they became distant. Patricia again felt the unpleasant past experience of rejection, which she recognized too well. She was five feet ten inches tall and weighed 260 pounds. She knew what was going on—she knew she was once again the victim of nasty prejudice, pure and simple.

Frustrated and disillusioned, she decided to pursue a career she'd observed closely in the attorney general's office. Patricia applied to law schools, and a couple of good ones accepted her.

Patricia thrived in the competitive atmosphere of law school. She had good grades, spoke up in class with thoughtful comments, and was on the prestigious law review. Her class had its share of "pushy, pompous lawyer-types," but there were a couple of female classmates she liked, and a few guys were respectful and friendly—though nobody asked her on a date.

After Patricia graduated cum laude, Sonya's husband, Peter, mentioned an opening for a lawyer in the local Department of Labor. She applied for the position and was hired.

Patricia gained respect as a lawyer there. For the first time, her homeliness didn't get in the way. The job required long hours of challenging work, and she loved every minute of it. The legal issues, her colleagues, and the atmosphere were all stimulating. Patricia was involved in mediating wage and other conflicts between management and workers in the public sector, and she showed a natural facility even in heated disputes. Corporations and unions both sought her to work for them. She loved the new feeling of being wanted and was happy staying where she was.

During a major strike negotiation involving union leaders and government executives, Michael Weiss, Esq., the union's strident lawyer, was insufferably pompous. He was articulate, but he couldn't resist demeaning the opposing representatives as "incompetent liars" in a tirade. Patricia firmly asked Mr. Weiss to restrain himself, and when he persisted, she said, "I must ask you, Mr. Weiss, to please shut the hell up!" This exclamation was followed by a round of applause and, later, by an apology from Michael Weiss, Esq.

When she and Michael had a drink at his invitation after the strike was settled, he praised her legal and diplomatic skills. "You put me in my place, and I deserved it," Michael said as he sat across the table from her, the hum of the busy bar droning in the background. A group of kids in their twenties was hanging out, laughing loudly and shouting above the music a couple of tables away. Patricia leaned across the table to hear Michael better, and she took the opportunity to size him up for the first time not as an adversary but as a man. He was slightly built and a couple of inches shorter than she was. His wedding band was clearly visible, as was his interest in her. Though opposed to the jerk she'd seen in sessions, she found him engaging, funny, and self-effacing. He lived in Manhattan with his wife; one of his children was away at college, and the other was married and had given him their first grandchild. He said that he was free that evening and wasn't leaving for home until the next day.

Patricia was astute enough to recognize a man hitting on her (for the first time!). She was flattered but had sufficient savvy to give Michael the message "Thanks, but no thanks." The seductive proposition excited her but also frightened her. She recalled the ribald conversations she and Sonya had shared, and she worried, *Did I just blow my one chance? What the hell was I thinking?* and, of course, *What does he see in* me?

Michael returned to New York, and Patricia uttered a few un-Catholic "Damns!" A few weeks later, Patricia was still working on forgetting Michael, when he phoned and asked if he could see her when he was to be back in town on a business trip the next week. She was excited but thrown into a panic: she wanted to see him again yet felt vulnerable and fearful.

Michael suggested that he see her on the way down to the hotel from the airport. Patricia agreed, yet questions bombarded her: *Am I too eager? Did I turn him off? What if he doesn't like me?* She felt like a schoolgirl. She felt tremulous, sweated, and breathed rapidly. She had to choose the right makeup, dress, and even attitude. She regretted her weight, wished she were pretty, wondered about Michael's motives ("What does he *really* want?") as well as her own motives ("What do *I* want?"), and worried about intimacy ("How?"). Catholic doctrine did not enter her mind at all. She phoned Sonya, who said, "Go for it!"

Michael arrived; the waiting was over. Patricia prayed to God to help her, recognizing the incongruity of asking God to help her indulge in sin. She poured her second glass of vodka and then Michael's favorite drink, Crown Royal—he'd told her last time, and she'd remembered. They sipped (she guzzled), had some hors d'oeuvres, made small talk, and then touched and kissed. They quickly became aroused and began caressing and exploring each other's bodies. Their physical differences precluded the usual clerical congress, but they soon found imaginative and effective positions ("Ways and Means—a great congressional committee!" they joked). They were passionate and pleasured.

The first thing Patricia did the next day was phone Sonya and shriek into the phone, "You were right!"

Michael had said early on that he wasn't going to leave his wife. Although she felt he was a bit too blunt, she got the message. She accepted these terms as the bad with the good, and for quite a few years, this limited relationship sufficed. She had her moments of guilt and resentment, but still, she looked forward to their meetings at her home or in his hotel. She knew she was doing wrong, but for once, she was going to please herself. She pushed the nagging idea that the affair was sinful or would lead nowhere out of her mind.

When her guilt about the nature of their relationship got to her, she would go to confession in a couple of outlying Catholic churches. She noticed that over time—years, in fact—the two priests seemed to be more tolerant. They didn't absolve her of her sins, but neither said she must cease and desist. They made no mention of eternal damnation, which she had expected and even hoped for on some level. Rosaries and Hail Marys seemed to suffice. She also saw a Catholic psychotherapist, who offended her by asking, "You want my permission to be a mistress?" Patricia wanted a committed love relationship, but she allowed her liaisons with Michael to continue.

Other than in this realm of romance, Patricia had never been more fulfilled. Her career was thriving; she was getting recognition and promotions. She became the director of conflict mediation within the Department of Labor and was called on for national policy deliberations. Her social life included a few close friends, including Sonya and the now-frail Peter. She went to dinners and concerts and vacationed with friends, and the occasional trysts continued.

Even while enjoying her career and social activities, Patricia still pursued her interests in the Catholic religion. She participated in prayers and masses as well as in volunteer programs. She studied at the central Catholic cathedral and diocese, where she had a good relationship with the bishop. She was friendly with some priests, nuns, and lay clergy and with many congregants, and the church community held her in such esteem that she wondered whether the Church was finally becoming more progressive.

But no, she was more disenchanted than ever with the male-dominated dioceses and the Vatican. "The pope and his minions were living in their own Dark Ages," she later told me. Though she once considered

Religion and Eros

Religion (i.e., the belief in and worship of God) and Eros (i.e., the need for sex and romance) are profound human drives, yet they appeal to different parts of our brain, body, and being. They are also often in conflict.

Patricia, however, was both God loving and sex loving. The struggle between our physical desires (e.g., pleasure, carnality) and the rules imposed by religion (e.g., waiting until marriage) are as old as antiquity. These are battles between our brains and our emotions and loins: religion and rationality versus desire and passion. Who among us has never been in this dilemma?

These struggles can feel epic in the moment to the conflicted person, yet there are often no absolute rights and wrongs. Those with absolute certainty of what people must do are usually outsiders who sit in uninvolved judgment. It is unpredictable what any individual will choose to do when confronted with the internal battle between lust and guilt. Can this ever occur without anyone getting hurt? Seldom.

becoming a nun, she now knew if she were to play an active role in the Catholic Church, it would be as a priest or even a bishop. She also knew this was impossible.

After enduring abandonment as a child and rejection as a teenager, she had come so far that she had to pinch herself. The Department of Labor appreciated Patricia as a talented leader and policy maker and implementer; she was the go-to person, a problem solver. She was a confident professional and a comfortable person. She regretted not having children, but she had made peace with this.

However, in her spiritual beliefs and in her womanhood, she still felt unfulfilled and at the mercy of men. These frustrations led her to make two important personal decisions.

The first had to do with Michael: she was now thoroughly dissatisfied with their relationship. Their sexual liaisons had become much less pleasurable, and he provided no real companionship. The rules of the game they'd agreed to were no longer viable. She woke up one day and realized that she'd lost interest in him. She was bored. She no longer yearned for more time with him. She was soon clearly aware that it was irrevocably over, kaput, whatever the *it* had been. In retrospect, she asked herself, "What was that all about?"

Michael, on the other hand, couldn't understand how she could give up their relationship with such "callousness," as he put it. He called her a few times a day, almost begging her to reconsider, but in Patricia's mind and heart, their relationship was finished. After seventeen years, she was surprised how easy (and important) it was to end the relationship. She felt free.

Her second decision was also profound. As much as Patricia loved the Mother Church, she knew it was really a "Father Church." She said, "The women there were only handmaidens." She was "allowed" to read to the congregation, but she could never offer sacraments, conduct Mass, deliver sermons, or be a priest.

When she discussed this issue with her friend Bishop Ferguson, his condescension appalled her. Their differences of opinion became less theological and more personal. He was visibly angry. "Just who do think you are?" he asked. Bishop Ferguson took her opinions as a personal rebuke of him. He told her she'd changed and showed a lack of faith and understanding of Catholic doctrine. He accused her of disrespecting the Church and of harboring "sacrilegious and dangerous opinions." Patricia left in tears, hurt and furious (as her mother had been a half century earlier). "The glass ceiling was a holy barrier," she said.

Patricia discovered that a highly contentious movement existed within Catholicism, dedicated to enabling women to become priests and even bishops. Patricia contacted a few outspoken women in the United States and Europe who were calling themselves priests. They were ex-nuns or religious-studies professors; some were married, some single, some straight, and some gay, and all were impressive, educated, and articulate. They were well versed in Catholic theology, and some were already giving the full range of priestly sacraments and services, although the Church officially granted these rights only to male priests designated by the Church. "Males anointing males," she said.

Patricia considered studying for the priesthood with these activist women, who were receptive and warm to her. "We were allies in frustration," she said. The Church called them renegades and sinners and threatened them with excommunication.

Patricia kept her senior position with the federal government, but she dedicated herself to becoming a full-fledged Catholic priest. She visited the Vatican and met with low-level priests assigned to her, who said her views were "antithetical to Catholic doctrine and to Christ" and showed an "astonishing ignorance of the Holy Trinity." One called her a heretic.

This is where we will leave Patricia Arbitson, this "big-boned," impressive, resilient woman whose life has taken numerous twists and turns in her sixty-three years. To quote her, "From a nobody, I've become a somebody," yet she's still wondering why her mother left her and if she will ever see her again.

The Four Bs

Now that we've read Patricia's story, let's take a look at how the four core elements of leading a fulfilled life fit together within the realm of the four Bs. Patricia's resilience played a major factor in how she became a success on a personal, emotional, and professional level, allowing her to leave a positive emotional footprint on many of the people in her life.

Being

Patricia was able to come to grips with her turbulent beginnings and managed to wall off (i.e., compartmentalize) her childhood difficulties and the many rejections and slights she endured. She recognized her frailties and faults, tried her best to accommodate or improve them, and, most importantly, came to appreciate her considerable assets and strengths.

She can now look in the mirror (real or metaphorical) and genuinely like, respect and even admire the person she sees there. At the age of sixty-three, Patricia feels grounded and comfortable in her skin and is not preoccupied with self-conscious thoughts or criticisms.

Belonging

After a childhood of rejection and isolation, Patricia now has become an adult who is an integral member of a number of communities of people in which she feels appreciated, liked, and wanted. She has rewarding relationships with close friends, her now-frail grandmother Sonya, legal colleagues, and many female activists in the Catholic Church.

Patricia has many friends. Paradoxically, she attributes much of her success in kindling and maintaining warm collegial bonds and a few especially close relationships to the unusual relationships with her grandmother (now elderly and infirm) and Michael (long gone from her life).

Believing

Even though her parents forced her to attend a Catholic church against her will as a child, Patricia's belief in God sustained her over many years. After her college graduation, when she had a prolonged stay in Italy and Rome, home of the Catholic Church, she had truly moving religious experiences akin to an epiphany of belief in the Mother Church.

Paradoxically, it was then and during many times since in the Church over the years that her beliefs became even more impassioned as her dissatisfaction with the male-dominated church hierarchy grew. (The ascendancy of Pope Francis has given her cause for optimism.)

She is the first to admit that Catholicism has enhanced her life and given her a strong system of values and principles by which she conducts her life. In many ways, her beliefs have also contributed to her sense of being and belonging.

Benevolence

Patricia is proud of what she has been able to get done in her important professional legal work in labor relations and specifically what she has accomplished for workers, companies, and society in her career. Even more so, she has been heavily involved with Sunday school for youths and Catholic outreach programs for the indigent. In addition, of course, she has been a major force for the liberalization of the Church not only in terms of the aspirations of women in the clergy but also in society in general.

Resilience

Patricia Arbitson endured daunting experiences as a child: her mother demeaned her and then deserted her, and her father was emotionally and physically unavailable and died soon after fobbing her off on her resentful grandmother. Her appearance brought torment from schoolmates, and she endured painful loneliness in her formative years and much of her adulthood. After a start filled with abandonment and rejection, she now has confidence and a personal mission.

Patricia didn't let her disappointments dictate her self-image. She remembers her difficulties but savors her accomplishments and contributions and her pleasures.

Patricia had "corrective emotional experiences" (a term coined by psychiatrist Harry Stack Sullivan) via her grandmother, religion, law school, colleagues, friends, and even Michael. She had inner strengths that buoyed her: she was bright, articulate, and well read and had interests in music and religion. She was self-effacing and had a redeeming sense of humor to deflect her slights and deflate others' nastiness. She wore her appearance and personality comfortably, with dignity and grace. Her intense relationship with God, borne under early duress, evolved into a meaningful source of strength.

Patricia was able to derive strength from situations that were painful. Her relationships with her grandmother, Michael, law, and religion could have ended disastrously, yet each enabled her to grow, derive pleasure, and overcome setbacks. Patricia is an avatar of resilience.

Emotional Footprint

As important as the good works she has accomplished are, Patricia has left a positive emotional footprint by contributing meaningfully and respectfully to others. Her relationships with her grandmother, friends, and colleagues have been warm and mutually beneficial. Even her relationship with Michael was mutually benevolent while it lasted and thereafter. Those whom Patricia touched recognize that she enhanced their lives.

2

Ken Stursberg

The Observer

The conductor enters the car, and people start handing her tickets. She smiles at you as she plucks the ticket from your right hand. "Quiet today," you say.

"Not really," she says, hesitating a moment. "It's just late for the rush, but it'll start all over again next shift."

You smile back at her, "the rat race never ends, does it?"

You think about the job interview, hoping once again to join the world of the working.

She moves on to the passenger in front of you, and you go back to people watching. There's a casually dressed middle-aged guy a few seats back who talks to everyone around him, going on about the beautiful weather we've been having, the latest in football, and the stock market, which is on an upward trend that you know will end soon, as it always does. He seems socially confident, as if he is a performer of some sort. The nearby passengers seem tickled by him and appear to enjoy his friendly overtures.

You listen to him glibly chat, but you sense seriousness beneath the apparent frivolity. There's a story there, to be sure.

The Rider

Kennie Stursberg was a bright child, but he never expected to amount to much. His difficult mother, Hilda, regularly and snidely called him a loser, and some of his teachers conveyed a similar message, perhaps more subtly. Kennie assumed they were correct in their assessments.

He was raised by impoverished Polish Jewish parents living in a tenement apartment house with other immigrant families. His father, Abe, had wanted to be an artist while growing up in Crakow, Poland, but now worked in a sewing-machine repair shop each day and was quietly lost in his art books when at home. Hilda was an unhappy, angry woman whose loud yelling fueled gossip in their tenement. When Kennie tried to get her attention by playacting and singing, she considered his behavior annoying and said, "You're one pain in the ass."

Self-Fulfilling Prophecy

If a child is told something negative about himself often enough, he might well come to believe it. The power of self-fulfilling prophecies in determining how children regard themselves is remarkable.

In a seminal study, "Pygmalion in the Classroom," teachers in a variety of schools were told at the beginning of the year what to expect from certain students, whom they didn't know. The researchers told them that some students were poor students, while others were bright. (In fact, their abilities were exactly the same.)

The results were disturbing. When the teachers' expectations were lowered, the kids' marks descended to meet them. The children prelabeled as bright had higher marks and showed more confidence. The teachers' preconceived attitudes actually dictated how the children viewed themselves and how they performed.

Other researchers have since replicated these dramatic findings in other settings. This illustration should serve as a reminder to parents, caretakers, and others with young people in their charge: Don't disrespect, insult, or demean the children you are looking after. Look for their strengths and reinforce them, and expect the best from them.

Kennie was an only child, but when he was ten years old, his parents suddenly told him that he would have to share his small bedroom with his seventeen-year-old distant cousin, Hymie, who was to arrive in a couple of days. After Hymie's parents were killed, just before the end of World War II, he had been placed in a displaced-persons camp in Vienna, and he was now being sent to live with Hilda, his mother's relative.

She was taking him in out of the goodness of her heart, Hilda said, but Kennie overheard her talking about a monthly stipend they would receive from JIAS (the Jewish Immigrant Aid Society). Kennie's parents sternly informed him that this was a done deal, the message being "Don't you dare complain!" He was upset but carefully avoided infuriating his volatile mother.

Hymie was a big and burly youth but seemed pleasant at first, and Kennie decided to make the best of the arrangement. The plan was for Hymie to go to the local high school, which had an ESL program for newly arrived immigrants, but he seemed to think he would learn English on the streets, especially in the pool halls and striptease joints. After a few months, his daily ritual consisted of sleeping in until late morning and then making his way to this "better" scene. He would return as the mood suited him, eat a late dinner prepared by Hilda, and then go to sleep. Hilda came to adore Hymie, which hurt Kennie even more, and she seldom pushed him to go to school or look for a job.

If Kennie had any lingering ideas that this arrangement might work out or even that Hymie was an estimable young boy, sharing a bedroom with Hymie dispelled them. Within a few months after Hymie's arrival, Kennie began to dread that bedroom, because it was there that Hymie's true colors came out.

He would crawl into Kennie's bed, under the covers, and proceed to have his way with him. These were variations on the venal theme of Hymie's satisfaction: filthy talk and groping Kennie's body, culminating in oral sex or anal penetration until Hymie achieved his panting ejaculation. Then there would be silence for a few moments, followed by a pointed reminder via brutal words and a gesture across his neck that any hint of disclosure would result in unimaginable carnage to Kennie's family.

While Hilda was telling Kennie to love his cousin, Hymie was inflicting those degrading acts on him. Kennie loathed and feared

Hymie, but he didn't dare tell his parents, because of Hymie's violent threat and because he was deeply ashamed. He thought, *Why would they believe* me? Kennie was sure his mother would blame him or say, "Kennie's crazy," or call him a liar. He was left with thoughts of dread and hatred and his dark, degrading secret.

Kennie spent his youth in this toxic atmosphere, but his internal life was his salvation. Kennie learned he could escape Hilda's tirades by using vivid flights of fantasy to bring him solace and even enjoyment. His private fantasies were colorful, creative, and safe. He could escape the misery at home and, especially, block out the pain inflicted by Hymie. Kennie mastered the technique of virtually disappearing from an ugly reality.

Hymie's molestations continued until Kennie was about to be thirteen, the age when he would have his bar mitzvah, which, in the Jewish tradition, meant he was deemed a man. Perhaps it was this milestone that emboldened Kennie to tell Hymie that if he ever tried to touch him again, he would stab him with a knife he'd hidden in the bedroom. (Hymie left their home soon after, never to be seen or heard from again. True to form, Hilda blamed Kennie.)

Child Molestation

Child molestation occurs all over the world in all kinds of families, ethnic groups, and social strata. Boys and girls are exploited and abused, often at the hands of relatives and trusted adults. The young victims have painfully mixed feelings of fear and fury toward the adult, and they feel shame and guilt for having "succumbed" to the malevolent advances of someone they trusted and cared for.

When children tell their parents of the abuse, the parents express horror and anger. Sometimes, however, they respond with disbelief, accusing the victim of lying or blaming him or her for having caused the ordeal. If the perpetrator is arrested and the family is wrenched apart, victimized children feel responsible. These acts are cruel rapes, but blowing the whistle is often fraught with conflict and complexity.

In Kennie's young life, these acts were coerced and painful invasions of his body and being. Molestation often causes years of emotional distress, problems with intimacy and trust, and even increased physical disorders in later life. If the acts are brutal and painful, repetitive, and under threat, and if the perpetrator is a supposed source of love, this is a recipe for severe long-term suffering.

School was another difficult reality for Kennie. Although he was bright, his negative home environment could have waylaid even a budding Nobel laureate. Hilda put him in the Hebrew Community Day School, where most of the students were first-generation Jewish immigrants who thrived in that atmosphere and where academic success was the only measure of worth.

But Kennie couldn't concentrate on schoolwork and studies when his personal life was so painful, and his mother and some teachers held his less-than-stellar academic record against him. Just as he did at home, he used his skills of disappearing into his daydreams, transporting himself away from the classroom, which was a boon to his mood but not to his academic performance.

In these escapist reveries, Kennie felt respected and loved. He pictured himself singing on a stage and reveling in the warm applause.

Despite his home atmosphere and school difficulties, he was well liked by classmates because of his warmth and sense of humor and especially because he was so self-effacing (unlike most boys that age).

He'd occasionally hint that his home life was miserable, usually with sarcastic asides. His sharing of vulnerability offered his friends a window into his inner doubts, which drew them closer, but he used humor to hide the extent of his *dybbuks* (meaning "demons" in Yiddish.) He did not share with them the terror that lurked in his bedroom. His friends used each others' apartments as surrogate families, but Kennie never invited them to his place. They thought the absence of an invitation was due to a lack of space, unaware of the misery lurking there.

In the eighth grade, Kennie discovered a unique source of fulfillment for himself, utilizing his vivid fantasy world. His English teacher, Miss Ida Reznick, offered him a major role in the annual school play, which was to be *Uncle Vanya*, by Anton Chekhov. During its three performances, Kennie stole the show, as his natural talent shone amid the young cast. In the Hebrew Community Day School at least, a star was born.

Kennie continued his acting in high school, where his passion and talent for theater stood out, and he participated in dramas, musical shows, and Gilbert and Sullivan operettas. He had a good singing voice, but it was his stage presence, his ability to project his energy to an audience, which was so winning. He was asked to join a community theatrical group, but Hilda dismissed his acting as a complete waste of time. Since he "obviously [had] so much time on [his] hands," she demanded that he get a job and contribute his earnings to the family. The missing income for Hymie's room and board had come back to haunt Kennie.

However, he did not let his mother deter him. Kennie got part-time jobs as an usher at a downtown movie house and as a gofer at a local radio station, both of which fueled his dreams even more. He graduated from high school with improved grades (his parents didn't attend his graduation), and he committed himself to two immediate goals: "getting the hell out" of his family's grasp and pursuing a career in the dramatic arts.

Even on his miniscule income, he was able to rent a small apartment with a high-school classmate. Kennie felt as if he had been released from purgatory; he breathed freely in his own home for the first time that he could ever remember.

With his drive for an acting career and the help of Miss Reznick and his high-school drama teacher, Kennie got into a community college theater school. He thrived there, eating up the curriculum: the history of theater, acting techniques, film and stage production, and directing. This was an exciting time for him, and his positive spirit energized other students and faculty.

He had left his mother's tirades and his cousin's abuses

Home as a Haven

In the best of worlds, our homes serve as havens from the stresses of the outside world. Without a sanctuary or safety zone, we human beings, like all animals, tend to fare rather badly. Havens provide us with replenishments of food, nurturance, rest, and respite from the pressures of the day. At their best, these havens solidify our personal niches in the world, where we can experience a sense of authentic self-acceptance (being) and feel we are a treasured part of a warm family or community (belonging).

If a comforting retreat is unavailable, we look to other constructive sources of comfort, such as reading, religion, music, exercise, television, the Internet, or psychotherapy, as ways of coping with a frenetic world. Escapes can also be overdone or even destructive, such as alcohol and drugs, which can be immediately gratifying but can come back to haunt the seeker of solace.

Luckily, we humans can use inner fantasies and flights of fancy to escape painful realities, just as Kennie did. When he heard an old German protest song, "Die Gedanken Zind Frei" ("Our Thoughts Are Free"), he said, "That's me!"

behind. He remembered them clearly, but they no longer plagued him. The theater was a salve to him, a source of fulfillment and an escape from demons, just like his fantasies of old. Kennie had found his niche.

Kennie had sexual desires and reveries, but he had no intimate relationships. He occasionally wondered if—and feared—he was gay because of Hymie's assaults, but all his sexual fantasies were heterosexual, and he was naturally attracted to girls. But he was scared. When he was attracted to a girl or when girls would come on to him, he feared he'd be humiliated if he couldn't perform.

However, in his college dramatic studies and performances, Kennie was excelling and receiving accolades. After his sophomore year, Kennie applied for the opportunity to spend an academic year at the renowned Academy of Dramatic Arts in New York, and the school accepted his application. As soon as the school year was over, Kennie bade farewell to close friends and faculty. When he phoned his parents, Abe had little to say, and Hilda was nasty—same old, same old.

Kennie loved New York, including its urban cosmopolitan atmosphere, the Broadway and off-Broadway theater districts, and the arts and music—"Everything!" He immersed himself in the drama school and reveled in its curriculum, teachers, and students.

Kennie's talents and enthusiasm did not go unnoticed, and the local academic and repertory theater circles were soon talking about him. About four months into the year, he was at a restaurant in Greenwich Village frequented by theater-school students and faculty, and a couple of Kennie's best-known professors invited him to join them in their booth. He was flattered by their attention and awed by their warmth and praise of him.

They urged him to remain in New York and offered to facilitate the transfer from his home college; they said they'd get him a theater-related job. They also strongly advised him to drop the suffix *nie* from his name, which they said infantilized him. From then on, he went by Ken.

Already enthused about his life in New York, Ken saw their offer as a godsend. One friend warned him about trusting his new patrons, but Ken surmised that his friend might have been jealous of his good fortune. He did briefly wonder if there was such a thing as a free lunch or if there was a quid pro quo, but the professors kept their word: he landed a front-office job in the theater school, and his home college enabled him to complete his degree in New York. Ken had to pinch himself. Deep in his heart, he thought it was all too good to be true, but he couldn't quite put his finger on why. Maybe, he thought, his experiences at home had made him cynical.

Ken was still dedicated to his studies and roles and was enjoying his time with the two professors. He was starstruck by their heady lifestyle, their beautiful townhouse on the West Side, and the elegant people in their circles.

At the restaurant one evening, they were even fuller of bonhomie and hinted that they would do even more favors for Ken. Then came two shocks: they told him they knew he was gay, which staggered him, and followed up with "So are we, so we understand your problems." They went on to share how much they cared for him and suggested that he move in with them. He would have his own private bedroom on another floor and full kitchen privileges, and he would be part of their active social lives. They would also provide him with a monthly stipend, and they added, "We'll have a wonderful time together."

Ken was offended and unsettled by their assumptions about his sexual orientation, but he was still hazy about their drift. Finally, somewhat annoyed, they spelled out their true intention: they wanted him to join in their love nest, a ménage à trois. They had confirmed his worst fears about his sexual identity.

Ken was stunned. He had believed their relationship was that of mentors and protégé, mutually respectful and caring. He felt betrayed, bewildered, and stupefied. He couldn't speak at first and then, using his acting skills (honed by these very professors), asked for time to think over their "incredibly generous offer." After a few forced jovialities, Ken said he had to go home. He was stunned; he felt as if he'd been raped yet again. *My fucking professors are as bad as Hymie!* he thought.

Back in his apartment, Ken wanted to throw up, but he couldn't; he wanted to cry, but no tears came. He was hurt and furious at the professors and even more so at himself. Tears soon came, as did nausea. He wanted to leave as soon as possible, but where would he go? Home? Where was *that*? He had read *You Can't Go Home Again* and felt there was no real home for him anywhere.

Ken knew he had to leave New York. He remembered that Alice

McNab, a warm American student who'd been in the theater program and was nice to him, had said, when she returned to Los Angeles last year, "Be sure to look me up when you're in California."

Ken decided to take her at her word, and when he phoned her from New York about possible plans of coming to LA, she sounded delighted.

Ken arrived in Los Angeles on March 1, a day of brilliant sunshine that contrasted with the weather he'd left behind a few hours earlier. Alice welcomed him and helped him get settled. They found a cute one-room coach house (once a servants' quarters) behind a large home in the Hollywood Hills.

Alice's father was an accountant for actors, directors, writers, and producers, and within a few months, he introduced Ken to several of them. Ken was at first starstruck, as newcomers to that scene often were. He met warm

> ## The Power of Charismatic Mentors over Youth
>
> Adults can wield Svengali-like powers over impressionable youth. These situations occur in intense belief systems, such as religious or ideological cults led by charismatic leaders, or in romantic seduction by manipulative older adults who exploit susceptible youths in the guise of love. Power, fame, style, and fortune are impressive and compelling forces to impressionable and needy individuals, who are swept off their feet by praise, professed love, and promises of happiness.
>
> In that mesmerized state of adoration and followership, vulnerable young people ascribe to the idealized person wonderful traits, such as compassion, honesty, and brilliance. However, they eventually realize that they largely imagined these traits and ignored their human faults. They then feel hurt, betrayed, and humiliated and become wary of their feelings and judgments about people.

and creative members of that community and began to feel comfortable. New York had also been wonderful at first, but his bitterness about the finale had soured that entire experience. He'd struck out in two homes, but he felt he might have found an emotional haven here. While at ease in this new community, he was wary and didn't yet trust his judgment.

Nevertheless, his time in New York had served him well. His charm, energy, and talents were impressive for a twenty-seven-year-old. He auditioned and won a couple of roles in the LA live theater scene and got an entry-level job at one of the major film studios. Ken was again excited but cautious.

Within a couple of years, Ken Stursberg had impressed people as a talented young actor, and he was trying his hand at writing a couple of film scripts with Alice. Her father, Fred, had taken a shine to Ken and hoped that Ken and Alice would become more than a platonic twosome, as did Alice. There were a couple of hurdles, however.

At the age of thirty, Ken was a virgin. He told me later, "I belonged in the *Guinness Book of Records!*" His sexual insecurities were increasingly nagging at him, but he rationalized that he was too busy for a relationship. Alice felt that Ken was not attracted to her or maybe was gay, but she said nothing.

Ken was attracted to her but was shackled by fear. Using his career as an excuse worked for a while, but that facade soon ran its course. He wondered whether he would ever have a relationship with Alice—or any woman.

Even some of Ken's friends began to wonder about his sexual orientation. He enjoyed being with women, but he wasn't a party animal; he seldom drank, and he had no interest in weed or drugs, which were easily available in Hollywood. Alice liked that he was different, but she was disillusioned. After two years of being kind of together, she'd had enough. She wanted to get married and have children, and she felt she might be wasting her time with him. Her dad said, "Face it—Ken is gay. You've got to start seeing other guys."

Alice decided to put her cards on the table with Ken. Sitting with him on a warm evening in a small seaside restaurant in Santa Monica, she blurted out, "Ken, what's going on with you and me?" Ken was startled; his first inclination was one of avoidance. He paused, summoned his courage, and steeled himself for inevitable humiliation.

They sat there at the restaurant for hours, talking late into the night, then walking, and then sitting in Alice's car. Ken shared, remembered, and cried; Alice listened compassionately. The night ended, and both of them, exhausted, fell asleep in Alice's home—she in her bed, and he on a couch in the den.

A bond of intimacy and caring had been forged, and to the relief of both of them, love was now tenuously in the air. They were sheepish and shy when they awoke. After a few moments of anxiety, Ken told

Alice that the weight of the world had been removed from him that previous night. They spontaneously kissed and made sweet, tender love.

Alice felt that Ken needed help to deal with some of his painful life experiences, such as his mother's rejection, Hymie's abuse, the two gay professors, and his insecurities. She introduced him to Jennifer

---

Get Thee to a Shrink!

Cynics say that the first response to a personal crisis in Manhattan and Hollywood is "Get thee to a shrink." People both praise and deride psychotherapy, which is seen by some as healing, by others as an exercise in futility, and by others still as an excuse for lack of individual accountability. Depending on the perceptions of different cultures, people might consider it inappropriate or even shameful.

Psychotherapies and medications can be critically important in the treatment of serious mental disorders, such as severe anxiety, depression, psychosis, bipolar disorder, and substance abuse.

But what about the problems of everyday living, such as the distress we feel when inundated by pressures and overwhelmed or when we get into repetitive, difficult situations or relationships? People use different ways of coping with stress: A mental-health professional (e.g., a psychiatrist, psychologist, counselor, social worker) might well be helpful, but there are other supports. Some people use friends or family as sounding boards for meaningful support and counsel. Others confide in their clergy leaders (e.g., rabbi, priest, minister, imam) or physicians, and still others confide in their hairdressers or bartenders.

Whether to see a therapist is usually a personal decision, but when troublesome symptoms (e.g., anxiety, anger, insomnia, sadness, confusion) become long lasting or severe enough to affect our functioning, this is a powerful reason to seek professional help.

Yet all over the world, even sophisticated families consult their astrologers or other seers when the going gets tough. Many people find solace and effective help in so-called alternative therapies, such as mindfulness, chakra healing, gestalt therapy, eye-movement retraining and reprocessing (EMDR), mind-body treatments, Zen therapy, and many others that exist nowadays.

While we can be more open-minded about alternative healing paths, we need to be wary, as there are many self-appointed "experts" who claim to have the answer to all emotional difficulties and disorders. But caveat emptor: hanging up a shingle (or using social media to sell oneself) does not confer expertise, and adopting the dictum "Whatever works" can prove to be dangerous. The public has to be protected from charlatans and dangerous practitioners. Stringent regulations of healing practices, including education and training, licensure exams, ethics, confidentiality, regulations, supervision, and monitoring are absolutely necessary.

Miller, PhD, an experienced psychologist she knew, and Ken took to psychotherapy with the kind of commitment he'd brought to the theater. He finally wanted at those *dybbuks*!

Ken and Alice married within a year, and in a few years, with their two young sons and daughter (Philip, Jeffrey, and Shana), they were living in a warm family atmosphere, which, for Ken, was a revelation. Alice was a loving wife and mother, exuding a serenity that moved him. He had not met anyone before who was so at ease with herself. This equanimity was totally absent in his own family of origin. He thought her inner peace likely stemmed from her loving family, but she attributed it to her belief in God. Ken could understand the former but not the latter.

The Significance of Belief

Nonbelievers decry religion as blind belief or the source of intolerance, the "opiate of the masses" (as Karl Marx said), and the cause of wars in the name of God and peace. There is no doubt that belief in a deity gives people immense comfort in times of pain and suffering.

The truth is that the majority of human beings have always had a need for a spiritual or nonmaterial dimension in their lives as a source of security, guidance, solace, and meaning. Believing often takes the form of a god (or gods) in different cultures, but it does not require a deity; it can also be satisfied by an adherence to other spiritual interpretations or searches, or an ethical value system, or one of many other profound attempts to address the meaning of our lives beyond materialism.

While Ken was working as an actor and doing scriptwriting and directing, he most enjoyed his roles as husband and father. He'd always wanted a warm family haven, the opposite of the suffocation he'd felt as a child, but now that he lived it, he had a feeling of desperation to maintain it and to protect everyone at home.

Ken kept in touch with his early group of school friends, most of whom were professionals or in academia, who visited from time to time. He and Alice were happy with their visitors, and they enjoyed spending time with their LA friends and with Alice's parents, who doted on their grandchildren.

Some of their friends and acquaintances had divorced, there were drugs and school failures among children of people they knew, and many people were losing their jobs in the vagaries of the fickle entertainment biz. Ken and Alice were spared these problems. Alice attributed their good fortune to God's benevolent guidance, but Ken felt it was due to Lady Luck. This worried him, for how long could one's luck continue?

He'd known hard times and wasn't going to be lulled into complacency by this peaceful interlude. Even with his family's health, love, and financial security, he took nothing for granted. He was aware of a vague unease, a surreal vigilance. He wasn't cynical, as Hilda and Hymie were, but he worried that feeling too good might invite an *ein horeh* (a Yiddish term meaning "evil eye," or "bad luck").

Their children were doing well: Philip, at twenty-two, was a student at Princeton; twenty-year-old Jeffrey had put off college and was trying to "find himself" by hitchhiking across Africa (to Ken's chagrin); and Shana was a freshman at UC Berkeley. Alice and Ken had time for movies, dinners with friends, and making love. Ironically, it was during romantic foreplay that a blip on the screen of their seemingly ideal life occurred: Ken was caressing Alice's breasts, when she suddenly cried out. She shuddered in a brief self-examination when she detected a lump she hadn't felt before in her left breast. Alice knew immediately what it was.

Her family doctor confirmed the breast lump and discovered a couple of smaller nodules in her lymph nodes. Her doctor referred her to Dr. Hilly Greenberg, a respected oncologist, whose biopsies revealed a particularly virulent type of breast malignancy. He told them the diagnosis just a week after they felt the lump during their tender, romantic moment.

Dr. Greenberg was kind and respectful, but he was the bearer of sad tidings: the diagnosis of stage IV breast cancer was extremely serious. The prognosis was guarded at best, he told them with sensitive candor. He offered data about treatment choices and discussed the pros and cons of each approach. Dr. Greenberg knew that all this new information in this stressful time had added to their confusion and anxiety and that they would need time to digest all he had said, so he scheduled another meeting.

A Doctor and Time

Dr. Hilly Greenberg spent vital clinical and personal time with Alice and Ken. He was a doctor's doctor: knowledgeable, respectful, and compassionate—exactly what we wish of our own doctors during times of serious illness.

In contemporary American medicine, time has unfortunately become a four-letter word. A critical element in a doctor-patient relationship is the amount of time spent together, during which the doctor gets to know the patients and discusses the diagnosis, treatment, prognosis, and implications of the illness and interventions. However, in many of the profit-oriented HMOs, time is the one ingredient most at risk. The more time the physician spends with his or her patients, the fewer patients he or she will see, and either his or her income will decrease or the HMO could remove the physician from its panel.

The word patient gets lost in business-ese: "health care as a widget." The practice of medicine has become corporate, driven by market share, cost cutting, productivity, and profit. Only the United States, of all developed countries, lacks a universal health program, yet Americans pay much more per person for their health care. A third of our population is uninsured (although that is now changing), and many families have gone bankrupt because of medical expenses.

That this country has allowed market forces to drive its once-vaunted art and science of medicine should be an embarrassment to us. The Affordable Care Act (Obamacare) is a good step in the right direction.

Alice and Ken's children and friends supported them, and stories of survival and the success of new research buoyed their spirits. However, Dr. Greenberg conveyed unpleasant realities: surgery was dicey because of inflammation and metastases, and her tumor was highly virulent (i.e., not responsive to chemotherapy or irradiation).

Despite Alice's physical deterioration, she appeared more at peace than her family. Her naturally strong personality and support of her family and friends were crucial, and she had her firm faith in a God. Ken was a lost soul, almost as if he himself were dying. He was unable to work, and his doctor put him on Prozac, a then-new SSRI antidepressant medication.

Alice tried to comfort Ken, reassuring him about "God's will," as she called it, but the idea of a protective Supreme Being was more than he could stomach. The anti-God rants of his family had stayed with him, and now he took them to heart. As he sat in a darkened room alone in the deep recesses of the night, he'd rail against God, cancer, evil, and the randomness of life that seemed to indicate there was no God. He remembered his mother saying and his usually silent father agreeing, "If God existed, why did six million of us die in the Nazi ovens?" *Yes,* Ken thought, *why* did *he let them all die?* Ken loved Alice for many reasons, none more than her spiritual grounding. Her belief in God had baffled him, but there was no denying that it worked for her. However, such faith did not work for him, especially not now.

When Alice died, Ken was distraught; his one font of strength had been removed. The end of a marriage to the woman who had saved his life left him feeling as alone and powerless as he had felt as a child. His caring children and Alice's family and friends surrounded him, but he withdrew from everybody, sometimes pushing people away. The effusive and warm Ken had become cantankerous and even insulting at times. Bitterness permeated everything he did, and people began to withdraw from him as much as he isolated himself from them.

Ken was still using Prozac and seeing Dr. Miller, who felt that Ken was depressed as a result of losing Alice. Ken was repeating behaviors he had seen as a child in his mother, Hilda. Rather than dealing with the pain of his loss, he'd become irritable. He was angry with Alice for leaving him, but he was ashamed about this reaction, which added to his sense of guilt. He was feeling miserable and acting offensively to avoid dealing with his sadness, and he was alienating the people he needed most. The medication was not helping and was contributing to his insomnia and irritability; Dr. Miller took him off it but kept seeing him in weekly psychotherapy sessions.

Within a few months, Ken's kids began seeing the "rebirth of Dad," as Shana described it. He was more energetic, positive, and trusting of others. While Alice's absence was palpably with him, he began experiencing pleasure in small things again.

Ken was in his midsixties when he started to put the puzzle of his life into some coherence. He was no longer waiting for the sky to fall. When he turned sixty-eight, Ken experienced something he'd believed was impossible: he fell in love. He felt exhilarated yet frightened. "It was ridiculous at my age," he said. He was somewhat embarrassed but proud he didn't go the Hollywood route of finding a young trophy wife.

An unlikely sixty-five-year-old Latina widow, Gabriella Mendoza, drew Ken's affections. Like Alice, she was warm and caring and had an abiding belief in God. Ken had fallen in love with two women who were spiritually and religiously oriented, while he himself ridiculed religious beliefs. "Go know," he said self-mockingly.

Gabriella was originally from Mexico, the daughter of mariachi musicians who immigrated to the United States when she was ten years old. She grew up in a barrio of Phoenix, Arizona, in a close-knit family. Gabriella had also been a performer in her youth (like Ken), singing and dancing with her parents at restaurants and special events. She graduated from a community college and then a university, eventually pursuing a graduate MFT degree (a master's degree in marital and family therapy). She became a caseworker for an agency and, later, a psychotherapist.

"Gaby," as Ken called her, was a widow who had been married to a Mexican-American importer of crafts and collectibles from Mexico. They had four children, three of whom lived in the far-flung Los Angeles area; the other lived in Arizona. After her husband died, Gabriella ran his business for a while, where she met Ken, who was browsing in one of their outlets.

Both sheepish about their new relationship with their grown children, they dated for over a year before they moved in together, and they married two years later.

Both are now retired and live in a small home in a multicultural area of Los Angeles. Philip and Shana are both married with children and live in the eastern United States, and Jeffrey, who is gay, works as a diplomat in Nairobi, Kenya, where he lives with his boyfriend.

The Four Bs

Ken's experiences show just how long it can take to finally achieve a true sense of self and to embrace your unique position in the world at large. He suffered greatly as a child. His mother's rejection of him as a person and the sexual abuse he endured from his cousin messed up his ability to develop a sense of being. It took his passion for the stage to bring out that sense of being.

As we've seen already, one or two of the four Bs can impact the others. In Ken's case, when he found his sense of being on the stage, his belief and sense of belonging followed. Still, it took falling in love with Alice for him to fully accept himself, and that, in turn, led to benevolence, particularly as he cared for his wife as her condition deteriorated. His resilience eventually enabled him to get through his grief over Alice's death and fall in love again.

Being

Now in his midseventies, Ken is at peace with himself. "Alice was the one who was at peace, never me," he says. He still remembers his dysfunctional family, Hymie's molestations, and his New York debacle, and he wonders about his life's journey—whether it was just a series of random happenings or if there was some kind of game plan. Alice would have said that God preordained his life, but according to Ken, "It was more luck than brains."

He has learned to cope with the fleeting stabs of sad memories. Sometimes he misses Alice so much that it "hurts [his] heart," but the rawness of the pain is receding.

At this stage of his life, Ken feels more comfortable than he can ever recall. He is no longer keeping up a frenetic pace to try to prove to himself or others that he is worthy. He recognizes his frailties and limitations, but he now respects who he has become and what he has achieved personally and professionally.

Belonging

Ken no longer feels like he did as a child, when he was the perennial outsider in a rejecting family or alienated from his classmates. He still feels accepted by the film community, Alice's surviving family, and a few old friends from his childhood.

He even feels comfortable in gatherings of Gaby's family, who show him respect and caring. They have provided him with an entirely different cultural experience and models of emotional intimacy. He is close to his and Alice's grown children. He feels that he is an important and loved member of different meaningful communities.

Believing

Alice and Gabriella both provided Ken with love as well as grace and warmth. They also both evinced a strong spiritual core, which one would expect would make them shun a professed nonbeliever like Ken. This speaks volumes about Ken himself, because these estimable women saw in him the essence of a true mensch—a caring, honest, and generous soul.

Though not a believer in God, Ken had values and ethics that he lived by, which were more important to him than the materialism of everyday life. Despite his pathetic family of origin and all his misadventures, Ken was a believer in goodness.

Benevolence

Ken has been an authentic, caring soul; the legacies he bestowed on this world are obvious in the smiles of his two wives, his children and grandchildren, his stepchildren, his friends, and his apprentices, students, and colleagues in his theatrical and film circles.

Resilience

Kennie was a child who lived through constant demeaning, rejection, and verbal and emotional abuse, not to mention severe molestation from within his own family. Those around him told him that he was an abject failure throughout his formative years, and for quite a few years, he came to believe the validity of that destructive message, which emanated from his supposedly loving family. He experienced other early setbacks along the way, including the painful experience in New York.

He was fortunate that he had a few caring friends and abilities to use both his vivid imagination and the stage as vehicles to escape his tormentors. Tom Stoppard said, "Drama opens a window into areas we otherwise dare not tread." Acting was much more to Kennie than creative fulfillment; it led to self-awareness, it protected him from pain, it was therapeutic, and it enabled him to be a remarkably resilient soul.

Emotional Footprint

Despite his sordid beginnings and other trials and tribulations, Ken made a positive emotional footprint over his lifetime. He participated in creating a loving family, he was kind to others, and he set an example of decency in his relationships and his work community. He won't leave a fortune to his survivors when he departs this world, but he will leave warm memories in the hearts and minds of those who knew him, and a quantum of goodness that increases the "civility in the ether."

3

Neville DaCosta

The Observer

You notice a tall, skinny black guy wearing a beret stand up a few seats down on the left. You know he's from the Caribbean, probably Jamaica, because of his accent as he speaks with the conductor. You see he's wearing designer sneakers, blue jeans, and a stylish leather jacket. He glances back at you and catches your eye just before he sits down again. For those few seconds, the two of you see each other, your respective humanity. You both nod, acknowledging the brief connection.

You wonder if the fellow is an artist or a musician. Something in the way he handles himself makes you think that maybe he is. The man's deep brown eyes reveal a sensitivity that you pick up on even in that quick exchange of looks, and as you consider the man, you realize there is much more to him than his cool outfit. What is it? He definitely has an artistic flair, yet his style doesn't quite jibe with this midday train journey, so you imagine he has had some hard times. Maybe drugs? You wonder if you're falling into the trap of stereotyping, and you feel uncomfortable about it. There is more to this guy, you think, and your imagination runs free, but here is his story.

The Rider

Neville DaCosta was preparing to die. The tall, slim seventy-three-year-old artist and musician was telling his old friend James that he had been diagnosed with liver cancer. "The doctor told me that it was hepatocellular carcinoma, which means the 'big *C*'. She said it was caused by my years of boozing and drug use. It's inoperable." He paused and shook his head. "It's a real bitch. I start on chemotherapy next week, but I don't think I'm up to it."

Neville told James that he planned to overdose on Oxycontin (a narcotic painkiller) he'd been stashing. James felt his stomach drop, but he kept quiet and let Neville keep talking.

Neville said he'd shared the news of his cancer with his daughter Sabrina, whom he was forging a late-life bond with, and her young son, Marcus, whom he adored. But he'd saved the suicide plans only for James, a jazz musician who himself was an ex-addict. He said he wanted only a few close people around him when he "snuffed out [his] life." James understood where Neville was coming from and wasn't sure that he wouldn't do the same thing if he were in his shoes.

An air of serenity pervaded Neville's California studio apartment, a small granny flat with a colorful garden tucked behind the elaborate home of a benefactor. The furnishings of his studio were sparse, but visitors felt surrounded by music, art, and warmth. Large, deep-hued, evocative canvases capturing the images of classic jazz greats, such as Miles Davis, Muddy Waters, and Billy Holiday, covered the walls. Other more surrealistic paintings reflecting Neville's spirit hung on walls or leaned in stacks.

There was a haunting painting of a beautiful Afro-Caucasian woman who looked alluring yet distant. Natasha had been Neville's lover more than forty years earlier, when they'd briefly lived together in Paris. In the painting, she stood semiprofile in the nude, holding brush and palette at a canvas that she and little Marcus, also naked and holding a brush, were creating together. This painting within a painting evoked Neville's deep feelings for his grandson and his long-lost lover.

Neville was born in Kingston, Jamaica, in 1933 to Edna, an impoverished but strong single mother. Shortly after Neville was born, his father disappeared in "a dark cloud of bullshit," as Edna called it, referring to the mixture of "ganjaweed, reggae, and Rastafarian junk in his bloodstream." Edna wanted a better life for Neville than the tough streets of Kingston offered. She knew they had to get away. If not, she'd go back to "using and hooking," as Neville called it, sometimes in pleasure when she was high but often in pain and sadness, and always in desperation.

Edna's distant aunt living in New York sponsored them (for a fee), and she and five-year-old Neville soon moved into a small walk-up apartment in Harlem. Neville recalls that time as a colorful blur, with a revolving door of people from Jamaica coming through, often with tumult, terrific music, and loads of weed and rum. Mostly, the visitors were warm and fun, but a few got nasty when drunk or high.

Edna worked a couple of cleaning jobs to pay the rent and dress and feed them, so she was often away from home, and Neville was alone much of the time. Drug use and fighting were common at school and on the streets, and he had to be on his toes. He loved to draw and play guitar; he had little in common with other kids there. The other children occasionally bullied him with macho taunts, but some seemed to like him. The teachers were preoccupied with reining in tough kids and raising test scores, but a few noticed his talents and encouraged him.

In high school, Neville felt harassed, sometimes running from bullies by day and, at night, running from tormentors during vivid dreams from which he'd awaken in a cold sweat. However, he found peace when he was playing his guitar, drawing, or painting.

After graduating from high school, Neville was at loose ends; he knew he had talents but was unsure how to turn them into a career and his "daily bread," as he called it. He tried a state college, but a couple of uncomfortable semesters convinced him it wasn't his scene.

The jazz scene—living as a night owl, attending performances, and meeting musicians ("the hangers-on, the wannabes, and the greats")—drew him. He wanted to play guitar with major artists but soon realized that despite his passion, he didn't have what it took. This realization was a bitter pill to swallow.

But Neville's talent in drawing and painting was burgeoning, and he used music, personal experiences, and vivid fantasies as his themes. He sold a few of his works to musicians, but the art community viewed him as a dilettante, resenting his facile movement from music to art.

Neville persevered and was gradually accepted, for a while moving between both creative communities, but he soon concentrated exclusively on painting.

Neville's local artistic reputation spread, and he began to gain confidence. He was debonair: tall and stylishly dressed, wearing a beret cocked to one side and ascots or scarves. He noticed the interest of many women, and he started dating, wining and dining, and soon bedding. The local art and jazz cultures were also nests of alcohol and drugs, and Neville experimented liberally.

As he indulged in these pastimes, he had difficulty concentrating on his work or sleeping soundly. He was having disturbing dreams with one recurrent, upsetting theme: He'd be walking along at ease, yet he'd sense danger lurking. He'd get nervous and pick up the pace until he'd break into a frightened run. Scary, bizarre human forms would appear, and he'd awaken sweating, relieved yet fearful.

When Edna died of a heart attack, Neville promised at her gravesite that he'd make her proud of him someday. For a few months, he worked feverishly at painting and drawing. He was on a mission to make something of himself.

In a nightclub about that same time, he heard the voice of Sylvia Buchanan, a blues singer with a wonderful sound like that of Billie Holiday. "I wasn't sure whether I fell in love with the maiden or her music," he said.

In contrast to Neville's rough beginnings, Sylvia came from a close-knit, evangelical Trinidadian family with a strict moral code. Her family saw themselves as "people of God rather than of the street," she said, referring to their misgivings about Neville. But Sylvia was sure she

---

Dreams

Most people roll their eyes when someone recounts a "fascinating" dream he or she had. Our own dreams, however, fascinate us; sometimes we clearly recall the plots, and other times, we remember nothing. We've all experienced mystifying dreams that made us wonder about their meanings. We forget most dreams, but some are repetitive and linger in our minds.

Dreams have played major roles in literary fantasies—for example, in Shakespeare's A Midsummer's Night Dream, in the Old Testament (e.g., the story of Joseph), in children's literature (e.g., Scrooge's ghostly encounters in A Christmas Carol), in opera (e.g., Radames's dreams in Aida), and on Broadway (e.g., Tevya in Fiddler on the Roof).

Sigmund Freud, the father of psychoanalysis, attributed symbolic meanings to dream content, and his ideas were in vogue for a while: cylindrical objects represented the phallus (penis), and round, warm symbols depicted the womb. Experts have since debunked these symbols, but the use of dreams as windows into our unconscious (i.e., hidden thoughts and feelings) is still important in psychotherapy.

Another pioneer, Carl Jung, used dreams to explore cultural and spiritual meanings. Dreams can provoke thoughts and feelings that can be highly significant. Recurrent disturbing themes (e.g., Neville's running away from danger) can be signs of troubling preoccupations, which can be fruitfully explored.

---

could turn Neville into a God-fearing soul, and for a while after they married, things were good: Neville was clean, and he painted and sold canvases and brimmed with energy.

However, that energy was soon directing him to the available booze, grass, and cocaine. The heady mixture of drugs and adoring women led to work slippage and carousing, and Sylvia feared she would lose Neville to these sinful temptations. Her parents warned her that his father "rode that same evil train."

But the birth of their daughter, Ella, gave Sylvia hope that Neville would settle down, and he did—for a few weeks. Their repeated pattern was that Sylvia would be hurt and furious, and Neville would express remorse, beg for forgiveness, vow to change, and attend church. He would convince her he'd changed, she would relent and forgive him, and then the dance would begin again.

Neville continued his slide, becoming physically and emotionally unavailable to his wife and daughter and even to himself. He created few quality paintings, and he failed to honor commissions. After he physically threatened a gallery owner who had berated him, the gallery owner called the police. A few days later, he swung his fist in anger at Sylvia, and she'd had enough: she got a restraining order and pressed charges. Neville put her deep religious values to the test, but she walked out hurt and angry, depleted but resolute. She knew their marriage was over.

However, in Neville's drugged haze, he felt certain that Sylvia and Ella would soon be back. When a court hearing mandated a three-month stay in rehab, Neville was sure he'd convince Sylvia of his remorse and commitment. Neville was in a vulnerable state of inner turmoil and chaos and in dire need of help, but he thought he knew better.

Neville mastered "the rehab game," as he called it: he was charming and impressive and demonstrated sincerity and dedication to a life of being clean. He mocked himself: "My credos were purity and monogamy!" He expressed remorse and shame, took responsibility for his destructive behaviors, and expressed strong motivation to get on the healing path.

After three months, he had convinced the staff that he was committed to a life of sobriety, AA meetings, and family values. "I gave them their own psychobabble," he said, admitting that he did not mean a word of it. He'd gamed the system by fooling others and harming himself.

Neville felt there was more to his self-destructiveness than alcohol, drugs, and moral weakness. The rehab staff "looked at [him] through drug-tinted lenses," he said. Neville didn't think he was an addict; he'd show them.

He pleaded with Sylvia, who was now in a serious relationship with someone whom she said gave her what he couldn't: love, trust, and God. She was angry and wanted to protect Ella from his influence.

She did not want Neville back, and he couldn't believe it; he was shocked. He longed for his wife and daughter; he felt shattered and even

"I Don't Wanna Go to Rehab!"

After a person's substance abuse has caused significant impairment, when there's been severe pain and damage to others, or when lives are close to shambles, claims of remorse and promises to reform forever usually follow. Often, however, drug use returns with a vengeance, and the family then places the individual in rehab (i.e., a rehabilitation facility). Amy Winehouse famously sang, "They tried to make me go to rehab, but I said no, no, no"—her plaintive cry on behalf of so many like her, with a tragic real-life ending.

Being forced into rehab is not the ideal pathway to getting help, but it's the most common. The user is placed in a setting he or she doesn't want to be in, to deal with an addictive disorder that the person often doesn't believe he or she has.

The patient has to follow a fairly uniform program of individual and group therapy sessions, therapeutic group meetings, and other interventions. The goals are to get the individual off all abusive substances, to achieve some insight into his or her problems, to accept personal responsibility for his difficulties, and to achieve self-acceptance and self-control.

These are all worthy goals, but the long-term success rates of many of these programs are not impressive. Some addicts have better outcomes in intense group approaches that are not based on a twelve-step model, while many others succeed in getting the monkeys off their backs while undergoing individual psychotherapy, sometimes in conjunction with medications that diminish their cravings.

avoided the art and music, which had always given him solace. He was preoccupied and filled with self-hate, and he began to use booze and grass to ease his pain through self-medication.

He avoided asking for help, but his friend James urged him to go to Alcoholics Anonymous. Neville had felt that AA was useless and based on "guilt and God." He had difficulty with the proselytizing he felt went on at AA, but he was desperate and agreed to attend some meetings.

At his first AA meeting, Neville met the flamboyant Mercedes, who immediately told him she was bipolar, with seeming pride. She wore this diagnosis like a badge of courage, regaling Neville with her history of extreme mood swings, paralyzing depressions alternating with hypomanic highs, hospitalizations, and the meds that helped her. Her attention and her sharing of this personal information flattered Neville.

She was divorced, she said, because her husband "couldn't take [her] wildness." Though she'd forewarned him, he and Mercedes began hanging out. She was verbal, funny, and a passionate lover, which helped get him out of his sadness. He enjoyed their emotional and physical intimacy and their shared love of jazz and art. Mercedes urged him to pursue his painting, which spurred him: he began another artistically productive period using Mercedes's energy to delve into new themes. He shuddered, recalling that Sylvia had also served that function once.

When Mercedes proudly announced to Neville, "I'm pregnant!" he felt snookered, because she was supposedly on the pill. In spite of misgivings, he agreed to marry her. Their daughter, Sabrina, was soon born, followed a year later by a son, Tony. For a while, these two healthy children seemed to settle both of them down.

For a few good years, Neville's career blossomed, his canvases were in demand, and meds enabled Mercedes to rein in her volatility. They attended AA meetings sporadically, but this soon ended. They saw a few friends and listened to jazz, he painted, and Mercedes enjoyed

Alcoholics Anonymous

It is true that attenders of AA meetings are encouraged to turn themselves over to a spiritual Higher Power, but Neville misconstrued AA's purpose and process. What he saw as guilt induction was the expectation that members accept their roles in the roots and resolutions of their problems. Acceptance of personal responsibility is the first step in moving toward sobriety and redemption.

AA and other twelve-step programs seek to end self-destructive behavioral patterns, and they teach personal ownership and accountability. Destructive, compulsive behaviors could be related to alcohol or drug abuse, overeating, abusive anger, uncontrollable gambling, or obsessional sex, but personal accountability is a key element for ultimate healing.

There is a debate as to whether these behaviors are a sign of mental illness or of moral weakness, hence the derision that members of these groups face. Either way, healing will not occur without the ownership and commitment of the addict.

The addicted individuals' behaviors hurt their family members, even when they are caring and supportive. Caring family members often hear that they are codependent (i.e., partly responsible for the perpetuation of the addiction), an idea that is too often invoked, akin to blaming the victim.

being married to Neville and a mom to Sabrina and Tony. For a while, their lives seemed serene.

Mercedes felt so good that she concluded she no longer needed her medications. She started missing doses, and her moods began to fluctuate unpredictably and suddenly, swinging between highs and lows; she could be angry and nasty and then pleasant soon after. Mercedes became moody, erratic, and disorganized. Neville was worried, but she reassured him that her mood swings happened every now and then. When he returned home one evening, Neville found the children watching television, and Mercedes nowhere to be found.

Two hours later, he received a call from an emergency-room social worker at University Hospital who said they'd admitted Mercedes to the acute psychiatry unit. She had made a serious suicide attempt and had been found on a city bus, unconscious after overdosing on Vicodin, an opiate-like painkiller. On her left wrist were cuts and dried blood from an unsuccessful suicide attempt earlier that day. Her psychiatrist said she'd been hearing voices and fearing attacks by others and had thoughts of harming her children.

Creativity and Madness

When Neville was putting oil to canvas, he found he was able to redirect his anxieties and use these energies in his art. Many creative artists with emotional disorders produced memorable works in the midst of profound torment.

Beethoven, Van Gogh, Pollock, Hemingway, Plath, and Jim Morrison—all creative geniuses—are just some artistic giants who suffered emotionally and shared that ability to harness their fears and pain and enter deep artistic zones. Their intense emotions stimulated their creative juices, and they embedded their souls in their art. Thomas Merton wrote, "Art enables us to find ourselves and lose ourselves at the same time."

Although one does not have to be tormented or disturbed to be a creative genius, there is a somewhat higher incidence of mood disorders among those with strong artistic inclinations. There are also many others whose emotional disorders paralyze them into inactivity. Finally, and most important, the majority of artists are emotionally grounded, stable, and happy.

After three months in the hospital, Mercedes came home overweight and slow moving, in part due to the medications. Neville expected her to be her old self, but this was not to be, and he knew they couldn't go on like that. She showed no interest in him or the kids, and her new attitude turned him off. They remained in a state of siege for a few months, waiting for the inevitable death knell of Neville's second marriage. He wasn't proud of it, but he knew he had to get away from her.

By the time Neville left, neither Mercedes nor the children were speaking to him. They blamed him for all the problems, as did everybody else. In their eyes, he had caused his wife's breakdown and the family breakup.

Mercedes had a serious psychotic disorder before they met, but others pilloried Neville as the cause of her illness. They ostracized him and blamed him for being a terrible husband, father, and individual.

The Blame Game

Human beings love to play the blame game. Gossiping and criticizing others seem to be part of our protoplasm. We find fault with officials who abrogate the public trust, clerics who are abusive, spouses who stray, celebrities who are destructive, and CEOs and bankers who are greedy. We blame our mechanics, doctors, neighbors, lawyers, and politicians. We even criticize our friends.

We cluck at the immorality and hypocrisies of others, mocking their frailties and faults, fascinated yet repelled by their lapses, while we feel pristine and superior. We seem to be less interested in examining our own darker recesses.

We derive pleasure from what the Germans call schadenfreude, secretly enjoying when miscreants cause their own downfall, savoring their humiliation.

None of us is pure and innocent. We are complex souls, and all are capable of crossing the lines of ethics, given the right (or wrong) circumstances.

At that painful time in his life, Neville felt like a pariah. Desperate to stave off depression, he wanted to get away from his accusers, and he impulsively booked a flight to Paris. He told his friends that he wanted to work on his art, but they suspected other motives as well.

Living in Paris as an American ex-pat had its compensations. He made some new friends in the Left Bank art and music communities, his high school French was improving, and he sold some paintings to tourists along the Seine. He was living the life of an *artiste et boulevardier* (i.e., painting, frequenting cafés, having philosophical discussions over wine, etc.). He loved it.

About a year into his Paris sojourn, Neville met the beautiful and mysterious Natasha. While her dark appearance belied it, she told him she was a Russian artist who had come to Paris from St. Petersburg to further her artistic studies. Natasha showed little interest in art or much else, but he was swept away. His romantic attraction was torrid. Hers was less so, but within days, she moved into his tiny flat in the fourteenth arrondissement.

It was romantic heaven for a few weeks, until the day Neville returned home to an empty apartment: Natasha and her belongings were gone, as were the jewelry he'd bought her, the American dollars hidden in the bottom drawer, his camera, and his beloved Fender guitar. Natasha vanished "after thirty-nine days of pleasure," he lamented as he recalled the whirlwind affair. He searched frantically, questioning her acquaintances, but his effort was futile. She was an evanescent spirit who'd taken over his entire being and vanished.

Neville was left bewildered, still yearning; he never heard from her again. He had placed his relationship with Natasha on a pedestal of magical significance, but his French friends just shrugged. She had used him and scammed him, nothing more. *"C'est la vie,"* they said.

Neville felt shaken and vulnerable and did not trust his own feelings or decisions, but he didn't sink into the throes of the depression he feared, and though tempted, he didn't use drugs. He recalled where drugs had taken him before, and he chose another course: he forced himself into the life he'd had before Natasha. He had no choice.

He confronted himself, worked at accepting responsibility for the demise of his marriages, and pined for his children. He resumed painting, playing guitar, going out with friends, and rekindling the spark of bonhomie that he'd exuded a few months earlier. He again reveled in the ex-pat lifestyle and even considered a permanent stay in Paris or a move to Provence.

Then his life in Paris came crashing down around him. The initial blow was the news that he'd contracted hepatitis B. Heavy drinking for years had left him with a damaged liver, but the hep B virus had likely entered his body years earlier via contaminated needles, when he was mainlining. Doctors diagnosed his fatigue and weakness as a flu bug until a young Algerian doctor at a community clinic made the diagnosis. The doctor put him on a strict medical and dietary regimen and reassured him that he could have a healthy life if he took the necessary precautions, including abstinence, which had not exactly been his forte in the past. But he made light of this: "Instead of vats of vino, I'd switch to carafes of caffe."

His lightheartedness was upended a day later by a short phone call informing Neville that his seventeen-year-old son, Tony, had been killed in a holdup at a liquor store. The police detective said Tony had been an innocent customer caught in crossfire. Neville rushed home.

Even in the midst of grieving, the rancor toward him didn't subside. In the eyes of Mercedes and others, Neville had caused this terrible turn of events. At Tony's funeral, the other guests shunned him. Mercedes wailed throughout the service, while his sad daughter Sabrina stared blankly into some other world.

Neville felt the cloud of hate directed at him, but a painful epiphany hit him: they were right! He even joined the accusations: "I fucked up my life. I hurt my wives. I caused Tony's death. I lost my daughter Ella."

After the funeral, Neville and Mercedes responded to their painful loss in their familiar patterns: Mercedes was hospitalized after another suicide attempt, and Neville went on a bender. Sabrina was used to her parents' different coping styles.

When Neville appeared in distress at James's door, James said Neville had to go back to the rehab center where he had been "cured" years earlier. Neville refused, saying, "I'm not an addict. I need something else." He was deeply depressed and thinking of ways he could kill himself, such as getting stinking drunk and blowing his brains out with a Magnum.

When he was on the verge of doing this, the phone rang. It was Sabrina, now a nursing student, the only steady rudder of the family, crying profusely. She was turning to him.

Someone else needing Neville was ironic: Sabrina and her father had been estranged for years and were now in need of each other's love and support. Neville hugged his grieving daughter, holding her close—it was the first time he'd done that since she was a baby. They comforted each other and commiserated. He confessed and cried about his life's debacles and his suicidal thoughts. Sabrina gathered her strength and told Dad, as she now called him, that she wanted to get him the help he needed.

She knew he needed to be in a compassionate place where he could face his inner demons and heal. Neville was hospitalized in a psychiatric inpatient unit, and Sabrina was in the weird position of having divorced parents admitted as psychiatric inpatients in different hospitals.

Neville entered the psychiatric unit voluntarily; no psychiatrist had to commit him on the grounds that he was a danger to himself or others.

He found the hospital jarring at first, but he worked with the therapists, his psychiatrist, the nurses, and the mental-health workers as well as the other patients. He was put on an antidepressant and was advised about possible side effects, such as diminished sexual performance. His mood improved, and he gave credit to the other patients. He learned that he wasn't the only one who had acted destructively, who was filled with shame, or who had contemplated suicide.

Neville remained there for four weeks. He felt appreciated there, and he actually enjoyed his stay. While he wanted to join the world outside, he was scared and was relieved when told he was going to a therapeutic halfway house.

He did well in that communal environment, even picking up brush and palette again and playing on a borrowed guitar. He remained there for two months, and on discharge, he was certain he'd maintain his new emotional and physical health. Yet he was wary. Throughout his life to that point, he'd harbored a deep-seated fear of failure. That fear colored virtually everything he did. He'd awaken at night in a cold sweat, having what he'd call an anxiety dream. The dreams were vivid and often scary, frequently featuring him in a high place about to fall. Failure was Neville's most powerful ghost, and it manifested itself in his relationships.

"I knew my life would never be the same." Both his ex-wives, Sylvia and Mercedes, wanted nothing to do with him; Natasha had abandoned him; he was estranged from his daughter Ella; and Tony was gone. All of this was almost more than he could bear.

He returned to his lifeline of the past. He gathered his palette, brushes, oil paints, and canvas and poured himself into the creativity that had been smoldering, awaiting expression for months.

His paintings from that period were darker than his earlier works, yet he sold a few evocative works. Neville had given up alcohol and drugs, and he continued to have his blood and urine levels monitored. "I did it for Tony," he said.

Recovering from all the losses was a tough road; Neville struggled with his guilt and grief for many months. His joie de vivre was slowly returning. He knew he was lucky to be alive. He reproduced these stirrings on canvas, where he was merging music and art, which resulted in some wonderful portraits of jazz musicians that proved to be popular with art dealers, galleries, and collectors. He was getting his mojo back.

Sabrina became a registered nurse and married a navy physician, Edward, and they had a son, Marcus, who was Neville's first grandchild. Neville and Marcus's bond was immediate, natural, and mutual. Edward's lack of presence or interest in his son facilitated the special relationship between grandfather and grandson.

Edward worked long hours when he was based at home, and he was often deployed elsewhere. He spent so little time with his son or wife that Sabrina concluded that his work was merely a convenient excuse.

Neville and Marcus became inseparable companions, listening to jazz, going to movies and galleries, painting together in Neville's studio, and talking all the time.

Over time, Neville tried to make overtures to Sylvia and Ella, his estranged first wife and their daughter, but they showed no interest. Neville was grateful that at least his relationship with Sabrina had been reborn.

When Marcus was six years old, the school called Sabrina about recent changes in his behavior. When Neville heard this, he railed at the teachers for not appreciating his grandson. Sabrina wisely listened to the teachers' concerns, which were significant: Marcus had been showing signs of difficulties at school in the areas of learning (including focus, concentration, and organization) and in his social behavior (including irritability and outbursts). His pediatrician diagnosed ADHD (attention-deficit/hyperactivity disorder) and prescribed Ritalin (a stimulant medication). The medicine aggravated Marcus's problems, and the doctor prescribed another stimulant and then another. As Marcus's behavior became more troublesome, the pediatrician suggested the possible diagnosis of bipolar disorder and suggested an evaluation by a child psychiatrist.

"That scared the hell out of me," Neville said, recalling the roller coaster of Mercedes. Neville demanded they get a second opinion, and Sabrina relented in order to placate her father. Marcus's physician reluctantly ordered further tests, including a CAT scan and MRI, and discovered that Marcus had a large temporal lobe tumor on the right side of his brain. The tumor was benign but dangerously located. A neurosurgeon at Children's Hospital operated on Marcus that same week.

Marcus had lost some normal tissue in the temporal-lobe area, and some scarring ensued, which led to some detrimental effects: Marcus's capacity for learning was affected, and he was having tantrums. Sabrina and Edward, already having serious marital problems, couldn't handle the pressure. A few weeks after Marcus returned from the hospital, Edward suddenly announced his transfer overseas by the navy. Sabrina was relieved to see him go. They never saw him again and later heard that Edward was living conjugally in Italy with another military man.

Neville was dedicated to Marcus's care and progress, and he became the overseer of Marcus's welfare. Sabrina was working full-time as a nurse, and she needed her dad's help. Over the next few years, he helped them both, and he arranged for Marcus to get into a special school, where he thrived.

Neville was acting as a responsible father for his daughter and as a surrogate father for his grandson, and he had never been happier. He was also producing the most avant-garde works of his career.

Then came Neville's diagnosis of liver cancer. In the beginning of Neville's struggles with cancer, his estranged daughter, Ella (Sylvia's daughter), whom he hadn't seen in over thirty years, suddenly reappeared. He was pleased but suspicious—and with good reason. She wanted to exploit her father's guilt to get money to support a drug habit. "C'mon—it's the least you can do," she said. She also mentioned she'd like some of his paintings after he was gone. He'd had it: he confronted Ella and got her into rehab ("the ultimate irony," he called it). At least this event opened some contact with Sylvia, his first wife.

Neville's last few years were in some ways the most fulfilling of his life. He was no longer drinking and was not in AA or rehab, in a hospital, under arrest, in altercations, or in an unhappy marriage. He had reconnected with his children, grandchildren, and one ex-wife. He had close friends and many admirers. He had a comfortable living and work haven, enough to eat, and sufficient clothing. Destructive behaviors no longer tortured him, and he was not running from bullies, the law, ex-wives, creditors, or nightmarish antagonists. He regretted his mistakes, but he wasn't besieged by remorse and self-hate. In the last months of his life, he was most concerned about his grandson, Marcus.

Two significant experiences were crucial in Neville's late life.

The first was his participation in monthly evening meetings of a group of eight men of about the same age. The venues were each of their homes, where the host supplied food and wine, which Neville never touched. They discussed their lives, pleasures, regrets, and aspirations. The members were a motley group, including a physician, a biology professor, a drug counselor, an actor, an entrepreneur, an author, and an artist.

These men were facing common life issues: losses of all kinds (e.g., family, friends, and opportunities), compromises in health, diminished strength and energy, looming mortality, and retirement issues. Now in their late sixties and early seventies, they had made mistakes in their lives, yet they were working to be better people. They were involved in their relationships, work, and activities, and their desire for love and sex was still strong. From different cultures, careers, and worldviews, they shared a kinship and intimacy that enhanced Neville, and he did the same for them.

The second experience was Neville's exposure to chakric meditation. When his oncologist had first diagnosed him with cancer five years earlier, she had put him on chemotherapy, though she had been pessimistic. She had also referred Neville to a healer in the ancient Hindu yogic techniques of chakric healing. In spite of Neville's cynicism, she began working regularly with him on the focal energies that he was emanating through his bodily tensions and his facial expressions. She would place polished stones on critical parts of his body to focus the inherent energies of his life-force centers, called the seven chakras. Whatever the theory behind chakric healing and despite Neville's skepticism, during each session and for days afterward, he experienced an inner calmness.

He was again enjoying his contacts with friends, the tastes of food, and the colors in nature. He was also painting, a clear sign to him of returned energy. MRIs and other examinations for a number of months showed the tumor sites diminished in size.

Was this progress the chakric healing, or was it the chemotherapy? Even his oncologist was inclined toward the former explanation. Neville learned techniques of meditation from his healer, and he meditated in his studio at least once daily. During the last months of his life, Neville was actually savoring his existence.

At the time of this writing, Neville's weight loss has stopped (he's lost sixty pounds), and the latest scans and MRIs have shown no new growth or new appearances of the tumors over the past few months. He has been playing the guitar and painting. He goes through periods of weakness and pain as a result of the illness and medications, and he experiences periods of intense sadness. But then he meditates, spends time with Marcus or friends, or paints and listens to music, and he says, "I'm not ready to go yet."

The Four Bs

Neville's story hinges largely on the many years during which he lacked a true sense of being. He ran from the ghosts of his past by losing himself in heavy drinking and drugs, yet his belief in his own abilities as an artist led him down a path that eventually allowed him to find the sense of being he lacked. His sense of belonging followed.

Resilience is at the core of the story. On the verge of suicide due to his terminal illness, Neville was about to give up. Yet the love of the people around him and his renewed sense of faith in creativity—his believing—enabled him to bounce back in the face of dire health problems.

Being

Neville has at long last achieved a genuine sense of being: he is finally comfortable within himself and authentically likes who he has become. He is no longer acting self-destructively or irresponsibly, is not using or abusing drugs, and is not manipulating people.

After a lifetime of loves offset by losses, and creativity undermined by carousing, he has come to terms with his needs to control his inner anxieties through behaviors that were hurtful to both himself and others close to him.

Neville has, through arduous work, been able to achieve a semblance of serenity.

Belonging

While he regretted his transgressions, it was in the last two decades of his life that Neville cherished the experiences with his healed old and new relationships. He has a deep appreciation for his family and friends, and significantly, he has become more interested in reciprocating and even initiating kindnesses in his relationships.

He made peace with those family members who wished to get close to him and with many of his artistic colleagues, new and close friends, and, most importantly, himself. For the first time in his life, there have been a number of years of mutual caring, respect, and needs met in his relationship. He perceives a naturally evolved sense of belonging.

Believing

Neville was never a religious man per se; he never attended church, and Alcoholics Anonymous turned him off whenever it invoked God in its tenets. But interestingly, he was actually always a believer in some kind of higher design. Whatever it was obviously never deterred him from untoward behaviors or carried the clout of a God who would punish his crimes and misdemeanors, but he never doubted that there was something out there in the vast unknown that was greater than his material surroundings. The power of creativity in art and music was something that he always believed in, and it was his life force.

In his later years, his spirituality and sense of right and wrong informed his behavior and his works of art and the music he loved. When he spoke of "soulful" jazz, he meant reaching a profound level of otherworldly consciousness. And his most moving paintings, even when they depicted real people, often conveyed to the viewer his deeper connection to a spiritual meaning—his sense of believing.

Benevolence

Neville learned from his errors and has actually grown because of some of them, and he has tried to make amends to those who allowed him that privilege. He is proud of his legacy of art works, but he is most gratified by his later-life generosity and sensitivity to others (i.e., his sense of benevolence).

He said recently, "After all the craziness in my life, the most important relationship and the one which taught me the most was with my grandson, Marcus."

Resilience

Neville had a rough beginning: his father abandoned him at birth, his mother sacrificed yet was often unavailable, and others abused and bullied him. Drugs and disappointments, failed love relationships, and losses inflicted their share of scarring. Neville ran away from fears, but he also ran from responsibilities and toward easy fixes. He experienced little introspection or inner peace, except when he was painting or playing music.

After self-destructive acts, behavior that hurt others, losses, treatment, and humbling setbacks, Neville finally started on a difficult uphill path toward resilience. Over the last few decades, Neville's relationship with the world evolved into one eschewing alcohol and drugs, meeting responsibilities, and demonstrating care and consideration for others, particularly Marcus and Sabrina, as well as friends and others. These laborious changes as well as working at expressing his innermost feelings through painting, music, and meditation helped him achieve personal growth and redemption.

Emotional Footprint

Neville's emotional footprint is a mixture of good and bad. In his younger years, Neville showed himself to be irresponsible and destructive to others (and himself), when he was carousing on alcohol and drugs.

It would be too much to expect that the pain he inflicted on others would simply evaporate over time. Just as he experienced at his son's funeral, his then-wife and her friends never forgave him for what they saw as dissolute and hurtful behavior.

As for those who had longstanding relationships with Neville, accompanying him through thick and thin, quite a few remained closely bonded with him and were even there in his last moments. Others whom he had befriended in his later (sober) years could only recall a loving, generous soul.

Postscript

Neville died a few weeks ago, after I wrote the material above. Neville was more at peace with himself at the end of his life than ever before. When his health allowed, he slept soundly. Close to death, Neville experienced rebirth.

His last few days in a hospice were a life–affirming experience for him. The atmosphere was compassionate and spiritual, and people who loved him surrounded him. "Neville had a glow at the end," one said.

Neville's circle of intimates and admirers was varied, colorful, and evocative, just like his paintings, a kaleidoscope of races and cultures, including his family, men's group, friends, longtime associates, admirers, and art collectors. All were there to honor and celebrate this wonderful man.

A downtown gallery displayed a public show of paintings and drawings, which included surrealism and jazz, spirituality and erotica, seriousness and whimsy. A videotape on a large screen of Neville talking and working attracted crowds just as if he were there, larger than life, in living color, animated and loving, as if he had never left.

4

Jane Whyllie

The Observer

Although the train car is practically empty, it is not quiet. The constant background noise of the train creates a sort of hum punctuated by the blast of the locomotive's horn, the staccato *clack-clack-clack* of the steel wheels on the tracks, and the whine and squeak of the airbrakes as the train slows at a crossing. Above the noise, you hear the occasional conversation.

The voices of two small children carry to you. The kids aren't misbehaving—they're just being kids—and the attractive young woman with them shushes them. You look more closely and note that the woman, probably their mother, is wearing a pearl necklace around her neck and a gold charm bracelet around her left wrist. Her sapphire-blue eyes are so arresting in their intensity that you couldn't help looking at her when she boarded the train a few stops back. Her grace, poise, and style caught your eye, making you wonder if she was some sort of celebrity. *But,* you think, *not on a train!*

You get the feeling that she has a bad-girl side to her or did in the past. You find the notion engaging, and it makes you a bit jealous as well. You've never strayed far from the beaten path. You've never taken major risks in life, opting instead for the path of least resistance, as many do. You wonder what it would be like to quit your boring job, if you had one, and trek up mountains. *Not a chance.* You wonder what it would be like to have an affair, and you realize this would trigger a heartbreaking divorce that would include financial and emotional ruin. You like the life you've led, for the most part, and you try to leave it at that. You sigh.

The woman appears to be unhappy, as if she's experienced loss. The death of her husband? Is that it? The idea of being alone in the world scares you. Loss has stricken you in the past. You turn away from the woman and her children and stare out at the wetlands. You feel empty for some reason, and you don't know why. To chase away your own ghosts, you think about the woman and her kids, imagining their lives in a way that distracts you completely.

The Rider

The first time Uncle Hughie made sexual advances toward Jane, she was just shy of her seventeenth birthday. Hugh Parker was the best friend of her father, Bruce, thus the *uncle* appellation. Jane remembers the incident as clearly as if it were yesterday. It happened at the annual Whyllie Thanksgiving dinner, attended by family and close friends.

Jane was seated at the elegantly set table next to Uncle Hughie, who quietly placed his right hand on her left thigh, softly stroking it while maintaining an animated conversation with Bruce. Jane was surprised but didn't flinch and carried on her pretense of interest in the conversation. She enjoyed the charade and the attention she'd neither initiated nor sought. She felt a rush and a sense of power over Hugh.

At Thanksgiving dinners, Bruce would loudly toast his "wonderful family," always mentioning their being blessed by a "cornucopia of plenty," his pompous depiction of success. And who was responsible for all this plenty? The socially prominent Whyllies personified conspicuous consumption, with their mansion and its manicured lawns and the luxury cars out front.

Bruce owned a large insurance company, and his wife, Sally, was active in the Junior League and charity balls. Jane's older sister, Mary, was an excellent student, outgoing, and popular. She was also a piano prodigy who started giving recitals at a young age. Their younger brother, Tim, also excelled in school and was a natural athlete. These four Whyllies—father, mother, Mary, and Tim—were attractive, accomplished, gregarious, and ambitious.

And Jane? She was neither a musical prodigy nor an athlete; she was an average student at best and kept to herself. Her parents had always described her as beautiful, often following the compliment with pointed criticism of her inadequacies. During Bruce's nightly drinking, he was particularly nasty to Jane, contrasting her with her accomplished siblings and criticizing her "bad attitude."

When Jane was fifteen, she was at home with her father one evening, and after imbibing a few scotches, Bruce mentioned how gorgeous he found her. Fathers often praise their daughters, but this compliment felt different to Jane. "It made me feel icky," she said. When he stroked her arm, she quickly recoiled. He made the uncomfortable situation worse by adding, "If I wasn't married to your mother …" His voice trailed off. He was clumsily coming on to Jane, confusing and offending her.

She said nothing to him or to anyone. However, when it happened again a few weeks later, she was repelled. "Mom wouldn't like that," she said, noting his blanching and quick, skulking retreat, envisioning his Sally's wrath. Bruce never revealed any of this to his wife, but he'd ask, "Why can't Jane get her act together?"

Jane did get her act together, but it was a different act from the one Bruce envisioned. She had blossomed early into a stunningly attractive young woman, and she noticed older men leering, including teachers at school, doctors at appointments, store managers, and even her parents' male friends. She learned that if she returned the gaze of attentive males and smiled, an unmistakable connection clicked.

Sexual Abuse

Sexual abuse leaves acute psychological wounds and chronic scars on its victims. Ugly, cruel acts perpetrated on children, often by older relatives or trusted friends (e.g., coaches, priests, etc.), are egregious experiences to endure, often relived by victims through painful memories.

Some abuse victims demonstrate resilience and achieve fulfilling lives. Whether severe long-term effects occur depends on the nature and severity of the acts, the relationship between perpetrator and victim, the inner strengths of the child, the attitudes of the family, and the availability of effective therapeutic interventions. These terrible acts are inexcusable: children must be protected, and predators and perpetrators must be removed.

Society's responses to suspicions must be judicious and thoughtful. While people should be vigilant, we must be careful to avoid a witch-hunt mentality: suspicion is not fact, zealotry is not rationality, and accusation is not guilt. False accusations have produced devastating results for the accused. If one makes an accusation, he or she must have strong evidence to protect both the alleged perpetrator and the children.

Abused children must be protected from further abuse and receive effective methods of care and treatment. But we need to be aware of unintended consequences: just as the false labeling of an individual as a sexual abuser is devastating, similarly, the label of someone as a sexual abuse victim can become an albatross, a permanent self-designation of victimhood.

A few men were emboldened to ask her for dates, but this attention bemused Jane, seldom offended her, and sometimes tempted her. By the time she was seventeen, Jane knew that she could use her beauty and flirtation skills to her advantage and that she had power over men: they were like Play-Doh in her hands.

The Thanksgiving thigh caress by Uncle Hughie was the first of a few similar advances, but Hugh waited until Jane's eighteenth birthday to begin—and consummate—his seductive campaign. He would shower her with dinners, concert tickets, jewelry, and clothing, and she would reciprocate with sexual favors. Jane thought that he was a foolish, dirty old man, but she liked the benefits and encouraged the affair. When her mother noticed some new possessions, she asked if Jane was selling drugs. Jane laughed and truthfully denied this (the sin of omission).

In the midst of a bitter argument a few days later, the "shit hit the fan," as Jane put it. She'd refused to attend a family dinner to which Hugh and his wife were invited. When Sally said, "What a pain you are!"

Jane exploded, "You really want to know where I got all that stuff? From Uncle Hughie!"

Sally screamed in horror, accused Jane of malicious lying, and collapsed in tears. At Sally's insistence, Bruce confronted Hugh, who denied the affair at first but soon owned up, blaming Jane entirely for seducing him. The Whyllie family was in shock. Sally severed all ties with Hugh and his wife, and Bruce downed more scotches than usual. He understood only too well why Hugh was drawn to his daughter.

This scandal caused huge ripples in the family and community: Hugh and his wife separated, the friendship between the families dissolved, and the church congregation was in disarray. Bruce and Sally barely spoke to each other; Sally secretly blamed her husband but wasn't quite able to pin down the reason.

Sally was miserable and ice cold to Bruce, who was often in a scotch-induced stupor. Jane's sister, Mary, moved into her own apartment downtown, continuing her piano studies and career. Tim was at college, focused on attending medical school. They all tried to avoid the unpleasantness at home, but they laid the blame at the feet of Jane. This hurt and enraged Jane. She considered their behavior a gross injustice, and she secretly wished that she could do something to get even. She bided her time, but deep inside, she simmered.

After high school, Jane tried college, but her heart wasn't in it. She worked at a few jobs in sales and public relations, jobs where a beautiful woman could be an asset. She left each after a few months, claiming it was boring. Bruce told her she was just looking for trouble.

In one area of her life, however, Jane was an unqualified success. Her affair with Uncle Hughie was her debut, the first of several relationships with generous suitors who were attracted to her. They lavished gifts, luxurious hotels, and even a condominium on her in exchange for her favors, her face, her company, and, of course, her body. Some of the men were successful businessmen or professionals, some were married and some were not, and they recognized they were using her. But the truth was that Jane felt *she* was using *them*. Jane's detractors disparagingly called it "la dolce vita," and she didn't disagree.

A few years as paramour to a parade of older wealthy men began to feel boring and unfulfilling. She felt as if she were Scheherazade or Jezebel, and she felt slutty. Of course, she was an unmitigated slut. She just didn't want to admit it to herself, not in a way that would induce her to change the path she was on. Drinking alcohol now reminded her of father's favorite self-medication, and she shuddered. She knew she was going nowhere; she had no career, interests, or friends—nothing.

What bothered her most was that for all her experiences with men, she had never met one in whom she had any serious interest. Their attention and gifts bored her, and she tried to avoid sex as best she could, which wasn't easy. Sex was her meal ticket. Sex gave her a sense of identity. At the time, it didn't matter if that identity sickened her and made her feel worthless, like a piece of rotten meat.

Jane felt adrift and alone. Her family had turned their backs on her; her relationships with her parents were tenuous at best. When she talked about this period in her life, she said that her sense of self-loathing was growing. Juxtaposed against the lives of her sister and brother, who were "busy being successful," she felt even worse. Jane felt starved for a close relationship. "I didn't have a single close friend," she said. "All I was good for was sex."

Jane recalled an upsetting dream: "I was on a motorcycle speeding down a mountain road. I hit the dirt side and lost control. I tried to get back on the paved road, but I spun, heading over a cliff, and I

The Paramour Game

The men in Jane's life were not exactly role models for a love relationship. Bruce was a pompous man who came on to his own daughter, Tim was arrogant and self-righteous, and Uncle Hughie was a lothario. And the men in the paramour game cared little for her other than as a plaything and showpiece. Jane got faux affection and material gifts at huge personal costs.

But Jane was hardly an innocent victim in the pas de deux between older males and young ingénues. Female youth and beauty turn on older, successful men. In this "contractual agreement," the Casanovas and the Jezebels both get what they think they need for a while. Men exploited Jane to make them feel good, but Jane felt she "wasn't good for anything."

The young women in these relationships with powerful men ultimately feel used, empty, and trapped. They need respect and trusting intimacy, and they get the opposite.

woke up, sweating and panicky." The dream was a metaphor for her life. "What the hell am I doing?"

Jane, at thirty-five, was seeing Malcolm, a forty-seven-year-old dyed-blond entrepreneur from England who owned a few bars in the Caribbean, courtesy of his late father's estate. She characterized him as a nice guy, good for a few laughs. They knew the rules of the game: Malcolm plied her with gifts, and others saw him with this beauty on his arm. By now, Jane wanted something better.

Jane accompanied Malcom to an immigration lawyer so that he could get his green card; they were referred to Sam Woolfson, a quiet forty-five-year-old lawyer (*Nerdish, Jewish,* she thought) whose office was stark, with no photos of family and minimal touches of color. Sam had a mild manner and was thoroughly professional, concentrating on Malcolm's legal issues. He barely noticed Jane, which annoyed her. She resented the attention Malcolm was getting, and she wondered why she even cared. Sam wasn't wearing a wedding band, she noticed. This unassuming man strangely appealed to her, but he didn't show the usual male interest she invited.

Jane phoned Sam's firm the next morning, asking for an appointment regarding a pressing need for a visa. At his office a few days later, Sam asked about the rush for the meeting. Jane fumbled with embarrassment and blurted out, "Okay, I just wanted to take you to lunch."

Sam was astonished, swallowed hard, and accepted the invitation, surprising both of them. He later told a friend, "I noticed her, but why would a beautiful woman have any interest in me?"

They hit it off while munching hamburgers. "Neither of us could believe it," Jane recalled. The Whyllies were upper-middle-class WASPs, while Sam's Jewish father had been a carpenter, barely eking out a living. Jane had experienced a luxurious and convoluted life; Sam's was studious and quiet. Neither of them had been married or in love; they had lost hope and endured loneliness and melancholy, and they were resigned to lives alone.

But here they were. Jane had never had two consecutive days in her life when she'd felt good about herself and her world. This unlikely couple was now in love.

Jane brought Sam home to meet her parents, and while Bruce and

Sally were gracious (he was sober; they were good with social niceties), they had misgivings about this match. They wondered what Jane saw in Sam and, even more so, what he saw in her.

They had never seen her so happy. She talked about loving Sam and settling down, but they didn't trust her motives. Jane was an un-employed courtesan—what could Sam possibly want from her? And he was so different from them: nerdy, unathletic, and Jewish. They held their tongues, knowing their irresponsible daughter was having just another fling.

When Jane announced a few weeks later that she was going to convert to Judaism and marry Sam, Sally and Bruce were speechless. Mary and Tim were also surprised and somewhat uncomfortable at first but soon warmed to Sam's gentleness. Their sister seemed so grounded, which was never a term used for Jane!

Jane and Sam married a few months later at a warm and decidedly un-Whyllie family wedding, a modest event with about sixty guests (a quarter of the number who'd attended Mary's and Tim's extravaganzas). They were married in the Jewish tradition: under a chuppah (canopy), with a rabbi officiating and a wrapped glass that Sam (and Jane) stomped on, followed by an exultant "Mazel tov!"

Within four years, Jane and Sam were living in a pleasant town-house with their two young daughters—Amanda and Robin—in a family neighborhood. They had good friends and a pleasant lifestyle and had what each had longed for and neither had imagined possible. Jane's parents accepted Sam, grateful to him for turning Jane's life around and especially for their granddaughters. The Whyllie family started spending time together, enjoying a new communal mood.

When Sam was in his early fifties, he noticed that he was getting tired, sleeping poorly, and feeling rundown. He put this down to a de-manding schedule and promised Jane that he'd cut his workload, watch his diet, and exercise; maybe he'd hire an associate. Jane felt reassured.

Sam's exhaustion continued. Within a few weeks, his doctor diag-nosed an advanced form of malignant lymphoma, which had already metastasized to his lungs. An attempt at a clinical trial with an exper-imental drug had no effect, and within three months, Sam Woolfson was dead.

Jane was devastated. Her family and friends rallied around her, but she could find no respite. "I couldn't breathe; every breath brought in sorrow," Jane said. Every muscle was taut, each move exhausting; her entire body ached. She was overcome with grief and an overwhelming sense of loss. The light of her life ("My personal savior," she said) had been taken from her. She feared her very essence had been removed.

The thought that their daddy wouldn't ever come home to hold them and play devastated the girls. Jane had to support them, but she had difficulty providing solace for them when her own world was shattered. She cried often, couldn't eat or sleep, and couldn't lift her spirits. Her despair was beyond grieving: Jane was in a deep depression.

Her brother, Tim, lost patience with her. "Just how long is this going to go on?" he asked with irritation. Tim insisted that she see a psychiatrist and made an appointment for her with Dr. Alan Hicks, a member of his medical staff and golf club. "Dr. Hicks is very busy and had to fit you in as a favor *to me*," Tim reminded her.

Jane resisted going to a psychiatrist, because her family had told her for years that something was wrong with her. Being a loving and loved wife, mother, and friend had convinced her that she was psychologically stable, but she feared her family's old perceptions of her as "sick" would be proven right.

She felt obligated to see Dr. Hicks, and their first session confirmed her worst fears. He was formal and cold, saying almost nothing while Jane spilled her guts out and bawled. He asked few questions and gave no sign that he empathized in the slightest with her pain. After about a half hour, he proceeded to sum up, saying that she was obviously depressed, adding that her depression was partly due to the loss of her husband but more so due to her past serious problems. He prescribed a daily antidepressant and told her to come back in a couple of weeks.

Dr. Hicks told Tim that Jane was a difficult patient. The psychiatric session felt to Jane as if Tim had imposed it as punishment for her years of bad behavior. In the midst of her mourning, the old feelings of being a bad girl and a failure had returned.

Tim's response to Jane was "Stop feeling so sorry for yourself!" He resented his wayward sister and was angry that she disliked Dr. Hicks. When his wife wanted to invite Jane's daughters over, he lost it. He'd anointed himself as *the* authority in the Whyllie family, and he cowed the others.

Ironically, the more Jane grieved, the less sympathy she seemed to receive from those closest to her (a paradox called "concentric circles of disbelief"). She felt her hard-won respect in the eyes of others was ebbing away. As if losing Sam weren't enough, she was fearful of becoming an outcast again. She was doubting the personal gains she'd made, and she wondered if Tim was right about her.

After a few weeks on the medication Dr. Hicks had prescribed, she'd experienced no respite from sadness and pessimism, and she feared she'd never experience happiness again. For the sake of her children, she felt she had to get rid of the feelings of deep pain, which she could feel in the pit of her stomach.

When Tim blurted out, "Get a life! You can't look even after your girls!" he'd gone too far. Even in her despair, Jane was profoundly responsible for her daughters. She loved them more than anything in the world, especially with Sam gone.

"You arrogant bastard!" she exploded.

But what if her brother was right? She felt her life imploding, but Tim's nastiness had energized her. She realized *she* had to turn things around, *she* had to regain her life, and *she* had to protect her kids. It was up to her and no one else. "If I lost my children ..." She couldn't finish the thought. She was sure she heard Sam saying to her, "Jane, you can do it!" Sam would want her to be strong and happy, the best possible mother to their daughters.

A friend suggested an older psychologist, Dr. Sarah Neufeld. In contrast to her last experience, this soft-spoken therapist listened intently. She commented that she recognized Jane's pain and explained that Jane's current fears had to do with the years of criticism she'd heard, her loss of control, and her low self-esteem. With the terrible loss of Sam, she felt sorrowful and isolated; she was afraid of not being a good mom and of regressing.

Dr. Neufeld reminded Jane how far she'd come. Sam would have wanted her to move forward, and her children needed her attention and love, but mostly, Jane needed to recover for the sake of her own health and happiness. Dr. Neufeld discontinued the antidepressant because it was not effective, but she spoke about the possibility of another medication, if necessary.

She stressed that Jane had already proven her resilience; she had turned her life around, and she could do it again. Jane sat up and said assertively, "I *will* get back on my feet!"

Jane chose a life-affirming path. She mustered her strength for her daughters, for Sam, and for herself. Whenever she asked herself, "What would Sam want me to do?" the answers came more easily. She knew she was a good and responsible mother: she loved her daughters with an intensity that scared her, knowing they represented a bridge to a kind of personal salvation, as Sam did. With her improved mood, the girls seemed to become lighter and energized.

Over the next months, Jane was pleasantly surprised to find the reawakening of her joie de vivre. Amanda and Robin were healthy and thriving in high school and active in sports and with friends. Jane rekindled friendships with girlfriends from her time with Sam and had a part-time job in a marketing firm—ironically, thanks to her father.

Her family and friends noticed the return of her positive energy. She was at relative peace with herself, feeling grounded for the first time since Sam's death.

In the decade since Sam had died, Jane hadn't dated once. She wasn't that interested, and dating had a connotation of the reckless lifestyle she'd indulged in years ago. She'd closed the door on that sensual scrum, but what if she still had those tendencies deep within her?

The Parody of Psychotherapy

Jane's appointment with Dr. Hicks was terrible. She had been fearful about psychiatry, but pushed by her brother, she went. In that meeting, Dr. Hicks was disrespectful and showed little interest, clinical acumen, or empathy. He barely inquired about her personal situation, feeling he already knew she'd had a troubled past. He made no recommendations for psychotherapy and said nothing about the indications or potential side effects of the medication he prescribed. He was the opposite of what a good psychiatrist should be.

Luckily, in Jane's next experience with psychotherapy, Dr. Neufeld showed interest, respect, compassion, empathy, and responsibility to her patient, all of which are crucial attributes for a good psychotherapist.

Jane worked on these issues with Sarah Neufeld with a sense of urgency, and the psychotherapy was invaluable to her. The progress she'd made since she met Sam was real and profound. Jane wasn't vulnerable to the seductions of la dolce vita; she knew she would never go that route again. Her past was like a surreal part of someone else's life.

In her midfifties, Jane found herself in a new situation. Her parents were now in their late seventies, and Bruce was drinking again, which usually led to anger. Sally handled his meltdowns by reminding him that he was a "drunken old fool." She went about her activities with her friends and especially her dear grandchildren, on whom she doted. Jane supported Sally in not putting up with Bruce's abuse but decided to finally confront her father.

Jane asked to speak with Bruce in private, and he was at first evasive and surly. He was actually frightened, but Jane's soft manner placated him. She spoke quietly, recalling the past sad times and conflicts they'd had. As was often the case, his bravado and pomposity were a facade: Bruce cried, begging her forgiveness for the way he treated her and recalling his diatribes at her, and he mentioned "mistakes." Neither of them referred to his seductive comments to her as a teenager, nor did they mention Uncle Hughie, but it was clear to both what they were discussing.

Jane apologized to her dad for her "crazy ways" as a young woman. They spoke for hours, holding hands and weeping. Bruce asked his daughter for help in making amends to her and Sally. Jane, of all people, was becoming the confidante and peacemaker for her parents.

Life's inevitable changes arrived, sometimes unwanted. Tim and his wife, Martha, were engaged in a bitter divorce. Jane's sister, Mary, had recently developed debilitating symptoms pointing to an anti-immune disorder. One of Jane's closest friends developed serious ovarian cancer. The onslaught of these problems of friends and family made Jane more aware of her own mortality. She felt vulnerable to the sudden changes in people's lives and wanted first to hug her kids, to protect them from life's difficulties.

Yet she recognized how convoluted all lives were and knew she was not alone. "No one is immune," she said. She knew how far she'd come and recognized the incongruity that she was now a helper and healer after being a so-called failure for so long. She spoke of this ruefully yet with charm, humor, maturity, and wisdom.

Jane's seemingly new personality and role in life felt authentic, natural. Family and friends were turning to Jane, of all people, in their hours of need, and she was able to reach out with warmth and empathy. Jane was a model of nurturance and stability. "I went from being the Whore of Babylon to a loving mother and a woman with her feet on the ground," she said.

The Four Bs

When a person has a negative sense of being, that negativity colors everything. Life is a painful exercise of self-reinforcing self-loathing, and no end appears possible. Jane suffered from a negative self-image, starting in her early childhood, and that made her susceptible to sexual exploitation and an inability to believe in anything positive in life. She also felt no sense of belonging within her family, and she embraced an absolute cynicism regarding benevolence. In her youth, she felt there was no such thing.

Then she met Sam, and everything changed. Love can be a true healing power. It can bring about change that seemed impossible beforehand. Sam's death devastated her, shaking her beliefs and her feeling of belonging. Only the love of her children, her sense of benevolence, and a skilled therapist kept her from going right over the edge. The four Bs played a major role in Jane's life, and they still do.

Being

"I feel grounded," Jane told me. Jane can finally look at herself in the mirror and see a reflection of someone she genuinely likes. She sees an older, wise person with scars and flaws, and she can certainly suggest areas for improvement, but she doesn't disparage herself and doesn't want cosmetic or emotional reconstruction. There is no guile, no mask; she doesn't wish to be someone or somewhere else. By embracing herself, she is more tolerant and empathic to those around her.

Belonging

"I can now say I have loved, and I've been loved," she said. But before she met Sam, Jane could not have uttered those important words. The truth was that she was ready. Jane would not have fallen in love with a "nerd" like Sam if she hadn't been dissatisfied and searching for something meaningful. She was on a desperate search for herself yet had felt alone in a crowd for years. She wanted a loving, meaningful relationship, and Sam and her kids released her natural ability to love, which had been locked up within her.

She came to feel that she was now an important part of many people's lives, appreciated and loved by them for her intrinsic good-ness. This essence of Jane had, in fact, always been a central part of her, but nobody had seen it, and neither had she. Her process of positive blossoming took many years and actually needed the hard knocks she endured, the falling in love with Sam, their children, and therapy to evolve into this natural maternal presence, belonging to many.

Believing

Jane told me, "I have an abiding faith in my values, and I feel guided by Sam's spirit. I don't know if there is a God, but I do feel that there is some force for goodness." Jane attributes her values and feelings of spirituality to Sam's ethereal guidance. But she became an earth mother because of her own strong core values long before meeting Sam and after he passed on. Her belief in a force of goodness emanated from deep within her.

Benevolence

"I know that my children, family, and friends think I've been a source of positive energy in their lives," Jane said. After years of scorn from her family, exploitation by men, and self-rejection, Jane, in her middle years, returned to her core. She has had a positive effect on the lives of many people, who appreciate, need, and love her.

Resilience

Jane evolved from a so-called bad girl into a courtesan and femme fatal and finally into a nurturer and earth mother. Many rejected her when she was a child and adolescent, then hungry men desired her, and her family and friends ultimately needed her as an intimate source of caring and bonding. Even her immediate family first scoffed at these changes they were witnessing, disbelieving what they were seeing with their own eyes.

Jane herself had difficulty putting this all together, but she has no doubts about the genuine nature of her progression. She knows how fulfilled and enhanced she feels as a mother, widow, daughter, sister, and close friend. She is the embodiment of resilience.

Emotional Footprint

I have no doubt that Jane has left a positive emotional footprint, but if tragedy had struck and she had died earlier in her life, her emotional footprint would have been seen as a complex admixture of positive and negative.

In her early life, Jane "lived down" to her poor self-image and the criticism of others. She could have ended up a trophy wife of a wealthy man, but her inner core of caring served as a compass for self-preservation and protected her from a lonely life. After her renaissance with Sam and since that time, her generosity of spirit and closeness to others ensured that others will remember her for her legacy of compassion and benevolence. This once pariah and seductress will leave a wonderful, positive emotional footprint.

She admits, with humility, that she is aware that she emanates warmth to others. But the contrast between her early years of seeming selfishness and the love she now bestows on others is difficult for her to grasp. "But you know," she says, "my heart was always the same."

5

William Nguyen

The Observer

Seated across the aisle from you is a middle-aged Asian couple. They're both dressed nicely but conservatively. You hear them talking seriously in low voices above the din of the train, but you can't understand the language they are speaking. The man, probably the husband, looks sad. His deep brown eyes glisten with tears about to stream freely down his cheeks, and you can see he's holding his emotions in check. His wife is holding his hands in hers, strength emanating from her.

You don't want to stare, so you look straight ahead, leaning back against the headrest and you wonder how many people have leaned on that same headrest. You hope that the cleaning crew cleans the seats, but you doubt it. Your mind focuses on the couple across from you, and you wonder if and how they came from a foreign land to pursue their American dream.

The Riders

The air in Saigon that day was so hot and humid that it was hard to breathe, and the mood was also heavy and ominous. It was April 30, 1975, when the Vietnam War ended chaotically after eight years of brutal conflict. Live television showed scenes of panic and confusion; countless noisy, smoky helicopters descended, and thousands of terrified Vietnamese citizens and hundreds of desperate American civilians and military personnel struggled to get on a flight in the rushed evacuation (Operation Precious Wind). Those left behind despaired, not knowing their future, fearing reeducation camps, prisons, or worse.

On that day, Captain William ("Vie^n") Nguyen, a pilot for the South Vietnamese Air Force, acted to save his family and himself.

Before the war, William and his wife, Thao, had lived pleasant lives. They, their five children, and William's mother, Hahn, shared a large home in an upper-middle-class neighborhood in Saigon. The gregarious William often wore his air force leather jacket, enjoying admiring glances at his strutting *Top Gun* appearance. He couldn't wait to leave the air force as soon as his five years of service were over, because had ambitious dreams of a career in business. Thao was more reserved and just wanted to be with their large family.

Over generations, Vietnam had experienced bitter wars with China and France, when the country was divided into North and South Vietnam. The early 1960s were a period of relative calm. While there were fractious politics and some military skirmishes, the lives of the Nguyen family were unaffected.

William and Thao were typical young parents, looking forward to their future and the success of their children. Both came from families that had been in Saigon for generations; they'd gone to school there and had large extended families and good friends. They loved Vietnam: the culture and colors, the food and aromas, the people and their language. They would never consider leaving the homeland.

Reality interfered with their dreams. The Vietnam War started in earnest in the midsixties, and William was redrafted as a fighter pilot.

For a while, their family routines remained unchanged except for more worrying and vigilance. But within a couple of years, the war came up close and personal, upending their lives.

Everyday living, routine chores, and errands became difficult and frightening. The family lived increasingly under siege, with armed guards stationed at the front of their house. Schools were closed, and Thao added teaching her children to her responsibilities. Their household grew extensively, including more family and close friends, and food was in short supply. William was gone for weeks at a time, but he managed—by contacts with Americans and bribery of South Vietnamese officials—to provide some extra food and clothing. The Nguyens and their boarders seldom ventured outside, where danger lurked and few could be trusted.

William was preoccupied with their safety, intensely committed to getting them out of the war zone, but Thao was afraid her children would be killed in any escape attempt, and she wouldn't hear of leaving her beloved Vietnam.

William shed his *Top Gun* stance and was disillusioned with the emotional poison and the destruction of the war, which had escalated into a mass conflagration with thousands of American troops propping up a corrupt South Vietnamese regime.

The Nguyen family suffered: two of the children were having panic attacks, another was sad, and none of them was interested in learning. If anyone got sick, there were few doctors, and getting to a hospital involved a treacherous journey. They experienced grinding hunger and fear, a terrible combination. Thao was the family's anchor, keeping everything together at home, while William was obsessed with plans for escape. He knew the layout of the local air base, including the whereabouts of planes and the armed guards, and he spent countless hours rehearsing the escape in his mind. At great cost, he bribed the guards at the air base.

On that day, he was ready. The choice was clear: life or death, now or never. William commandeered an F-111 jet on the base; packed it with Thao, his five children, his elderly mother, and relatives and friends; and flew away from the oncoming enemy and, sadly, from their beloved homeland. That same day, Saigon fell to the North Vietnamese

Army and the Viet Cong. The war over, they were safe, but for the Nguyens, there were no celebrations.

They landed two hours later at a military base close to Suvarnabhumi International Airport in Bangkok, Thailand, where they were promptly taken into custody. Within an hour, the planeload of human cargo was trucked at gunpoint to a detention center three hours north in Chiang Mai. Relieved of their money and valuables, they were placed in barracks behind barbed wire, forced to sleep on cots in plywood dorms and eat rice, soup, and vegetables. At least the children were safe, and they heard no sounds of artillery.

Eighteen hard months later, they were informed that they and a few hundred "boat people" from Vietnam would be released with all charges dropped. The US embassy provided modest sums of money, but the guards made it clear that they would have to be paid in order for the release orders to stand.

The detainees were given a choice of countries where they could settle, and for William, it was a no-brainer: "I fought for them, suffered for them; now I want part of the American dream." He had a distant cousin in Los Angeles and was excited, but his family was more dubious, fearful of the American reality. While America might have been the land of opportunity, they had heard it was a land of racism and violence.

William had saved them from a horrible fate in Vietnam, so in spite of their misgivings, his wishes prevailed. Within three weeks, the entire Nguyen family found themselves on a military transport plane bound for Los Angeles.

Adjusting to the United States was not easy. After a few weeks with William's cousin in LA, the Nguyens moved to a working-class area in East Los Angeles. The children were plunked in neighborhood public schools, knowing no one, speaking no English, and looking different from the other students. Some kids were friendly, some held back because of difficulty communicating, and a few teased or bullied.

William's mother, Hahn, worked in a coin laundry, cleaning and selling soap and incidentals for which she received occasional tips. Thao got a job as a cook in a Vietnamese "greasy-spoon" restaurant in a small strip mall, working long hours and receiving a pittance from

Quest for Betterment

The comfort, security, and love in people's homes enhances their lives, if they are lucky enough to have these crucial elements of living. However, over the millennia, thousands have wandered from their homes for a variety of reasons. On foot at first, then on horseback (or on camels, caribou, oxen, or donkeys), later by carts and boats, and then in fuel-propelled vehicles on land, sea, and air, exploratory curiosity (wanderlust) has always characterized our species.

But aside from geographic curiosity, the vast majority of these voyagers have left hearth and home to escape danger and to search for a better and safer way of life.

Exploitation and threats have contributed to migration, as have abject poverty and fear. Safety, economic opportunities, and better health and education for children have also been forces for immigration, especially to the United States. Millions of refugees and citizens from hundreds of other countries have sought the American dream and continue to do so. This country's shores have always beckoned, and the Statue of Liberty has served as a beacon of hope for immigrants and refugees the world over.

the owners. Ambitious *Top Gun* William got a job as an attendant in an upscale health club, cleaning, handing out towels to members, picking up their trash, being ignored, and facing occasional verbal abuse.

William had some facility with English, which he had picked up in the air force. Thao, the linchpin of the family, learned almost no English, because she said, "I don't want to!" She seldom ventured outside her home or the small restaurant kitchen. She was proud of her identity as a Vietnamese citizen, and she was the one family member who kept her Vietnamese first name in America. Yet she maintained a spirit of positive energy and grace that was enormously helpful to the family.

The customs of their new homeland sometimes proved difficult for William and Thao. The children had been obedient when they'd lived in Vietnam, but immersed in American schools, they'd picked up English easily, as well as "lip," or an attitude. Their new assertiveness unnerved William.

He and Thao were tied to Old World family values, and they saw their children's behaviors as disrespectful. When William felt them questioning his authority, he would take a tough stance, which made his children indignant and argumentative.

The unassuming Thao was able to stem these roiling feelings with her nurturance and understanding, but she could be demanding and tough. They might argue with their dad, but Mom was not to be trifled with. They respected her for her natural dignity and grace as well as her strength. They wouldn't dare give her lip.

The Immigrant Experience

Most of us are descendants of immigrants, either recent or long past. While each immigrant's story is unique, the process of leaving a homeland and being thrust into a new way of life can be daunting. When poverty, little education, a new language, and few marketable skills complicate this experience, immigrants can feel invisible and often toil in poorly paid jobs.

Even if they have some resources, novel sounds, signs, dress, foods, values, and customs that are jarringly different confront them. They have to relearn social behaviors taken for granted, such as voice tone, eye contact, hand gestures, and the distance between people.

Immigrants tend to gather in familiar groups—family, ethnic, and racial clans. Working, playing, and relaxing among familiar people is comfortable. The separation of cultures dissipates after a generation or two, but melting pots go only so far; ethnic communities exist in all countries with diverse cultures and immigrants. People gravitate to those with common roots and traditions, and they experience a sense of belonging.

Anti-immigrant attitudes dissipate with personal experiences with newcomers. Contacts during pleasant times (e.g., meals, parties, or sports events) and during stressful times (e.g., losses, illnesses, or accidents) enlighten and educate people about their similarities. So-called foreigners, it turns out, are just like us.

Immigrants enhance our society. Immigrants have enriched our culture, music, business, sports, science, education, industries, cuisine, and more, just like the contributions your forebears (or you) made.

As the Nguyens settled into a comfort zone of familiar routines, even Thao and William began to relax.

Then a calamity occurred: William's mother, Hahn, was working alone one evening in the Laundromat, when an armed young hoodlum entered and demanded cash. She quickly gave him all she had: a few scrunched dollar bills. The thug, unhappy with the paltry amount, yelled obscenities and beat her with his handgun. A passerby across the street witnessed this horrific event and called 911.

The police were there in minutes but were too late to save her. Beloved Grandmother Hahn Nguyen, who had been a central part of their lives, died in an ambulance on the way to the hospital. Her killer, probably high on drugs, vanished.

The Nguyens had seen brutality during the war, but this terrible crime and the loss of their mother and grandmother brought unbelievable agony. William felt betrayed by America. The cruel irony of having escaped a war zone to save his family by dragging them to America only to have his mother viciously murdered weighed heavily on him. The family was paralyzed and wanted vengeance. There was to be no avenging, and the grief was unbearable.

Comfort eventually came from a number of sources; their deep family bonds and the memory of their grandmother gave them strength. Thao reminded them, "What would Hahn want from us?"

William's family, the local Vietnamese community, and a couple of nearby church congregations supported them in their grief. At William's work, club staff and members expressed their sympathy; a few went out of their way to hug him. Thao's bosses at the restaurant treated her with some softness and gave her a few days off.

They felt touched by the generosity of neighbors, a mixed group of Caucasians, African Americans, and Hispanics, who brought over flowers and food. This outpouring of warmth from people they barely knew moved them.

A few months after Hahn was buried, the Nguyens moved to another area, far from the Laundromat. Within a couple of years, the five Nguyen children had adapted well to their new country and way of life. The oldest, Bob (Bao), was a nineteen-year-old freshman in college; the next three—Hugh (Huy), seventeen, Ann (Anh), fifteen, and May (Mai), fourteen—were in high school; and Thomas (Tha'nh) was in junior high. They were all above-average students, and they enjoyed participating in sports and music with Caucasian Americans, but they gravitated to the Vietnamese community.

Hahn's death made their family ties even stronger and gave them confidence in their heritage. While they applied for American citizenship, they remained committed to their Vietnamese identity.

William's old dreams of being a businessman received the impetus he needed from Thao. Her cooking at the restaurant was so good that it had become popular, but when the owners offered her a meager raise after years of strenuous labor, it was too little too late.

Thao proposed to William that they open their own Vietnamese restaurant. "Only better and more successful," she said.

Thao's vote of confidence excited William; she appreciated his people skills and strength of character. With her encouragement and permission, money borrowed from the bank, and loans from two club members, he jumped to the challenge, enthusiastic about finally having his own business. He had great plans for the restaurant—where it would be, what the décor would look like, whom he'd hire—but Thao laid down the law: "We will do this, Vi^en, but only if it is run by our family. We will choose the location and decor together. You and Bao will do the hiring together. You and I will do the finances, you will be the maitre d', the children will be the waiters, and I will be the cook."

William was taken aback but was actually calmed and comforted by her strength. She'd given him his marching orders, and as a military man, he had to obey. He recognized that Thao was the linchpin and essence of their family. The Nguyen marriage facade followed the Vietnamese tradition of the husband leading, and they were comfortable with their version, with Thao as behind-the-scenes overseer and William as the front man. The symbolism of tradition was important, and Thao wanted William to feel respected.

Their new restaurant, called Hahn's Vietnam, was located in a middle-class neighborhood close to a major freeway. The whole family pitched in to renovate the empty leased space and transform it into a modern, softly lit, warm place with upholstered booths, plants, an aquarium tank, and Vietnamese art adorning the walls. The kitchen remained small and tucked away in back, a private and personal space that Thao preferred. She remained the unseen force in the restaurant, just as she was in the family.

The first few months after Hahn's opened its doors were agonizingly slow. William was worried sick: he couldn't sleep, had no appetite, and was losing weight. He contemplated going back to the club for off-hour work. They sent neighborhood modest flyers and bought local newspaper ads, to no avail. The bank was calling in its loans, as were the two unhappy club investors. They tried incentives, such as special meal deals and coupons, but nothing worked, and they began to consider bankruptcy, which they felt would be humiliating.

The Nguyen children also worried about the restaurant but were more concerned about their parents. Bob, now twenty-five, called his siblings together for a private meeting on a Tuesday evening (their slowest night) while William and Thao were at the restaurant. At the meeting, they discussed their parents' sadness and what they could do to help. The prospect of being saddled with debt weighed heavily on them. Bob was their leader. "This is about Mom and Dad, their health, and the memory of Hahn. We have to help," he said.

They all took added jobs in addition to their schoolwork and work at the restaurant, and they cut back on other activities. Bob, who was in graduate school pursuing an MBA, took a job as a copyeditor at a local newspaper. Hugh, who was working as a telemarketer, increased his hours. Ann and May, both in college, worked for a catering company at parties and events, and Thomas, a high-school senior, worked as a salesclerk in a sporting goods store.

The kids remained loving and diligent, but their absences from home made Thao and William suspicious; they worried that the children were getting into drugs or other problematic behaviors in America.

By nature an optimist, William felt as if he were living under a dark cloud, expecting the worst. Even Thao said, "Maybe we should close the restaurant and go back to Vietnam." Coming from her, these words seemed even more ominous. They'd had enough of the financial hemorrhaging, the constant worry, and waiting for the inevitable end of their American dream.

The children saw this desperation and offered to work even harder to help keep Hahn's afloat. The children's dedication brought William and Thao to tears; they felt as if they'd failed their children. William was merciless in criticizing himself. "I was a total loser, as you Americans call it," he said years later.

Another twist of fate ensued. Just as they were about to let Hahn's Vietnam fail, seventeen months after opening its doors, the Nguyens detected a quickening of Hahn's pulse. More customers were coming through its doors, first a trickle and then a stream—an unmistakable trend.

Word-of-mouth reviews were the initial impetus; delighted customers spread the news that the cuisine was exquisite and the atmosphere serene. Strong reviews followed in the daily newspapers and other media, and then the local social networks put the word out: Thao Nguyen was a genius chef, William Nguyen was a great host, and the waitstaff, the Nguyen offspring, were terrific. By about the time of their new year (Tet), that stream had become a flowing river. Hahn's Vietnam had arrived.

Walking into the restaurant today, nineteen years after it opened its doors, fills visitors with sensory pleasures. The Nguyens have redone the decor, but the same warm atmosphere greets everyone, including wafting aromas of Vietnamese cuisine with French touches. Hahn's now seats about 130 diners when full, which is most lunchtimes and evenings, and their take-out business is huge. Awards and laudatory newspaper and magazine articles adorn a corner wall.

William is still at the front, welcoming diners with warm smiles, while Thao is still unseen in a somewhat-enlarged kitchen, creating her culinary delights, but now with a staff of three sous-chefs (who do exactly as she says). The five college-educated Nguyen offspring work some evenings in the restaurant when not at their jobs or with their families. Two nephews from Canada, a niece from Holland, and another niece from LA have joined the Nguyens and work at Hahn's.

William, at sixty-five, continues working and listening to the admonitions and advice of Thao. The Nguyens are a close family, and Thao and William see their children and seven grandchildren regularly. William is an avid tennis player and a popular member of the club where he was a locker-room attendant many years ago.

He and Thao have been back to Vietnam three times in the past ten years, and they've reconnected with the land they left behind so dramatically almost forty years ago. William has promised Thao that when he retires, they will spend at least half of each year in Vietnam. His retirement income will be modest, but given the exchange rates of the dollar and the Vietnamese dong and the different costs of living, they should be able to afford a small villa and even a couple of servants. They are looking at properties outside of Ho Chi Min City (their beloved Saigon).

The Four Bs

William's sense of being first came from his commitment to duty in the military, but it also came from his commitment to family. In fact, without that commitment, he would have been adrift, and it's unlikely that he would have been able to orchestrate the escape from Saigon. Yet when William escaped with his family, he lost his sense of belonging. After he arrived in the United States, his loneliness and isolation increased. He'd lost his sense of being, belonging, and believing. Any vestiges of benevolence left within him began to fade into oblivion as the family's hardships worsened.

In short, William lost his faith, and it plunged all the other four Bs into great turmoil, submerging them in the breaking surf of adversity. What finally turned things around was the cohesive family unit he and his wife had built, even as the kids were Americanized and less inclined to toe the line in terms of the values of the Old Country. The restaurant represented a wholesale investment in believing, and it also created a true bond, a sense of belonging, within the family and within the larger community as a whole. William was remarkably resilient, especially when it mattered most. It is like that for many people. When the chips are down, that's when you'll really see what you're made of, and chances are that you won't be disappointed.

Being

William's long journey wasn't easy, and there have been sorrows and trials along the way, but he has reached a point in his life where he is grateful for every aspect of his existence. He feels immense pride that he was able to save his family from the horrors of the war at their doorstep decades ago, and he is grateful to Thao, whom he knows enabled his accomplishments; his healthy and loving children; and his adopted land.

He knows he has imperfections and faults, but perhaps he needed his early *Top Gun* bravado to overcome the obstacles thrown at him by the war and life's subsequent tough circumstances.

In his later years, he became more tolerant of others and himself and more at ease. He is comfortable in his skin, having achieved a grounded sense of being.

Belonging

William is surrounded by his close, loving family, now expanded with grown children, their spouses, and his and Thao's grandchildren, all of whom live relatively close by, in the Vietnamese tradition. There is deep, mutual caring in the family, allowing a feeling of comfort and acceptance.

His tennis friends and a few Vietnamese expats complete his most intimate circles, and in all of these relationships, he experiences warmth and sharing; they all help each other in times of celebration and in times of difficulty. Mainly, he feels acceptance, comfort, and security, which is the epitome of belonging.

Believing

William was brought up in mixed Catholic and Buddhist traditions, neither of which was imposed on him in a doctrinaire manner. He and Thao celebrate Christmas, New Year's, and Tet as well as a few other mixed holiday rituals with their family. They are not churchgoers, but both believe in the ultimate power of a God of some sort. They also live according to the simple principles and values of hard work, education, and respect for others, which guide their day-to-day lives.

Benevolence

The Nguyen family all grew up in an atmosphere of generosity and caring for others. The neighbors, church members, and perfect strangers who visited and helped during their mourning when Grandmother Hahn was killed represented the kind of behavior they themselves extolled and demonstrated. In Vietnam and during their escape, many others in their community became part of their household and family. They are genuinely kind, generous people, contributing to others and having respectful interactions in their everyday lives.

Resilience

How do we describe a man who has lived in a war-ravaged country, protected his large family from serious threats, escaped, lived with them in a sparse foreign refugee camp for two years, immigrated with no money to America, worked menial jobs for low pay, endured his mother's murder, and started a restaurant that was failing despite arduous work and was on the verge of closing?

Well, I describe William Nguyen as a resilient soul.

This military man and fighter pilot was not going to allow the setbacks of life to defeat him. He dug his heels in, jutted his jaw, and tried that much harder to overcome his painful reverses. He showed courage, perseverance, commitment, dedication, a protective instinct, and belief in himself and others.

Emotional Footprint

William and Thao believe in simple credos: education, work, the primacy of family and loved ones, and mutual help and respect for others. This has been the sine qua non of their existence, and those they have touched even superficially or who have had social or business dealings with them have almost invariably walked away with smiles on their faces.

It should be obvious that William's aggregate emotional footprint is overwhelmingly positive.

6

Alexander Secomb

The Observer

Y ou feel restless and decide to go to the restroom. You get up from your seat, carefully balancing against the swaying motion of the train, and you make your way toward the rear of the car. As the train rounds a curve, you inadvertently bump into the shoulder of an older gentleman wearing a sports jacket and a tie. He's wearing plastic-rimmed black glasses that distort his eyes, his gray-streaked dark hair is thinning, and his face shows the erosion of time in the form of creases on his cheeks that furrow into distinct frown lines.

"Sorry," you say as you grab the overhead baggage rack to keep from falling.

The man, who looks professorial, lowers the journal he's reading and glares at you over the top of his glasses. "Just watch where you're going, okay?"

You glare back at him. There is no reason for him to get uppity, and you mirror the annoyance he shows you. The guy is apparently an unpleasant human being, a real jerk.

"Get a life," you mumble to yourself, and you continue down the car to the restroom. You close the door and check yourself in the mirror. The job interview has you feeling nervous, and you try not to think about it. As you leave, you pass that irritable jerk, and you size him up. He looks like a professor and you can see by the journal he's reading that his field must be math or maybe physics. He seems like an uptight, rigid, demanding guy; you don't like him.

You're careful not to touch him on your way by, though you're tempted to. But why make trouble when you don't have to? Sooner or later, trouble finds us of its own accord. As you sit down again, you think about the encounter. The antipathy recedes, and you wonder why people act in certain weird ways. It must be, you think, that it's about what happens in someone's life and how the person responds to events in and out of appreciable control. You wonder about your own life and how you got to be the way you are, and then you look out the window. Sometimes introspection just doesn't cut it. Sometimes it's easier to run away, even if it's just in your mind. Sometimes being an ostrich is the best way to go—until it isn't.

The Rider

Alexander Secomb had always been smug about his life and himself. He was a successful professor of physics who lived with his wife, Tanya, and his three children in a large home near the downtown university campus, where he could bike to his office at the High Energy Physics Research Institute (HEPRI). Their privileged life-style gave him some pleasure, but it was more important to him that others ("the gallery," he called them) envy the Secombs' idyllic life. However, they didn't.

Alexander was a loner, uncomfortable and impatient with others. He and Tanya socialized with friends of hers, but he had few personal friends. He was demanding of others to the point of being abrasive. He was cerebral rather than emotional, preferring his own company to that of anyone else. Colleagues abroad respected him, but colleagues at the institute avoided him.

Alexander came from modest and sad beginnings. His parents died in an automobile accident when he was fourteen. He and his younger brother, Jerrold, went to live with their father's brother and his wife, who had no children. They were welcome there but always felt like visitors.

Alexander was a brilliant student, and he was important to the family since Jerrold had been diagnosed at birth with cerebral palsy. His drive to achieve became even stronger after the tragic loss of his parents. He had an edge to him and could be impatient and overly assertive, frequently offending others. He pushed himself to succeed, but he wanted to be better than others. He received his PhD in theoretical physics at the young age of twenty-four, congratulated but not with affection.

The Secomb family's stability was shaken early. Alexander was in Geneva for a physics conference where he was a featured speaker, presenting his latest research. There he met and had an affair with a young graduate student at Basle University, who was in awe and soon in bed with this academic star.

When Alexander returned from the conference, Tanya sensed something was different in their relationship, but she didn't suspect her husband of an affair. A colleague at HEPRI who had attended the conference told Tanya about the tryst. "I care for you, and I don't want you to get hurt," he said, hurting her in the guise of being helpful.

Alexander's plea that it was "only a one-night stand" pained and infuriated Tanya. His depiction of a perfect marriage was a sham.

There were two separations over a few months after Tanya insisted that he move out, each lasting a few weeks in which the family was beset with confusion and melancholy. Many months of marital counseling sessions followed these separations. The Secombs regrouped, emotionally bruised, no longer as joyful or loving and, to be sure, not as trusting.

Their oldest child, Andrea, was bright and strong-willed, often arguing with Alexander, standing up for herself and her siblings. She experimented with pot and alcohol in her early teens and dated a couple of older boys, which infuriated her dad, who wanted the semblance of perfection from his children. Andrea marched to the beat of her own drummer, but Alexander couldn't get her rhythm.

Their middle child, Tamara, developed a rare illness (lymphade-nopathy) that caused an oozing of fluid from her lymph system, and as a result, her legs swelled enormously, greatly impairing her mobility. It took years of medication and physiotherapy to improve this condition. Somehow, however, Tamara was a resilient soul, excelling in school, having many friends, and projecting an air of happiness. Tanya called her "our Miss Sunshine."

Then there was their baby—their son, Joshua—the apple of his father's eye. Alexander adored his youngest child from the day he was born, saying Joshua was the perfect child. For a while, Joshua lived up to that description: he was attractive, scholarly, athletic, and engaging. Andrea and Tamara loved their younger brother but teased, with some bite, "Joshua is on a pedestal."

Alexander was successful in his research, but he disdained his colleagues at HEPRI. The culture there was one of scholarly ferment, which competition and nasty one-upmanship sometimes overshadowed. There were constant squabbles and backbiting among this "rarefied collective of brains," as Alexander called them. Tanya accurately likened it to a girls' high-school class, with its cliques and conflicts. While he said it was a toxic culture, he was convinced he played no role in that toxicity, but his colleagues saw Alexander as an arrogant lone wolf whose sense of entitlement and disdain was destructive to everyone.

Tanya saw this unpleasant side of Alexander usually when events were not going exactly as he had planned, and nothing seemed to bother him more than that. Even a minor alteration in plans could set him off. When he sensed obstacles in his expected seamless path, Alexander seemed to take on a new personality and a new face: it became dark, his eyes squinted into a focused glare, and his veins bulged, showing cold anger and even rage. He frightened Tanya sometimes ("Who *is* this man?" she recalled thinking), but she said nothing to anyone.

True to her generation, Tanya decided to grin and bear it. In spite of Alexander's fling and his difficult personality, she loved him. And with children, a mortgage, reputations, and responsibilities, what was she to do? Toss it all? Jeopardize her children's lives? She held on to images of their days of courtship and early marriage, wishing, hoping the "real

Alexander" would return. Tanya felt trapped. Still, she loved and waited.

Alexander also felt trapped. He was unhappy in the emotional scrum at work and considered leaving HESPRI. But how could he give up his tenured post, his travel, and his reputation? He didn't want to sully his all-important image. He tried to convince himself that people had to live with the bad and the good. "These are the vicissitudes of life, aren't they? I just had to hold the fort."

By putting Josh on a pedestal, Alexander was pressuring his son to live up to his expectations, but Josh wasn't driven like his father, and he resented being pushed and even felt bullied. He avoided private talks with his dad because he usually felt worse afterward. Alexander was obsessed with his son's success and was angry that Josh wasn't committed to "making it." The fact that he was doing well in school and was easygoing and popular was irrelevant to Alexander.

Who Is My Spouse?

Tanya is not the first spouse to look at her mate of longstanding and wonder if she really knows that person. The same individual whom she fell in love with and shared intimacy, children, laughter, and tears with over so many moons was often a stranger. We've all seen examples of scoundrels publicly exposed, yet their spouses have professed ignorance of their mates' behaviors.

We all want to look our best, presenting positive facades to conceal our defects. We have complex personalities, and we show different faces in different situations. We are presumably our most authentic selves at home, where we can relax, but as Tanya put it, "It ain't necessarily so."

Many marriages of longstanding are mutually fulfilling, but in others, an implicit social contract exists, in which the partners maintain a public and private kind of peace treaty, with little meaningful sharing and intimacy. They live in parallel under one roof, perhaps even sharing a bed, with little or no physical or emotional contact. The title of Hugh MacLennan's novel Two Solitudes captures that superficial closeness and intimate estrangement.

As Josh got older, Alexander had another concern: although Josh hung out with a warm group of male and female students, there were no hints of any romantic interest, unlike with some of his friends. Tanya convinced Alexander that Josh would soon find the right girl and be swept off his feet, but privately and intuitively, she harbored other thoughts.

In his junior year of college, Joshua told Tanya that he wanted to take some time off, perhaps to do something different for a while. She was surprised since he was on the honor roll and appeared to be content, but she humored this whim, thinking, *This too shall pass.* She didn't want to ruffle her husband's prickly feathers, so she avoided sharing this news with Alexander.

That whim did not go away. On a weekend home from college, Josh mentioned at a family dinner that he was thinking of taking a leave from his studies and was reconsidering his life's goals. Change in routine was Alexander's least favorite thing, and he glowered at his son but said nothing.

That evening, the family gathered in the den to watch a DVD together. The atmosphere seemed pleasant enough but abruptly changed when Alexander stood up, turned off the TV, and faced Josh. He was so frightening that it appeared an alien poltergeist had overtaken him. The kids hadn't seen this level of anger from him, and even Tanya was taken aback. Alexander seethed for tense moments and then, red-faced, neck veins pulsating, exploded, "What's *wrong* with you? How can you do this?"

The family was quiet and confused. Andrea assumed her usual role, attempting to protect her brother, but her father's furious glare and exclamation of "You, shut up!" silenced her. They all cowered. Joshua, hurt and angry, went to his room. He gathered his clothes and books, walked past the family group, closed the front door behind him, and drove the two hundred miles back to college.

Over the next couple of weeks, the tension remained high, but to salvage a family Christmas, with Tanya's encouragement, Alexander calmed down and agreed to forge the icy stream between him and Josh. They took a walk together to have heart-to-heart and make peace. He apologized to Josh for his outburst a couple of months ago and wanted to learn about his son's plans.

In the late afternoon, with the snow gently falling and fireplaces aglow, Josh was touched by and accepted his dad's apology. He tried to explain what he'd been feeling. School was fine, but he felt incomplete; he'd lost his zest for life. Alexander wanted to rush in and solve (his "M.O."; *modus operandi*); he said he recognized Josh was depressed, and he knew a psychiatrist who could help. But the look on Josh's face made him stop his gratuitous sops.

Alexander and Perfectionism

Alexander was brilliant, obsessed with details, and somewhat of a loner; had poor social skills; and was easily irritated, especially when unexpected change occurred. These personality traits along with his stubbornness, inflexibility, and insistence on perfection in everyone and everything might nowadays get him diagnosed as having a variant of Asperger's syndrome, a complicated and somewhat controversial diagnosis that some feel is overattributed to kids who are different or "nerdy." Asperger's is considered to be a part of the autism spectrum disorders, but it is usually reserved for children and adults who, while better functioning than autistic young people, still have relatively poor social skills, might show remarkable facility with certain subject matter (math, for example), and tend to be loners or "computer geeks or junkies." It is a diagnostic term, but like many others, it is sometimes used to stereotype or demean someone who is more engaged in private intellectual pursuits than social activities.

But Alexander had another attribute that is not typical of Asperger's: he was usually well controlled in social situations, keeping his angry feelings under wraps. As opposed to someone who often erupts in emotional outbursts, Alexander was usually reserved and quiet. He was like a dormant volcano: his moodiness was akin to escaping steam, and his temper was apparent as verbal sparks spewing, but when internal pressure built sufficiently, there were unexpected eruptions of rage, his personal lava.

They walked quietly in the fresh, powdery snow, Alexander listening carefully, waiting for some shoe to drop. "Dad, I think maybe, um, I don't know. I may have fallen in love." Alexander was ecstatic but remained silent. Joshua went on. "The person I love is an assistant professor of anthropology."

Alexander knew the rules against faculty-and-student liaisons, but he was relieved. Alexander controlled himself, pleased with his own sensitivity. He said, "These things happen and can be resolved."

Then Josh blurted out, "Dad, my lover is a guy."

Alexander had long professed ideas of tolerance and acceptance of gays and lesbians as deserving of all rights, but these convictions seemed to evaporate suddenly. He felt as if he had been personally wounded. He knew that he should try to understand, provide sage counsel, and express love and support for his son. He should have, and he wanted to, but he couldn't.

What came out was yet another torrent of outrage: "You're not gay! You're crazy! How can you do this to me?"

They walked home through the unseen winter beauty, avoided touching, both seething, both wounded.

Alexander's fulminations frightened Josh. Alexander's aspirations and needs were thwarted and his rigid personality exploded, enveloping and searing father and son.

The rest of the holiday was awash in platitudes; they did not revisit the elephant in the room. Soon after Josh returned to school, he informed his family that he'd taken a one-year job as an English teacher in South Korea, in a town one hundred kilometers south of Seoul. He wouldn't finish his junior year, as the college had granted him a leave of absence. He was committed to this decision, and it was not negotiable. He did not want or need to see a psychiatrist, and he said he knew exactly what he was doing.

Three months later, they received a terrible call from Korea: Josh had been found dead in his room after an apparent overdose of antidepressant medication. "There was no sign of foul play, and there was no note left by the deceased," the impersonal voice said.

My Gay Child

Even in this day and age, with gay and lesbian marriage gaining acceptance and making inroads in many Western countries and American states, there is still strong opposition among fundamentalist religious people and other groups. But even progressive thinkers who espouse gay rights, when confronted with their own offspring coming out, often feel concern and discomfort.

They might worry about possible difficulties, such as rejection, discrimination, threats, and other hurdles in the paths of their sons and daughters.

In unusual instances, however, there is the kind of outburst exhibited by Alexander. In his case, the explosiveness had less to do with the issue of homosexuality than it did with the shame of *his own son* being gay. He worried Josh's revelation would affect the family image, lead to Josh leaving school, and, most importantly, upset Alexander's rigid program and game plan for his son (and for himself).

Alexander's self-image was so enmeshed in Joshua's success that anything that detracted from Josh's accomplishments was a profound blow to his own sense of self (a phenomenon known as a "narcissistic injury").

Profound sadness, bewilderment, and pain engulfed the shocked family.

Suicide

The loss of a loved one is always difficult, but the suicide of a child gives emotional pain a new depth of meaning. Few experiences in life are as deeply heartrending and scarring. Parents feel their worst nightmare is that something terrible might afflict their children. Even the potential for this happening brings shudders, and if it actually occurs, they experience deep, mournful despair and profound grieving that transcend all reality.

Such a tragedy is soul searing, impossible to fathom, and impossible to forget. This enormous blow can precipitate psychological, medical, and social problems in survivors. In my forty years of working in the mental-health field, the losses of children are the most incomprehensible to grasp and cause the most excruciating anguish and agony.

When the death of a child is due to suicide, the parents' immediate state of shock is always mixed with doubts about what role they played in leading to the tragedy. In most large cities, there are support groups for the family survivors of this immense and, unfortunately, not-uncommon tragedy.

The suicide of a spouse is almost as devastating. The surviving spouse knows that the tragic demise was the result of a deliberate, self-destructive act borne out of immense personal suffering. Surviving spouses often blame themselves and wonder if they could have done something to prevent the tragedy.

But willful suicide represents a tragic end of perceived choices and hope. In an era when some jurisdictions condone assisted suicide and when groups (e.g., the Hemlock Society) and books espouse free choice in electing to end one's life, there is always agony and sorrow.

Many suicidal individuals who made serious but failed attempts to end their lives were grateful for having been prevented from completing that act of finality, including those who were comatose when they were revived and later expressed appreciation for their lives. When there is a suicide, there is an excruciatingly painful aftermath for the loved ones left behind.

I have also witnessed, along with family members, sensitive and respectful assisted suicides of terminally ill adults who were ready to leave this earth. In every one of these instances, there was a period of intense suffering in the desperate person and in members of the family who helped end the misery. They still experience intense grief and mourning, as after any death.

The death of someone close makes us face the pain of losing that personal relationship and confronts us with our own mortality. In the case of suicide, mourners experience these feelings more profoundly; confusion, stress, sorrow, and guilt are magnified. Nagging questions linger in those closest to the deceased, especially "Could I have done something to prevent this?"

Alexander Secomb was never the same after Joshua committed suicide. For years afterward, Alexander obsessed over two thoughts: *Why?*—a plaintive question—and "Not *this* beautiful child, not my beloved Josh!"—a poignant lamentation. He had idealized and idolized his son and couldn't believe he was gone. No matter where he turned, he thought he saw him. Their last conversation played over and over in his head—every word, every nuance. His agony was palpable to everyone; he directed his anger at himself and at God. Though he'd long given up on the existence of God, he now railed against him.

Alexander knew why Josh had taken his life: the act was, without a doubt, due to his own terrible inability to be there for his son. "I failed as a father and as a human being," he told me.

These thoughts and their last painful conversation before Josh left for South Korea haunted him. Alexander dared not share with Tanya the details of his rage and rejection of Joshua. He wanted to unburden himself to her, but he was mortified and fearful. He was his own prosecutor, judge, and jury, and the verdict was irrevocably and deservedly "guilty." He deserved nothing less than severe punishment, even execution.

Life was feeling increasingly burdensome to Alexander, though he tried to cope. He and Tanya threw themselves into the healing process, urged on by friends. They went to psychotherapists, and they joined a therapeutic support group for grieving parents, all of whom had tragically lost a child. With the aid of a cognitive-behavior therapist, Alexander practiced the arts of compartmentalization (i.e., walling off areas of concern), reframing (i.e., thinking in more constructive terms), visualization (i.e., imagining experiences of serenity), and meditation to improve his mood. He found the group experience the most helpful; sharing his loss and pain with others who had similarly suffered was especially meaningful and helpful to him.

He hunkered down at work, resolving that the petty squabbles wouldn't get to him, that he would remain above the fray. A colleague noted that Josh's death sapped the venom from him. He was less arrogant and surly, so colleagues who had reviled him felt sorry for him. He walked more slowly, his voice was softer, he made eye contact, and he even seemed to notice people, unlike in the past, when he'd apparently existed primarily on another planet.

He was rethinking his siege mentality at HEPRI, expressing to a couple of colleagues his regret for being a "pain in the ass," as he put it. The sight of this sad, broken man who, ironically, was now approachable startled them, and Alexander, in turn, was surprised and moved by their concern and sympathy.

Andrea was living in Philadelphia with her boyfriend while in a radiology residency at Penn. Tamara, a talented writer, was working in advertising on Madison Avenue in New York, aspiring toward a career in the art world. Both sisters were busy, but their feelings around Josh's death and their difficult father, while no longer raw, were still hurtful.

Aside from their mourning, Alexander and Tanya faced the new reality of being empty nesters, rattling around a large home filled with family memorabilia. They went through the motions of normalcy while aware of feeling emotionally and physically uncomfortable with each other. Some of their friends wondered about the viability of their marriage, and a couple raised their concerns with Tanya.

Life made its own course correction. Tanya was puttering in the garden on a warm June day, and Alexander was reading the *Sunday Times,* when he experienced a sudden sensation of heavy pressure in his upper chest and back. At Tanya's insistence, he took a glass of water and retreated to the bedroom. The pressure continued, and he felt weak and tired and began to sweat profusely. Despite his protestations, Tanya called 911. Within an hour, Alexander was hospitalized with a diagnosis of acute coronary artery thrombosis (i.e., a heart attack).

Aggressive treatment reduced the gnawing chest pain and some of the fear and brought his pulse and blood pressure to within normal limits. However, an angiogram and an MRI showed almost total blockage of his coronary arteries, with fatty plaque obstructing blood flow to his heart muscle.

He was sent to the OR, where surgeons placed stents (plastic tubes) in three coronary arteries to keep the blood vessels open. Alexander had defeated the death knell.

Both Andrea and Tamara rushed home, and Tanya maintained a vigil at her husband's bedside. After a week in the hospital, Alexander returned home to recuperate under Tanya's watchful eye.

His visitors were surprised by his good spirits and admired his courage. This social display of well-being relieved Tanya, but when he was alone with her, Alexander was distant, even cold. She was hurt, especially when he was full of bonhomie with visitors. She wanted to let him have it for his two-faced behavior, but she didn't dare show her feelings, fearing she might cause another heart attack. She was frustrated and angry and felt trapped again.

Alexander hadn't told Tanya that he'd caused Josh's suicide or about his self-loathing. The more he kept this dark secret from her, the more negatively he acted toward her. His icy demeanor was so painful that she became less sympathetic and began distancing herself.

She shared her frustration with friends, her daughters, and her therapist. They all said that she was encouraging his nastiness by staying in the relationship, that she was codependent. "If I hear that word again, I'll scream!" Tanya said bitterly, seeing it as an in-vogue judgmental criticism from them.

They all agreed that she should move out on her own. Tanya didn't want to—she still loved Alexander—but she finally gave in, hoping her absence would shake him up and make him realize the stakes. When she told him of her plans, he denied being cold to her and expressed his love for her. She weakened her resolve, but his nastiness soon returned. If she was upset, he said, perhaps *she* was the real problem. That was the moment of truth: Tanya decided to move out.

Tanya was excited about her move to a lovely condominium on the water, when life intervened once more: Alexander developed new symptoms. He felt fatigue and weakness with severe muscle pains in his arms and legs, even when he was getting up out of a chair or walking up a few stairs.

Alexander's doctor had put him on a new medication (a statin) to reduce his blood-cholesterol levels. Lab tests revealed that he had high liver, muscle, and kidney enzyme levels, indicating significant damage to those organs. (These were side effects of statins, which occurred in a small percentage of users.) Alexander's doctor took him off these meds, but the liver damage was severe and irreversible, and Alexander would likely need a liver transplant at some point.

Tanya's well-laid plans were upended. "Man plans, and God laughs," she said, recalling the adage ruefully. Alexander needed her, so she wouldn't be moving.

During the next two years, Alexander and Tanya felt they were in a "medical jungle," with tests and procedures tying them in knots and danger lurking everywhere. Innumerable physicians, nurses, and technicians poked, probed, and prodded Alexander. The sheer numbers and varieties were overwhelming: liver biopsies, blood transfusions, immunological studies, antibiotics, CAT scans, MRIs, renal angiographies, EKGs, EEGs, and more. This period was draining emotionally, physically, and financially. It spite of being well insured, they had to justify their needs each step of the way to their HMO, and their co-pays were significant. The worries about finances were, in themselves, detrimental to healing.

Alexander had become considerably warmer to Tanya. She subleased her condominium and resumed the role of nursemaid wife with renewed commitment. Her daughters and friends thought Alexander's new symptoms were a blatant ploy to keep her at home. They swallowed their feelings of mistrust and anger, though they questioned his motives.

Tanya had resolved not to put up with Alexander's crap any longer, but he miraculously (her friends said manipulatively) metamorphosed into a grateful, caring partner. This was soon after Alexander finally shared with Tanya the burden of his private shame: "My last talk with Josh and how I killed him," he said through anguished tears and sobs.

Tanya was not shocked. She was grateful that he confided in her, and she hugged Alexander for the first time in many moons. He fell asleep, and he awoke to find a note from Tanya, which he read through tears: "Dearest, I knew for years that Josh was gay. I sensed you blamed yourself for his death, but you made it impossible to speak to you. Josh told me what happened that night. I don't blame you, nor did he, I am sure. My love, Tanya."

Tanya's words lifted an immense emotional weight from Alexander. The physical pressures he'd felt for years on his back, chest, and shoulders dissipated. He could breathe normally and without oppressive heaviness for the first time since Josh died. His mood lightened; he felt released from bondage.

Stress, Emotions, and Our Bodies

People under severe stress are more prone to developing emotional disorders in reaction to the stressors. This is true for recent difficult events, but even painful experiences that occurred many years earlier can appear later as psychological disturbances, such as anxiety and depression.

In addition, external and internal psychological tensions can also influence and cause physical symptoms and disorders. If these are severe and longstanding, those who feel particularly burdened are more likely to develop bodily reactions.

Every organ system of the body can be vulnerable to undue tension, although each of us might react differently. Heart and blood vessels, the digestive tract, the nervous system, muscles and joints, pain sensitivity, the immune system—no part of the body is immune to the effects of chronic, severe psychological stress.

With this in mind, we try to make the environments of families, schools, and workplaces more comfortable; we encourage recreation, good nutrition, and physical exercise, and we engage in meditation, yoga, mindfulness, massage, and self-enhancing techniques. Many medical centers have recently established centers of integrative medicine, recognizing that body and mind affect each other and are integrated parts of one major remarkable system.

Our own genetic makeups vary, and some are more prone to stress than others, but the more we're able to reduce stressful events in our lives, the better we can withstand the effects and improve our lives.

But if our attempts aren't working and the pressures get to be too much, seeing our physician, nurse practitioner, or therapist can be an important step to enabling us to say "Whoa!" to ourselves and to slow down and, yes, smell the flowers.

The period after a heart attack is often difficult, but for Tanya and Alexander, it was a healing time. They felt closer and again enjoyed each other. Alexander appreciated Tanya's attention, and his newfound warmth moved her. Their daughters were pleased but wary, and a couple of her friends still thought he was toying with her to keep her in servitude. Two confronted her, but Tanya was at ease with her decision, and she wasn't going to let them dissuade her. She was sure Alexander's words were authentic.

They became affectionate, Tanya recalled, saying, "I felt young again."

Tanya noticed Alexander diminishing: he was losing weight, sleeping for hours, and increasingly weak. He was progressing up the national list of liver-transplant recipients, but an exact genetic match proved difficult to find.

Tanya remained at his side, as did Andrea and Tamara. When he died in his sleep a few nights later in Tanya's embrace, she was sad but deeply comforted that she and Alexander had rekindled the love between them. What she had been wishing, hoping, and waiting for over many years had finally come to pass.

The Four Bs

As we've seen, love is a magnificent healer and instigator of change. None of us can live a satisfying life without love of some sort. It needn't be romantic love, though that's the most common form between couples. Love can be between friends or even colleagues. The point is that to love means we must move beyond ourselves to envision the other person in a sensitive way, and that ability in itself necessitates a certain degree of compassion, a small sense of being, believing, belonging, and benevolence. In fact, love is the embodiment of all four Bs!

Alexander had trouble with the people in his life because he failed to see the humanity of others, and he failed to acknowledge his own needs until the last few years of his life. In many ways, his intangible legacy was not positive. The emotional footprint he'd left in the sands of his time on Earth remained indelibly negative, but in the end, he was resilient in the face of his own travails. He ultimately was able to see beyond the limits of his past and embrace the future, however limited that might have been in terms of time left in the hourglass.

Being

Alexander's rigid personality was part of his nature from an early age, spurred by his genetic inheritance and modified by the tragedies in his life and his innate intellect, drive to excel, rigidity, and perfectionism. All of these factors played significant roles in the evolution of his personality. He was as demanding of himself as he was of family, colleagues, and students. He was a major professional success, but he was arrogant, aloof, and abrasive.

Alexander never quite reached a successful sense of being, as tied up as he was in knots of perfectionism, the drive to achieve, and demands on others. He was hardest on himself but made others pay for this. His satisfaction with himself did not appear until shortly before his death.

Belonging

Tanya gave him unconditional love for years until his affair, and his selfishness and outbursts rocked their marriage. He antagonized his children, and they all moved away. The self-blame for his son's suicide never attenuated. When he fell ill, he mistreated Tanya and almost succeeded in sending her away, but her love never wavered, and it led to the reawakening of his humanity and love.

As difficult as he often was, Alexander did feel close to Tanya and his children. He never doubted his allegiance to his nuclear family unit, try as he might to continually push and pummel them. At the physics institute, he was a de facto part of the academic community, even if estranged, and it was not until the tragedy of Josh's death that he became an integral part of that community.

Believing

Alexander was not into believing. He had been a confirmed atheist since his parents were killed when he was fourteen years of age. God had no place in his thinking or hoping. He was scientific, intellectual, and rational, and he dismissed any thoughts of spirituality or extra-material existence with derision. His value system and his world were simplistically black and white, with no grays. Ambiguity made him uncomfortable, even anxious.

Alexander's life would undoubtedly have been easier for him (and others) if he could have left some room for grays and ambiguities.

Benevolence

Respect for others and generosity of spirit were not things people would have immediately equated with Alexander. There is no doubt, however, that his contributions to the scientific literature and their industrial and health implications made a lasting positive legacy to our world.

His two remaining children—his flesh and blood—and, of course, Tanya are all estimable people whose presences warm the rooms they enter.

Resilience

Alexander's life was not a bed of roses. It's true that he was bright and materially comfortable, and he always had the benefit of creature comforts (e.g., food, a warm bed, hygiene). But he lost his parents at an early age, his only sibling was severely brain damaged, his beloved son committed suicide, and his health deteriorated.

Alexander was not an easy man. Over the course of his complicated life, he antagonized his wife, children, colleagues, and friends. But Tanya continued to love him, and others recognized his brilliance, even when he was demanding and nasty. Thus, it was not until relatively late in life that he was able to show vulnerability, to allow himself to open up to his family and others. His personal fortifications had been so entrenched that he prevented just about everybody from getting close to him and, more so, prevented himself from easing up on himself, especially after Josh died. So his resilience was limited: at the end of his life, his defenses finally wilted, but it was perhaps too late for anyone but his dear wife, Tanya.

Emotional Footprint

Alexander did indeed disturb the equilibrium of other people, affecting their moods, self-esteem, and relationships, and that legacy might well have added a lasting dose of emotional negativity to our world. His wife, Tanya, however, is obviously a biased judge of Alexander's life. She accompanied him on his convoluted journey, sharing many of her husband's achievements and frailties, and she often bore the brunt of his nastiness. In spite of this, she told me "one big thing" she had known through all their years together, all the trials and tribulations: she never stopped loving him.

And then he died. Is this how we do justice to the span of a man's life over seventy years? To quote Peggy Lee, "Is that all there is?" Alexander's emotional footprint was mixed, as all of ours are.

Postscript

Tanya opened up years later to her daughters, who were trying to better understand their late father. She told them that she'd still loved him despite his faults, and she offered some strong negative and positive opinions about him.

"At his worst, I was furious with him, I felt trapped, and I just had to escape. But I knew the essence of him, and it was caring. Even when he was impossible, I still felt loving. Josh's death nearly killed him. But Alexander helped raise our kids, so many people admired him, and he left an important body of research.

"When we were young, his brilliance, his wide interests, and, yes, his love, excited me, and you know what? This is the way he was at the end. I accompanied him on his journey through life, and I feel fortunate," Tanya said.

Her daughters and friends felt that Tanya had to think this way in order to make sense of her devotion to Alexander and maintain her self-respect, given the pain he'd caused her. Psychologists call this "cognitive dissonance," explaining how we need to protect ourselves by rationalizing contradictory feelings and thoughts.

But Tanya understands this concept and disagrees vehemently. She is an intelligent, self-assured woman whose views of her husband, their marriage, and her life are serious and mature. In spite of the trials and tribulations, she appreciates the pleasures and achievements. These are not a self-protective ruse: Tanya is comfortable and grateful for the years and love she shared with the troubled Alexander. "That's life," she said.

7
Jose Alvarez

The Observer

The train leaves the wetlands and rolls into a station five stops away from the terminal in the city center. The landscape is urban, with brick housing projects sprawling out on every side. You know the buildings are for low-income people and were built in the early 1970s. Neglect is obvious in every aspect, from the colorful graffiti sprayed on entire sides of vacant warehouses to broken chain-link security fences and trash heaps in front of residential complexes that even the cops try to avoid, especially at night. You're glad you don't have to get off anywhere near this neighborhood. The gangs roam freely, and dealers sell drugs at virtually every corner. Shootings are common. The violence is worse here because the tax base dried up long ago with the disappearance of the factories, and the local government isn't able to afford adequate policing or rehabilitation, let alone basic public services.

You hate to admit that you are slightly uneasy as a tough-looking Latino guy in his late thirties steps aboard from the platform. He's wearing a black T-shirt and black slacks and is tattooed all over. He looks a like a Spanish ninja, and you smile at that image. The man is holding a couple of books in his hand, and you think that's a bit weird. Gangbangers aren't known for being bookworms, yet this guy apparently is one. You realize that you're stereotyping again.

The guy passes you and slows a bit to look down at you. He's seen you staring at him. He's seen the fear in your eyes.

"Nice day out," he says, shooting you a warm smile.

He's got perfect white teeth, you notice, and he's got a twinkle in his intelligent brown eyes. "Uh, yes," you say. "A nice day."

He moves on and takes a seat a few back from you on the same side of the train you're on. This guy seems to exude self-confidence, which you admire, wishing that you had more self-confidence yourself. You wonder if the man has an interesting story, and you imagine how his life might have been, how it has twisted and turned, and where it is going.

The Rider

Except for his hands, face, and feet, you can see no untattooed skin on Jose Alvarez's body, which looks like a semiabstract canvas of continuous colored symbols of his mother, his girlfriends, his gang, and religious icons. Jose isn't tall, but his stocky, muscular build and his seeming glare project a warning: "Don't fuck with me."

Jose was born in a barrio of Southeast Los Angeles to Maria and Jesus Alvarez, then illegal immigrants from Mexico. Jesus was an itinerant day laborer who got jobs by waiting on designated street corners with other migrant laborers for the hiring trucks to come by. A foreman would hop out and select a lucky few who would spend the day picking vegetables under a blistering sun in the fields of the Central or Imperial Valleys of California's agricultural belt. The arduous work paid below minimum wage, and there were no benefits then (in this pre–Cesar Chavez era). Jesus was often gone from the family for days, living in crowded barrack-like quarters, often with no electricity or indoor plumbing. He gave his earnings to Maria, keeping a paltry amount for himself.

Maria was religious and worried about her life in Los Angeles. They had little money, and she missed her family in Juarez, but she was most concerned about Jose. They lived in a small dwelling in a dangerous, gang-filled neighborhood. Gang membership was based on race and ethnicity, which, in that area, consisted of African American, Latino (usually Mexican), and Vietnamese, with a smattering of gangs from varied backgrounds, including Samoan, white bikers, and Filipino.

By the time Jose was eight years of age, older gang members had already made it clear that they expected him to join El Mexicanos, whose members were steadfastly loyal to each other and to the urban blocks (turf) in the neighborhood (hood) they controlled. Even when Jose went to school, gang members often watched him so that he wouldn't stray.

Yet Jose felt protected and secure in this atmosphere. He had strong bonds with his homeboys, whom he considered family, and he looked up to the older leaders, who were in their upper teens and early twenties. The members flaunted their heritage and were united in protecting their "property" (girls and their turf) and in hating the enemy gangs, which were racist, corrupt, and vicious, justifying the need for El Mexicanos.

Jose was bright and soft-spoken, and after establishing some comfort (safety), he was engaging and warm. At first, he was a loyal gofer in the gang, which gave him reputation points at school and in the hood for being with the honchos.

As he got older, the members relied on him for his intelligence and creativity in any mission. These could involve intimidating and threatening others, using behaviors like staring down, insulting, swaggering, threatening, and signing. Others included tagging (graffiti), stealing cars, dealing drugs, robbery and shoplifting, weapon use and smuggling, and fights with other gangs. These activities all reminded their enemies of their presence and power and defended their honor. Jose soon became a go-to person, one of the gang honchos.

Maria and Jesus saw so little of Jose that they were terrified, and with good reason. He reassured them, saying he loved them and telling them not to worry, but they felt him ebbing away and feared they were losing him to sinful forces. They sought advice from their priest, who commiserated and urged prayer.

The little boy who had been the pride of the community was becoming a full-fledged gangbanger; his life centered on the gang and his homeboys. His school attendance and grades began to slip, but he was still able to maintain a 2.8 GPA with minimal effort. Home and school gave him a semblance of credibility with his parents and the church community.

Jose felt safe in his gang, but the outside world was feeling more treacherous. He was constantly on the run from the police, other gangs, or both. He was preoccupied with running, hiding, ducking behind bushes or between cars, or losing himself in crowds. He became an expert in interpreting the sounds of gunfire: he could discern what caliber and kind of weapon was used and which enemy was closing in. Perpetual vigilance, attention, caution, scanning, and evading were his radar. He'd mastered these arts, but he told me later, "I was scared shitless."

Why Do Youths Get Involved in Gangs?

Kids join gangs for a wide variety of reasons. Not all gang members are mean dudes. Some gangbangers are aggressive, antisocial bullies even before they join the gangs, and the gangs serve as an outlet for them. They often come from troubled families in which chaos and abuse are common. Others get a thrill from gang-sponsored risk taking, from the danger and violence. A smaller number have symptoms of psychological or psychiatric disorders.

But many of the members join because they want to; gangs give them acceptance and a close community of comrades wherein they feel respect and loyalty (belonging).

The leaders and their important missions impress the young recruits. The gangs give them an overriding goal and a dominant meaning to their lives. They have faith in the values and believe in their credo and goals (believing).

Still other members have to join the local gang because of peer pressure or threats of punishment if they don't or for protection from their enemies.

Still others need to join because their lives at home, in school, at work, or on the streets are empty or abusive. Many gang members experience personal enhancement and security they get nowhere else (being).

Gang members share values, rituals, and goals. They feel more confident and comfortable than they ever felt before. They feel accepted, respected, and liked by members they can count on. They feel they are being true to their ethnic or racial heritage, and they feel they're part of a cause—something important and worthwhile. They feel they are serving their communities and protecting their families, their friends, and their people. We can see all four Bs right there.

After a federal immigration amnesty in the 1970s, Jesus's employers were convicted of egregious abuse of their workers. Jose's parents received their green cards, and they moved to a larger home, but Jose's gang life was so encompassing that for a while, he was unaware of any of these events.

The constant vigilance and estrangement from his parents began to eat at Jose. Increasingly, he thought, *This is no way to live*, and he contemplated getting out of the gang. But fate intervened when the police stopped him because he looked suspicious, and they charged him with driving without a license. They knew he was an El Mexicano and arrested him for past misdemeanors. He angered the cops when he refused to rat on his homeboys, an act of betrayal Jose would never do, and because he'd been in juvenile hall a couple of years earlier. He was sent back to juvie, but during the wait for his court date, he turned eighteen, which meant a transfer to adult corrections. "Two years in state prison," the judge said.

He recalled three thoughts: *My poor parents, Those fucking cops,* and *Better they get me than another gang.*

Juvenile hall had not prepared him for the culture of adult prison. The gang rivalries were hateful, and tough criminals and guards made life terror filled and miserable. Threats and violence took their toll on Jose: he couldn't eat or sleep, he was losing weight, and he was exhausted. He was frightened and demoralized, and he wanted out—not only out of prison but also out of the gangbanger way of life. He contemplated going back to school to make his parents proud, but he knew that if he shared these thoughts with anyone, he'd be seen as a wimp or, worse, a traitor, and many inmates would threaten him.

Reverend Alice Lipton, the pale, bespectacled prison chaplain, came by with some books on a cart while Jose was lying in his cell. While she spoke quietly, the confidence and strength she emanated struck Jose. His usual pattern of relating to women was through macho posturing, but he later told me that he liked her in a different way. And he was right; he did. Alice made a big impact on his life. Her first step was to rid him of the attitude that got in the way of any positive sense of being. They talked about prison, his life, his family, and God. Although he was a Catholic and she was a Methodist, Jose could confide in her, sharing his private fears and hopes.

Over the next few months, Jose looked forward to their conversations, like a starving man awaiting food. Some meetings were profound, and others were less so, but they were all meaningful to him. His friendship and discussions with Rev. Alice, as he called her, made him even more eager to get out of prison. He planned to get his high-school equivalency certificate and go to college. With the reverend's encouragement, he wanted to return to his parents, to school, to church, and to God.

Fickle fate intruded. Jose heard that Roberto and Manuel, two of the homeboys he'd grown up with, had died in a shootout with a rival gang right in his own neighborhood. Jose felt sick and saddened, and more so, he was full of rage, wanting vengeance. He scrapped his plans for a new life. He had only two months left before his release, but retribution was now his priority. He wanted to kill the fucking murderers, he said, and his descent into darkness accelerated. He wouldn't speak with Rev. Alice, feeling she couldn't begin to understand the pain and fury in his heart. Chaplain Alice Lipton viewed this change with dread; Jose was now unreachable.

On his release, after signing the papers arranging for probation, he was single-minded. Not stopping at his parents' home, Jose went straight to his gang's main hub, where the others ecstatically received him. They made plans for the bloody vendetta. They opened a hidden cache of automatic weapons stored in preparation for just such a war. They planned a surprise assault on the other gang—one so explosive that survivors, if there were any, would never forget.

Fortunately, that bloodbath never came about, because an embedded mole informed the police. As Jose and his compadres gathered at a predetermined meeting place in a rural field, their cars full of weaponry, their hearts filled with hate, and their blood filled with inner adrenaline and outer alcohol and amphetamines, dozens of police officers in full battle gear suddenly surrounded them and arrested them. Jose was sentenced to five years in a more secure prison in a remote part of the state.

This joint was maximum security and tougher, yet it felt less dangerous to him than the last one. Jose had learned the ropes of prison life: how to avoid confrontation, how to avert one's eyes when required, how to negotiate, how to threaten, and how to fight if there was no choice. Jose was adept at protecting his flanks and his skin because of his social artfulness and his facility with more diplomatic channels, such as the ability to befriend and convince, bribery, confidence, and respect—but never fear. The other prisoners respected him as a natural leader, but he had no interest in leading anyone in prison or outside. Still, he remained vigilant.

While not as threatening, this prison experience was more humiliating. He was angry with himself for being carried away on an emotional wave of vindictiveness. And for what? Part of him was actually grateful for the arrest; the battle would have led to carnage with no winners—only losers—and the cycle of violence would have continued. He was ashamed he'd learned nothing from his talks with Rev. Alice, and he was sure he'd lost her too.

Jose had begun reading again and writing to his parents with affection and apologies, saying he missed them. Around the time of his first Christmas in the new pen, Jose received a wonderful gift: a handwritten holiday card from Chaplain Alice Lipton. She recalled their wonderful talks in the past. She asked about his well-being and his plans for the future and wanted to know if she could visit him again soon. She signed the card "Rev. Alice."

Their visits started up again, and Jose was committed to not letting her—or himself—down again. He took correspondence courses, studied hard, and received his high-school certificate in just over a year. To his embarrassment and pride, the prison authorities made a big fuss over his accomplishment. They held a ceremony in the mess hall, which Rev. Alice, the prison warden, the guards and staff, and many of the prisoners attended. They brought out his parents as a surprise, and Jose cried.

With some trepidation, Jose wrote to his homeboys in the barrio to tell them the news. Most of them took pleasure in his achievements, since he'd proven himself as a gangbanger and would always be one of them, even if he were moving on. A few, however, felt that he'd sold out.

Jose was released after two years in prison, and he was dedicated to working on his dreams for the future. He lived in his parents' home and started attending church. He also stayed in close touch with Rev. Alice. He went to the local state college while holding down a part-time job at a fast-food Indian restaurant.

He had been turned down for the first three jobs he'd applied for, and he knew the rejections were because of his record. On the next application, however, the questions were direct, as were the answers: "Have you ever been arrested? No. Have you ever been convicted? No. Have you ever served time? No." Luckily, that restaurant didn't do a background check.

The Ethics of Lying

Can Jose be forgiven for lying in these circumstances? Most of us tell the truth most of the time, but as Cecily Bok showed in her book On Lying, we tend to fib as well. Ethical behavior dictates that we tell the truth, which usually makes one's life much simpler. (As Sir Walter Scott wrote, "Oh what a tangled web we weave, when first we practice to deceive.") We teach our children to tell the truth, and in court, we promise to tell "the whole truth and nothing but the truth."

But should one tell the truth if it will endanger him or her? The unsatisfactory answer is "It depends on the context and the danger." For ex-cons, this is not a philosophical discussion; it is a crucial dilemma since their answers can determine their fate. They have to respond with a yes or no to questions about prior arrests or imprisonments. What would you and I do in this situation? Which answer will do the least harm (or the most good)?

The ability to accept the inherent grays of life instead of absolute right versus wrong is a common challenge in our lives. Most of us learn to live with inherent ambiguities in our lives, and no one is infallible. This is why we have ethics committees in medical centers, universities, and many other venues. "It depends" is an increasing fact of life when we make critical decisions.

In my opinion, Jose's lying in this context can be forgiven.

As an ex-con in school, Jose had anxieties about himself and his abilities, but he began to find his rhythm. He liked his college major, social studies, and became interested in a career as a counselor or teacher. He was strongly encouraged by Rev. Alice and by a few professors who found him committed and creative, a breath of fresh air in their classes. He dreaded that his past would be revealed and his dreams shattered. Even after he graduated with honors, he feared that it was just a matter of time before his past came to light. He even worried about his extensive tattoos. They covered his arms and neck, and many people immediately identified them with gangs. On the other hand, he tried to reassure himself that the younger people he wanted to work with wouldn't immediately think he was a banger just because he had tats. Still, he'd sometimes take walks to clear his head, and the fear came hovering around like a wasp.

He steeled himself and applied to graduate school in a master's program in marriage and family therapy (MFT). He decided that if interviewers asked about his background, he wouldn't lie; he would look them in the eyes with respect and dignity and tell them everything. Jose did exactly this, and all five graduate schools he applied to turned him down, even though his marks and references were excellent.

His prison record intimidated admission committees, whose attitude was "Once as criminal, always a criminal. What if word got out?" They worried about liability, litigious parents of other students, and donors revoking their pledges.

Jose was despairing, and Rev. Alice too was losing her optimism. He was reluctant to put himself out there again. Rev. Alice urged him to apply to one more graduate program, where the dean was known to be a flexible and progressive thinker. He reluctantly agreed.

Jose was scrupulously honest about his prison record. He was articulate, committed, and humble, and he brought laudatory letters, his academic record, and strong references from the prison warden and chaplain as well as his parish priest.

It worked: the dean and admissions committee took a courageous chance on this unusual applicant who impressed them in spite of his background of poverty, gangs, violence, and prison.

They never regretted their decision. Jose was not only a straight–A student, but he was also a gifted clinician. He was no longer incognito on campus; the students and faculty knew his past. Two years later, Jose was selected as the graduating class valedictorian. He received a standing ovation from the university community and their guests, who included his parents, Rev. Alice, some home-boys, his parish priest, and his last warden.

During his internship in a hospital setting, Jose's energy and commitment again impressed people. A physician there intro-duced him to Roberta, an attrac-tive divorcee who was an assistant professor of social work at a nearby university. Roberta also had a convoluted background; she had grown up with abusive, alcoholic, evangelical parents.

This unlikely couple hit it off and were so swept away in love that they married a mere six months later. The wedding was held in the chapel of Jose's parents' church in the barrio, and the wedding guests included Hispanic church members, aca-demics, gangbangers, clinicians, family, and friends. By the end of the evening, the occasion (and the flowing tequila) had transformed

Alcohol in Society

We know that alcohol use is as old as ancient history and that those beverages usually fuel convivial celebrations all over the world.

Alcohol often makes people feel good. It is a potent disinhib-itor, enabling drinkers to tem-porarily overcome shyness and social constraints and to some-times behave in untoward ways. It is part of evening meals in many cultures, it plays a role in some religious rituals, and it's almost a universal element in celebrations. In moderation, alcohol is one of the great equalizers, enabling conversations between rich and poor, humble and haughty, shy and effusive.

However, there is a high correlation between the use of alcohol and the occurrence of destructive behaviors, such as domestic abuse, fights, accidents, rape, suicide, and homicide. Serious physical and psychological disorders are as-sociated with excessive drinking, as is addiction.

Can we legislate abstinence or even moderation? It has not been for lack of trying, but we've not been successful in myriads of prevention and intervention pro-grams. Prohibition was a failure in this country, and even in countries that forbid and punish alcohol use on religious grounds, alcohol is available and widely used. Our human desire to drink beer, wine, and liquor seems boundless.

these diverse strangers into a lively singing and dancing crowd with a communal joie de vivre of old friends. Jose referred to it as *"una fiesta buenissima."*

Two years later, Jose had a clinical position at a university counseling clinic, Roberta was promoted to associate professor, and they were proud parents of a sweet girl, Juanita, and a cherubic boy, Jorge, who looked like his father.

Two problem areas in the marriage appeared fairly early on.

The first was Roberta's difficulties with Jose's allegiance and love for his homeboys and girls. When he attended a funeral for one of his closest friends who had been killed in a shoot-out, Roberta was angry.

They fought, and Roberta said of Jose's friend, "He was a gangster! Why do you care if he's dead?"

"This is who I am!" Jose said. "If you don't like it, then why are you still here? You knew who I was when we got married!"

Jose later told me that Roberta's "hardness" continued to eat at him. And worse, when Jose's father died suddenly of a heart attack, Roberta expressed her resentment that his old friends were at the funeral. Things went from bad to worse. Roberta didn't seem to have an ounce of tact.

"Your scummy sisters and brothers!" Roberta shouted. "I don't see why you even asked them to come!"

Jose was aghast. "This funeral is about my mother's and my loss, not yours!" He couldn't believe her callousness, and he couldn't forgive her.

The other sore point in their marriage was Roberta's diminished desire for sexual relations or even affection with Jose. He had been used to easy sex in the gang, and he considered himself a good lover, proud that he satisfied all his girls.

When their sexual embraces dropped in frequency and pleasure, Jose put it down to the kids, busy schedules, and fatigue. But after a few months of deterioration, Jose broached the subject with Roberta. She blamed his dissatisfaction on his insatiable sex drive and his experiences with whores. She was attacking both him and his home girls, her words designed to hurt him deeply.

Neither of them wanted to rock the family boat at that time, but they became distant. Over the next couple of years, Jose attended the funerals of two other homeboys, and he invited some old friends to his children's birthday parties and other functions. Roberta was, of course, furious.

She increasingly ignored him, she showed no interest in his work or life, and their sexual relationship disappeared. She moved away emotionally and physically from him and even the children. Jose urged Roberta to go with him to see a marital therapist, which she brushed off as a "useless exercise."

At a homeboy party fueled by tequila, he had furtive sex with an ex-girlfriend, which he saw as necessary for his machismo. When the woman called their home asking for him, Roberta asked about the caller, who had sounded evasive. Jose decided to come clean, partly due to guilt and partly as a message to Roberta. "If I get no sex from you, I'll get it from someone else," he said to her.

This infidelity shook the foundations of their marriage, but not in the way Jose had expected. Roberta showed no rage or tears and made no accusations. Instead, she coolly informed Jose that she was sorry it had come to this and said she was going to leave because it was the "right thing to do." It didn't add up to him.

She then added, almost as an afterthought, that she was in a serious relationship with someone. Jose was momentarily relieved that he understood, and he felt they could work on their marriage.

But she twisted the knife: "Jose, I'm in love with Linda Cornover." Linda was an openly lesbian faculty member and a close friend of Roberta's.

Jose was shocked, sweating, and tremulous. "Are you trying to kill me, Roberta?" A cascade of questions were roiling his mind: *She is leaving me? For a woman? How long has this been going on? What about Juanita and Jorge? And our friends? And colleagues? And my mother? And my homeboys and girls? How will I manage without her? What about my reputation?*

He was bewildered, frightened, and angry.

Roberta was out of the family home and living with Lindy two weeks later. Obviously, she had planned this move. She told him she'd realized she was gay years ago and that her relationship had been going on for over a year. Jose had just given her the opening she needed.

Her decision to abruptly leave him and the children appalled him. All her nasty comments about his sexual needs and his homegirls had been a ruse. The dishonesty, cruelty, and humiliation were devastating. He told a friend that her actions "hit [him] like a train."

Jose was angry with Roberta, but mainly, he was ashamed of himself as a man, husband, father, and lover. He felt like a failure in the eyes of family, friends, his gang, colleagues—everyone. His self-doubts returned. Would everybody see through him and realize that he was a fraud? A loser? Would they mock him?

A judge granted Jose primary custody of the children; Roberta was moving to a city a hundred miles away, and they wanted to keep the children in their home and local school. (She also had expressed no interest in being a primary parent.)

In spite of the turmoil, Juanita and Jorge appeared happy—their grades didn't plummet, they had friends, and they got along well with each other and their dad. Jose poured his heart and soul into caring for them.

He got them up each morning for school and showed positive energy and good cheer. Rev. Alice visited regularly and became close to the children, especially Juanita, who called her Aunt Alice.

Jose knew he had the support of his friends and colleagues, which gave him comfort and courage. He had been set back on his haunches emotionally, socially, and financially. His depressed mother had moved in to help look after the children, but it was clear that her own ill health required his support. He had to find a more affordable, larger home.

Overwhelmed with new responsibilities, Jose worked hard, which helped him deal with his sadness. "I just didn't have time to fall into a deep depression. The kids were depending on me; so was my mother. I needed money to keep us going," he said. Jose was all about dedication and responsibility. He didn't have time for the pleasurable activities he'd once enjoyed, and for a while, he didn't miss them.

Self-Questioning and Despair

Most people go through some periods of self-questioning and sadness, because life, at times, presents dilemmas that challenge us and affect our minds and moods. Sometimes serious problems confront us, and at other times, our melancholy might be due to chemical imbalances, hormonal changes, illness, exhaustion, or the stress of coping with our frenetic schedules.

In periods of stress and sadness, we might find ourselves lying in bed wide awake at night or in the cold gray of dawn. In that mood, we are prone to worry, review our past and present, and contemplate our future. We usually get through and overcome, but sometimes we enter periods of despair. In those moments, we fear failure or worry that the fragile house of cards we've spent a lifetime creating will come crashing down. Our related fear is that our inadequacies will be exposed, followed by humiliation. They will learn our frailties, and we will be the emperor who has no clothes.

These fantasies of failure are not unusual when people are in particularly difficult times. They often disappear as the day begins and our moods lift, but if these persist and impair our functioning, they can be signs of depression, which should be evaluated and treated.

Two years later, Jose was still completely involved in his family and professional duties. His old spark hadn't returned. Each time his friends tried to fix him up with a date, he declined politely. He was still smarting from Roberta's abandonment and was reluctant to get into another relationship. He had a few dates and some sexual experiences, but they were mere diversions that left him feeling empty.

He received promotions at work, with increased administrative and supervisory responsibilities in addition to his clinical workload. Jose appreciated the clinic's confidence in him and the salary raise, but he was still the epitome of "all work and no play."

Juanita was a twenty-year-old sophomore in college, eighteen-year-old Jorge was a senior in high school, and Jose was committed to protecting his children from society's dangerous temptations and vices, which he knew well. But his kids felt stifled by his overprotective umbrella. In addition, his mother was becoming more infirm and needful of his attention. His friends wondered if they would ever again see his radiant smile.

A producer from the local public-broadcasting station phoned and asked if Jose would be interested in being interviewed for a program on the descendants of illegal Mexican immigrants, a hot topic in political and journalistic arenas and in the public eye. He was reticent at first but agreed as a contribution to the community. Jose's family and his gang and prison experiences were in such contrast to his current situation that National Public Radio was intrigued.

At this broadcast, Jose met Natalia Estevo. Originally from Mexico City, she was a resident alien (green-card holder). She had an MA in anthropology and an MBA and worked for NPR, reporting on Central and South American issues. As the anchor for this special series, Natalia was assigned to be the interviewer for the segment on Jose.

Natalia's beautiful Latino features and intelligence struck Jose, and his articulate and self-effacing manner in the interview captivated her. After the recording, they had a warm conversation, which surprised him. "She was a big-time media woman, and I was an ex-con," he said. "She was totally out of my league."

Natalia had had her own dangerous experiences in Mexico City: her prominent family had been subjected to threats and attempted kidnappings, and she'd covered the violence there for worldwide media, so she was familiar with gangs and cartels. They discussed their experiences, exchanging stories about gangs, enmity, fear, love, and grief.

They spent hours together. Natalia expressed her love for Jose long before he reciprocated. "I was sure she'd drop me if I told her everything," he said. But Natalia was winning him over. She had an easy relationship with his children, and she was caring toward his mother.

Jose fell in love in spite of all his fears. Jose's children, Rev. Alice, and his friends agreed that the best part about Jose being in love was the return of his smile.

Natalia moved in with Jose and his family. Both Juanita and Jorge are now away at college and are doing well. Natalia and Jose are collaborating on a book tentatively titled *From Inside and Out: Gang Culture in the Western World*.

During his turbulent early years, Jose had positive experiences crucial to his development. He had a caring mother, a hardworking father, meaningful relationships with his homeboys, and strong ethnic identification and religious beliefs. He was bright and had an engaging personality and a sense of loyalty and fairness. Even in the gangs and in prison, others respected him. What carried Jose through the tough times were his motivation and confidence in himself and the respect and help of others, especially Rev. Alice. She was his guiding light and mentor, his inspiration. He went through many profound and painful experiences and has much to be proud of, but he knows that he had crucial help. Once again, we see that nobody does it alone.

The Four Bs

If you go on basic statistics regarding inner-city gangs, Jose should be dead. At the very least, he should be in jail doing a lifer. He had everything going against him except for one thing: his sense of being and his belief that he could do better. It's hard to figure out where these core elements come from in a young person in Jose's position. He had no role models to emulate. Yet he was able to stand up in the harsh prison environment and take responsibility for himself and for his past transgressions. He'd done the crime, and he'd do the time.

Reverend Alice played a big part in his turnaround, once again revealing how important the influence of others' benevolence is on other people. Without her, Jose might never have achieved the success he enjoys today. Without her, he might not have had the strength to recover from his failed marriage. Jose was wise enough to understand that he couldn't successfully complete his journey alone and that he needed help. He got that help but only because he opened his heart as a profound sense of being enabled him to see the world in a positive manner, ushering in the other four Bs to make him the whole and serene man he is today.

Being

Jose has been through a lifetime of inner and outer turmoil, starting at a young age. He has a realistic appreciation of himself, with "all [his] warts," as he puts it. Jose is proud of what he has accomplished against stacked odds.

He feels more comfortable now that he is on personal and professional paths to fulfillment. He is no longer running from gangs, feeling embarrassed about his tattooed appearance, or feeling like an "outsider looking in," as he once described himself.

Jose finally accepts his limitations without self-blame or guilt, and he still strives to improve them. As—or more—important, he appreciates his considerable leadership abilities, intelligence, and ability to reach others, whether in teaching, psychotherapy, or friendships. He has achieved an authentic sense of being and now considers himself happy.

Belonging

Jose is devoted to his wife and children, his mother, his homeboys, and his new friends. He is loyal and steadfast to those who are important to him and is respectful to colleague, acquaintances, and others. He feels like an integral part of different groups of individuals, such as his family, the homeboys, the professors and students at the college, and the clinic staff and clients. In each of these circles, he feels cared for and respected by others, and reciprocally, he cares for and respects them. He has a strong sense of belonging.

Believing

Jose was brought up in the Catholic Church but strayed from the church during his gang days. Ironically, a Methodist chaplain (Rev. Alice) facilitated his return to God and Catholicism.

He is not a regular churchgoer, but he has an abiding faith and belief in his God and tries to adhere to the principles laid down by Catholic teachings and doctrine, but he finds them somewhat challenging and hypocritical. He has a friend who is a priest, with whom he enjoys discussing the rights and wrongs of the church. Nevertheless, he is encouraging both his adult children to go to church and is looking forward to taking imminent future grandchildren to Sunday school. He finds that believing helps him deal with the trials and vagaries of life.

Benevolence

Jose has positively affected and enhanced the lives of many different people and in widely different contexts. He was always deeply caring toward his parents, even when estranged, and ultimately returned to them more loving than ever. He has been loyal and generous to his homeboys, setting an example of "making it" and "going straight" for them and their children. He has been and continues to be a doting, protective father to his children; a devoted husband; a warm friend to Rev. Alice and others; a kind colleague and teacher; and a talented therapist. Just about all who know Jose look upon him as a benevolent soul.

Resilience

Jose Alvarez's story is symbolic of the remarkable resilience of human beings. I've met many who have been impressive in their comebacks from the depths of despair or degradation, but his life stands out as inspirational.

As a child in an impoverished immigrant family living in the barrio amid warring gangs, Jose had a tough child and adolescent existence filled with violence, drugs, and imprisonment. During that time, he was estranged from his parents, endured beatings and gunshot wounds, and knew no peace. He became a distant son to his parents, a loyal friend to his homeboys, and a danger to his enemies. This period was followed by severe upheavals in his life: his first imprisonment, the vendetta to avenge the deaths of his homeboys, his reimprisonment, and, finally, the betrayal and breakup of his marriage.

Yet he ultimately broke free from the shackles of gang culture, went back to school, became a gifted clinician and teacher, raised two healthy kids, cared for his mom, and fell in love again.

He was able to mobilize his inner strengths, grasp the outstretched arm offered by Rev. Alice, and incorporate positive lessons of life he learned in all his previous relationships with his parents, colleagues, and even his homeboys to achieve his remarkable resilience in the face of major obstacles.

Emotional Footprint

Jose Alvarez endured dangers and hardships and long ago hurt others in misguided escapades as a gangbanger. But even then, he showed responsibility, loyalty, and love for his fellow members and his heritage. Whether at home or on the streets, in prison or in his family, in school or at work, this intriguing man left a legacy of a positive emotional footprint.

Now in his late fifties, Jose's life is still a work in progress, but over the last decade, he has been a model of resilience, redemption, and compassion.

8

Eduardo Morales

The Observer

You're counting down the stops now, and you see that you have four to go. You try not to glance at your watch, but you can't help it. It's about eleven o'clock in the morning, and your interview is at noon. You calculate the time it's going to take to walk from the train terminal to the address you need to go to, and you figure you've got plenty of leeway. You're just happy the train is on schedule. You've had enough bad luck lately. It's about time something went right.

A passenger stirs in front of you. You see that he's a Hispanic man in his later years and that he's wearing casual slacks, a nice shirt, and a sport jacket that doesn't quite fit correctly. He's holding a cane as he gets shakily to his feet. You wonder if you should ask if he needs help to get something down from the overhead baggage rack, but he's not going for the rack. As he passes, you figure he has to use the restroom, and that's exactly where he's going, slowly, as he limps along.

The man's creased face looks haunted, as if the ghosts and inner demons we all struggle with are in great abundance within him—as if he's had more than his share of trouble, pain, and loss. However, there is a sense of calm in him as well. You can feel it. It's almost as if he has fought wars and been brave enough to make something from the wreckage.

The Rider

Eddie Morales, a gray-haired man dressed in a sports jacket and slacks, stood in front of the White House amid a boisterous crowd. Cops looked on, many of them nervously, as he and his friends waved placards in a demonstration for increased benefits for war veterans. He stood out because the other participants were all younger and dressed in T-shirts and jeans. He walked with a limp and had a carved cane with military insignia. He was one of the only veterans in the crowd old enough to have served in Vietnam.

Eddie was born in Colombia seventy-three years earlier. He spent his childhood in Bogotá, Caracas, Buenos Aires, Paris, and Madrid because his father, Emilio, worked as a *charges d'affaires* in Colombian embassies. The family moved to the United States when Eddie was fifteen.

Decades earlier, Eddie's grandfather Ramon had immigrated to America from Colombia, married an American woman, and fought for the US Army during World War I. After the war, Ramon lived in Oakland, California, but he returned to Colombia when federal authorities grew suspicious about alleged shady business dealings. In Colombia, he lived on a large, beautiful estate, cultivating two main crops: coffee and coca leaves. Ramon obviously made considerable money, but as the family lore went, he was never convicted.

Emilio evidently inherited his father Ramon's facility with dubious business ethics. At whichever embassy he happened to be posted, Emilio laundered money on behalf of some Colombian special interests. The Colombian government discharged him from the diplomatic corps when he was stationed in Madrid, which prompted the family's move to the United States. They settled in a suburb of Oakland, where Eddie's grandfather Ramon had lived years ago.

Eddie couldn't remember his father having a regular job in America except for a stint in the US Army in 1944–45, which enabled automatic

US citizenship. Emilio was involved in unknown Colombian businesses, and Eddie recalled hushed phone calls, which scared him but also excited him.

Yet Emilio was a hard taskmaster to his sons, demanding that they study hard and stay out of trouble. He used words like *duty* and *honor*, which Eddie felt was hypocritical. Eddie wasn't interested in his high-school studies, which he found difficult, but he was a gifted tennis player, and the school team welcomed his skills. His classmates called him Fast Eddie because he was always on the move; he was restless and couldn't sit still in class or concentrate on studying. His parents despaired, and teachers criticized and berated him. The truth was that Fast Eddie felt slow in his classes. What the teachers saw as laziness was his inability to focus on reading and schoolwork.

Attention-Deficit/Hyperactivity Disorder

In today's world, Eddie might well have been referred for a professional evaluation and an individual education plan (IEP). A learning disorder or a psychological problem might have been suspected, and a psychologist could have assessed him in order to discover the cause of his restlessness and lack of focus.

Many young children like Eddie, who show hyperactivity, poor concentration, and attention problems, are diagnosed in elementary school with attention-deficit/hyperactivity disorder, a common diagnosis nowadays. A doctor might have put Eddie on some form of stimulant medication, medicine that is commonly prescribed and can have some beneficial effects. But back when Eddie was in school, children like him were seen as bad or dumb or lazy.

We can't know if ADHD or a learning disability caused Eddie's difficulties in school. However, the frequency with which these diagnoses are applied to children (usually boys) and the widespread use of medications with young children trouble me. Some studies show initial positive changes, but there are occasional side effects, and the long-term effectiveness is debatable.

Children with ADHD can often benefit from behavioral-management techniques at home and at school, sometimes in combination with medications or psychotherapy.

Fast Eddie couldn't slow down; he burned off energy to feel better about himself. Without intervention, these children might seek areas of success away from the demands of school, sometimes in other outlets, such as sports. Occasionally, they might indulge in risk-taking behaviors or seek short-term relief by using over-the-counter or street drugs. Eddie eventually used both these methods.

Eddie kept his relationships on a superficial level. He used his charm and cultivated a pose of toughness at school and on the tennis courts. He wasn't able to fool himself; he was afraid of school and felt like a failure. He felt stupid.

Eddie barely graduated from high school. His older brother had gone on to college, but Eddie said, "School is for suckers!" He wasn't keen on studying extra hard and preferred to pursue tennis, hoping to become a teacher or pro. He also soon discovered that alcohol and marijuana gave him a buzz, reduced the pressures, and lifted his mood.

Eddie's laziness exasperated Emilio, and he insisted that Eddie join the Army Reserve, as his brother had done, a reminder that stung Eddie. Both his grandfather Ramon and his father, Emilio, extolled honorable military service; the walls of their homes were festooned with medals, mementos, and photographs of Ramon's service in World War I, Emilio's service in World War II, and his brother's service in the Korean War.

To avoid this haranguing, Eddie finally joined the Reserves, which turned out to be "a snap," as he put it. His duties were few, and he made "a few fast bucks." Much to his father's chagrin, the Army Reserve enabled Eddie's way of life.

Emilio pushed harder, and to placate him, Eddie took a job as a used-car salesman on commission. To his own surprise, his charm and edge made him a great salesman. Within a few months, he mastered the fast-talk

---

Family Lore

The lore handed down in some families is often an amalgam of fact and fancy. There is typically an inflated legend of the remarkable genetic stock, combined with outstanding personal characteristics of the family's forebears.

The stories accentuate accomplishments and courage, and they understate failures and omit nefarious events. They are meant to mythologize the older family members and enhance the images and pride of the current name bearers. These stories are meant to keep the heritage fires burning, to serve as goals of achievement and role models for the children, the future generations of the incipient dynasty. Pride in one's heritage can certainly serve to motivate, but when combined with an explicit or implicit unfavorable comparison, it can weigh heavily.

sales pitches, and his cars started moving off the lot, many of which were overhyped and defective. Bernie Strickland, his boss, saw in Eddie a younger version of himself. "You've got moxie" (i.e., assertive drive), he told him. Bernie increased Eddie's commission, added a modest salary, and soon began to use Eddie as a personal assistant in the business end of things.

At an auto-industry convention with Bernie in Las Vegas, the attractive and outgoing Flora, a recently divorced and talented sales-person, bedazzled Eddie. "She could put me to shame," he said. They dazzled each other and married within a few months, together making a formidable marketing duo.

In the midst of heightened love and enthusiasm, their ambition flourished, as did their greed. They decided that Eddie would leave Bernie and that they'd begin a new business that Flora had long been planning. The business was an illegal operation that they agreed was foolproof. They smuggled medications and street drugs from Mexico, which they sold at an inflated profit in Southern California.

This enterprise boomed, and they spread their sales to Arizona, New Mexico, and Texas. Giddy with newfound wealth, they felt on top of the world. Within three years, they—together with their two young sons, Ernesto and Claudio—were living in a large hacienda with a pool and his-and-hers Mercedes. He wanted to show the world, especially his father, that he'd made it big and didn't need a damn thing from anybody.

But drinking, using weed and cocaine, gambling, and partying began taking a toll. They argued—Eddie criticized Flora's spending, and she nagged about his absences and high living. Flora wanted to be more available to her little boys. She'd been the brains of the illicit operation, but she pulled her energies from the business and from Eddie. Things started to unravel.

Eddie enjoyed his risky lifestyle and failed to see that his family and livelihood were in jeopardy. Fast Eddie was living up to that moniker; he knew no self-imposed braking or moderation.

He couldn't have coped with a traditional nine-to-five job even if he'd wanted to. He needed to keep moving and always felt under pressure, but he never convinced himself that he was worthwhile.

Eddie's parents were again disenchanted, and Flora showed him little interest or affection. He realized he couldn't manage the complex criminal operation on his own. Losses and debts accumulated until he realized he had to pack it in.

Eddie went back hat in hand to Bernie Strickland, now a respected businessman who was the owner of three auto franchises and newly prominent in the Jewish community. Bernie was wary because Eddie had quit on him, but Eddie's past success and his contrition convinced him to take a chance.

However, Eddie's sales abilities had suffered from his high life and low mood. After a few lost sales and failed promises, he was out of a job. He and Flora had to sell their home, and they moved with the boys into a small condominium. In the eyes of Flora, his parents, and himself, Eddie was a failure.

After a few months of "wastefulness," as his father called it, Eddie's family met with Eddie in a sort of misguided intervention. More angry than sympathetic, they criticized his irresponsible behavior. Because of the family's military history, Eddie's family ordered him to enlist in the US Army. Eddie tried desperately to avoid this, pleading with his father and promising Flora, all to no avail. The family's honor came first.

As fate would have it, the decision and the pleading were moot: Eddie's Army Reserve battalion was called up to go to Vietnam.

According to the US Army, the Reserves were battle ready and could be called to war on short notice. "Everybody knew this was bullshit," Eddie reminisced. These part-time soldiers were unprepared. "We were scared shitless," Eddie said.

A captain told them they had a choice: "You can fight for your country, or you can run chickenshit away." No Morales man would ever be a draft dodger or deserter. Eddie knew he was going to war in Vietnam.

Within two months of training, including two weeks at Fort Dix, New Jersey, focused on heavy conditioning and munitions use, Eddie was in Saigon. Twenty-four hours later, their unit was in Da Nang; in another twenty-four hours, they were in Ankhe; and within less than a day, he was on patrol as part of a platoon with nine buddies on an advanced reconnaissance mission.

Climbing down ropes slung from a low-hovering helicopter, they dropped into a battle zone about twenty miles from HQ, and their mandate was to report on troop movements, armaments, and anything that "smelled, looked, or sounded like trouble."

Their mission was to ferret out locations of either the Viet Cong (VC) or the North Vietnamese Regular Army and then report back. They were told not to engage the enemy, which was a relief to most of them: they had been warned about the ruthlessness of the "Geeks," as they were referred to in a demeaning manner. Eddie pictured some dark phantom out there in the jungle, ready to devour him. He was terrified, suffocated by overwhelming fear. "I couldn't breathe; it was eerie. I peed in my pants; other guys shit in theirs," he said.

During their first few missions, they were exposed to the results of collateral damage. They saw injured civilians, including women and children, in destroyed villages. They were told, "It was the Cong." Even more frightening were the rumors of grotesqueries the VC inflicted on captured American soldiers.

One soldier said, "The Cong are paying us back for what our napalm and Agent Orange did to them," but the other guys shouted him down.

Andy Colson, the quiet, bespectacled platoon leader, then spoke in his Oklahoma drawl with a calmness that eased their anxieties. Andy told them he'd joined the army because he believed in the American cause. He'd been in 'Nam for all of five months and was now a seasoned veteran. He repeated the old adage "War is hell" and added, "Let's just do our jobs, and we'll all be okay." The presence of someone in authority helped sooth and anchor them. Further soothing came in the form of "sweet weed" they smoked every day at the base and on patrol.

On a mission soon afterward, a sniper popped out of a tunnel long enough to fire a single burst from an automatic weapon, killing Andy immediately. The sniper vanished into the complex maze of tunnels covering hundreds of miles of territory. The men were terrified, and a voice of an officer at HQ crackling over a battlefield phone promoted Eddie to replace Andy. "I was near panic!" Eddie recalled.

The traumatic assaults on all their senses overwhelmed them: in every cell and sinew of Eddie's body, in every breath he took, in every nuance of movement, there was exhaustion, vigilance, and a relentless fear. Eddie had no choice or time to think about his sudden designation as leader.

Back at base camp, Eddie was thinking this was a great honor he had to live up to, with the lives of the men now largely in his hands. When he lost a couple of platoon buddies in a landmine explosion near Da Nang, Eddie cried and was embarrassed, but the men seemed to move closer to him.

He wanted to share these experiences. He wrote a few letters to his family, to Bernie Strickland, and even to old tennis teammates, trying desperately to connect with someone. His father responded with a praising note but little else. The message was clear: they didn't believe him, or worse, they didn't care.

Eddie had never felt a close personal bond with anyone until he met the guys in his platoon; he liked them, and they depended on him. He was pleased to discover he was a good listener, and a lot of the guys felt comfortable confiding their personal concerns to him. He took pride, even some pleasure, in this imposed role: "I never admitted this to anyone, but after a while, I enjoyed what I was doing in 'Nam."

Eddie was more focused and fulfilled in the cauldron of Vietnam than he had ever been, and in his role, he felt pride and even, paradoxically, some inner peace.

The few letters that Eddie received were perfunctory responses, indicating little real interest or personal sentiments, and they made him feel worse. Eddie envied the men who were opening messages of love and longing. How he yearned for those messages.

In the eleventh month of his yearlong tour of duty, Eddie was slated to return home, and it jarred him that he would miss his buddies. The army wanted their experienced soldiers to stay for another tour, but few chose to do so. When they offered a higher pay incentive for multiple combat missions (MCMs), Eddie signed up. Flora felt that he was out of his mind, but Eddie's dad, Emilio, experienced a rush of pride.

Flora didn't realize that Eddie dreaded going home, where he felt like a loser. Eddie was aware of the public turmoil about the Vietnam War, how society derided and shunned 'Nam vets. But he felt he was

Comrades-in-Arms

Wartime camaraderie and bonding of soldiers is as old as war itself. This isn't exaggerated nostalgia; it's an authentic experience of soldiers thrown together in the heat and grotesqueries of battle, sharing fraternal love, pain, and sorrow. These relationships are intense and meaningful and can last a lifetime.

For soldiers like Eddie, whose past was unfulfilling, these wartime relationships can be vitalizing and enhancing. The bonds are based on living in close quarters on a 24–7 basis, with shared, deep emotional and physical experiences. The fears they experience, the carnage they witness, and the injuries and losses they endure together stay with them for years afterward.

Many soldiers experience feelings of sadness, guilt, anger, and shame after their return to civilian life—feelings mixed with accomplishment and pride. These shared experiences serve as an emotional epoxy, sealing the special bonds between soldiers.

Eddie's wartime comrades were his first intimate friends, closer to him than his family. He genuinely cared for them, and they reciprocated those feelings with an intense loyalty. Eddie was their respected leader, a model of maturity, calm, and confidence, like an older brother or a father figure. He was finally living up to the Morales lore, but who would believe him?

needed there—not to help win the war but to protect his comrades-in-arms. Finally, he was good at something! Even in the terror of battle, Eddie felt a sense of community and camaraderie he had experienced nowhere else. "I felt better ten thousand miles away in that jungle than I did back in the States," he said, and he wasn't alone. Many soldiers felt the same way.

On a crisp, sunny late-December day almost a year into his second tour of duty, Eddie was leading a routine reconnaissance mission. It was his fortieth mission, and although they were vigilant, the platoon that day was jovial, looking forward to a special Christmas Eve dinner and gifts back at the base. Copters dropped the soldiers off, and they regrouped and began their patrols. They came across a quiet hamlet of about two hundred or so huts, with a few men, women, and children milling about, eyeing them with curiosity and some suspicion but no overt hostility or fear. All was quiet.

He heard a sudden, loud yell from a boy, and then sheer bedlam broke out. Hundreds of VC soldiers entered the hamlet from all sides, shooting and tossing grenades. There were loud explosions; hovels in flames; acrid, dark smoke; terrified screams from children and mothers; bodies; and the smell of burning flesh. Horror! Then angry soldiers pounced on him, kicking him, and he felt the sharp stabs of bayonets and blows to his head and body and then darkness and eerie quiet.

The MASH unit couldn't handle Eddie's serious injuries, and he was airlifted that night to the base in Ankhe and then immediately to Saigon. Within less than a day, he was again airborne, this time to the army hospital in Frankfurt, Germany, where he was immediately sent to the operating room. This was the first of seven major surgeries he would have over the next year and a half. Powerful bayonet thrusts had shattered his right femur (the major thighbone), his abdominal cavity was a mess of gastric wounds, his large and small colons were in ribbons, his forearm bones were badly splintered, and he was in shock and delirious, with a high fever, dehydration, and serious infection.

Eddie learned afterward that during that last chaotic battle, almost all the civilians in the hamlet had been killed. Of his eleven-man platoon, four soldiers had been killed outright, and four were severely wounded. The other three were physically intact but in various states of emotional shock. Both the US Army press and the North Vietnamese media claimed this battle as a major victory.

For the next year and a half, Eddie was a physical and emotional shell of a human being. Long and painful recuperation and rehabilitation followed each difficult operation. He was bedridden for five months, then in a wheelchair for a year, and on crutches for months after that. He was finally discharged from Walter Reed Army Hospital in Washington, DC, almost nineteen months to the day of the firefight in that unnamed hamlet.

Flora had already sued for divorce, and Eddie had neither the energy nor the resources to contest it. He received an occasional vitriolic letter from Flora's lawyer, and from his children, he heard nothing. His Purple Heart and Bronze Star for valor in battle convinced only his father of his worth as a human being, a small consolation.

After two years of medical care and rehab, Eddie felt emotionally depleted. It was 1972; he walked with a permanent limp, his body ached, he was sapped of strength, and though exhausted, he had trouble getting a good night's sleep. The physical problems, he said, "were nothing compared to [his] mind." He was sad and withdrawn yet on edge, and he kept reliving that last battle in daydreams and nightmares. He would awaken suddenly in his dark room, soaking in sweat but unable to remember what had occurred. He saw a couple of psychiatrists in the clinic, who wanted to put him on more medications, which he refused. "I was taking so many meds for my pains that if I added any, I'd have been a zombie," he said, and he was probably right. He needed to find his own sense of being, belonging, and believing. He needed to find the benevolence within himself to reach out to others who were hurting just as much as he was.

An orderly who befriended him at Walter Reed told Eddie the diagnoses he had seen in his confidential medical chart: "personality disorder" (his disturbed "character"), based on his history of drugs and illicit activities; "recurrent depression"; and "war neurosis," an old term referring to emotional breakdowns due to exposure to battle. In those days, society saw this affliction as a sign of cowardice or malingering. (The diagnosis of post-traumatic stress disorder, or PTSD, was not as yet a defined psychiatric disorder.)

When Eddie finally returned home, he discovered he had no home. He tried to use his disabilities as a badge of courage, explaining why he was having trouble coping with life, but when people heard that he was a Vietnam vet, he sensed a taint of unpleasantness. "What's the matter with you?" and "You're not the only one who had it tough" were a couple of the comments he heard. *Welcome home,* he remembers thinking, fingering his medals.

Returning to Flora and the boys was not an option. He knew he'd badly screwed up as a family man, and now he didn't have the energy to be a husband and father. Eddie was almost relieved that his family had removed themselves from his life. He'd heard about other guys from his battalion who were involved in domestic violence, alcohol and drugs, divorce, and suicide.

Post-Traumatic Stress Disorder (PTSD)

Post-traumatic stress disorder (PTSD) is a psychiatric diagnosis that has become commonplace both in clinical work and in the media. It refers to the serious emotional reactions of individuals who have been exposed to frightening, life-threatening experiences. Symptoms often include intense mood changes, flashbacks, hypervigilance, withdrawal, avoidance, nightmares, insomnia, and fears. Dramatic behavioral changes, such as substance abuse, belligerence, and suicide attempts, can also occur.

Clinicians introduced the diagnosis of PTSD after the Vietnam War (too late for Eddie). Nowadays, the diagnosis is applied to traumatized soldiers returning from war zones (e.g., Iraq, Afghanistan), as well as to individuals who have suffered from severe trauma, such as child abuse, brutality, terrorist attacks, or natural disasters. It can be a profound disorder, reflecting the damage inflicted on human beings who have been confronted by extreme threats to their lives and loved ones.

The impressive resilience and coping skills of human beings can get them through even the most cataclysmic of disasters, but sometimes these skills are not enough. While experts have developed effective treatments for PTSD, the unfortunate reality is that such treatments are not always available in both military and civilian life.

A less-appealing perspective to this diagnosis is that it has become "in vogue" and is sometimes automatically ascribed to any individual who experienced abuses or tragedies. However, sometimes mood or behavioral problems preceded the traumatizing event. With the bar lowered recently for returning soldiers to have this diagnosis applied, there is concern that doctors use it in the absence of valid criteria.

This misuse is especially prevalent in legal disputes. In the pursuit of damages for having suffered, a potentially large financial award to the victim (and his lawyers) can cause one to emphasize pain and suffering and even feel symptoms more strongly. An explanation for this phenomenon is "secondary gain," which refers to the unconscious desire or need to exact punishment and to reap financial rewards for having suffered unduly.

Psychiatrists and other mental-health professionals should diagnose PTSD only when the clinical facts support the diagnosis. The facile use of this diagnosis can paradoxically act as an obstacle to treatment, giving the patient a permanent label as having suffered unduly and been permanently damaged.

He was ashamed of the way he looked and sounded. "I was pathetic," he said. The pain was visible in his eyes; the depths of despair and self-loathing were palpable to anyone who saw him then.

He'd fought for the United States, but he hadn't yet fought for himself. He was referred to a VA outpatient psychiatrist, who was a nice guy but was so busy with patients that he had little time to spend "just" talking to Eddie. He tried antidepressants, which made him feel worse; his misery continued.

Home from the terrors of war and largely healed from his physical wounds, Eddie should have felt relieved, but here, he wasn't the respected leader of men in combat. He felt paralyzed. His father made some overtures to him, but Eddie was ashamed; he had no family, no job, and no prospects.

With his head down and his tail between his legs, Eddie swallowed his pride and went back to Bernie Strickland. This time, he displayed no bravado: he was tearful, humiliated, and almost begging Bernie for a chance. Bernie was astounded when he first saw the thin, limping Eddie, recalling the outgoing young man with a flair for sales. Eddie told him about his war experiences and hospitalizations, his estrangement from his wife and kids, and his personal misery. Bernie said, "I must be *meshugeh* [crazy], but I take *rachmoness* [pity] on you. You fought for our country, so I'll give you a chance, but don't expect any special favors." He hired Eddie as a car salesman on a commission-only basis: he received no salary and was no longer Bernie's right-hand man.

Eddie was scared and wanted desperately to make it. He was tentative at first, but within a few months, he was turning over enough cars to pay his bills. He worked long hours seven days a week, seeing no one outside of work, pushing himself until collapsing into bed each night, exhausted. But he was feeling better about himself, doing honest work, holding his own, and earning his keep. He exhorted himself: "You did it in 'Nam; you can do it here!" In some ways, making it back home was harder than fighting in the steamy jungles. In the jungle, the rules were simple: you fight, and you sometimes die. You protect your friends. On the used-car lot, the only rule that seemed to matter was closing the deal, regardless of what he had to say or do to get it done.

With his increased moving of cars, Eddie's mood improved, and within a few months, he was closing even more sales. This time, however, he showed potential buyers a respectful patience, which set him apart from many of the other salespeople. He wasn't Fast Eddie or Slick Eddie. He didn't manipulate or mislead customers, and he steered them away from bad choices—something he'd never have done when he was younger and out solely to make his mark on the world.

Success was a salve to Eddie. The book *Been Down So Long It Looks Like Up to Me* by Richard Farina struck him as perfectly describing him. He was so used to problems that he had trouble believing his "up" was real.

He received warm letters from two of his platoon soldiers in 'Nam, both thanking him for his leadership and for safeguarding them. Eddie recalled when and where these guys had been injured, and he cried, "Me?"

As his depression lifted and his energy returned, Eddie tried to take up tennis again. He hadn't played in years, not only because of injuries but also because he remembered himself as a brash young player. Now, even with his limp, he could hold his own on the court. He was especially proud that an old and gimpy guy could defeat some younger men.

Eddie moved to a two-bedroom apartment in a modest complex that had a pool and a tennis court. He had a manageable income from his sales and his monthly military pension. He began to meet other tenants in the development, many of whom were single or recently divorced. He was feeling more vigorous and optimistic and starting to think about making friends, maybe even dating, a thought that hadn't crossed his mind in years. "I wasn't good enough for a half-decent woman," he said.

Lucy Ambruzzi was a thirty-one-year-old widow who had moved into Eddie's apartment complex with her seven-year-old daughter after her husband died of cancer. Eddie met her in an inauspicious way: he was looking for a lounge chair at the pool and sat down on Lucy's chair while she was playing in the water with her daughter, Audrey. Lucy and Audrey returned to find Eddie sitting on her chair, which she'd reserved with a towel, and Lucy was annoyed. Eddie was embarrassed and apologized, making a hasty retreat to his apartment.

Lucy had become more protective of Audrey since her husband passed away. Her parents were close to her and took care of Audrey when Lucy returned to college to become a high-school English teacher. But Lucy still worried.

The next time Lucy saw Eddie, he was sheepish and flustered, again apologizing, which she found touching. They were different: he kept conversations at superficial levels and was alone in life, while Lucy was serious and involved with her daughter and parents. Perhaps at an earlier time, they wouldn't have been interested, but now they felt drawn to each other.

They married a year later, and Eddie turned out to be a responsible and warm family man this time. It was not something he worked at; he felt devoted and grateful to Lucy and loved spending time with her and Audrey. His father, Emilio, began to visit Eddie again, now proud of his son, a decorated war hero and a hardworking and caring husband and father.

It was Emilio who broached the subject of Eddie seeing his sons, Ernesto and Claudio. Eddie was embarrassed about his earlier failure, and he knew that Flora was now in a stable marriage and had no interest in seeing Eddie. He had been thinking recently about his sons with feelings of guilt and longing.

Emilio brought an old, unsent letter addressed to Papa Morales and written in neat, childlike cursive writing in short sentences: "Dear Papa, We hope your wounds are better. We miss you. We want to see you." Eddie broke down sobbing, his copious tears expressing the regrets of his life and remorse for his past selfishness, the ways he hurt people, his loss of comrades—everything.

Eddie's sons were now adolescents; they'd written that letter a few years earlier and had given it to their grandfather. Their vague memories of Eddie were less of a daddy than of a hazy father figure. Flora's early anger had dissipated after she married Donald, a quiet churchgoing man who was a good stepdad to her sons. Eddie had receded from their thoughts, but when Ernesto and Claudio got older, they asked their granddad about him. When Emilio gave Eddie the letter, Eddie asked if they still wanted to see him.

The stars aligned: Eddie wanted to see his sons, and they wanted to see him. Emilio was the facilitator, and Flora and Donald were cooperative. The boys were excited yet anxious. The reunion of Eddie with Ernie (Ernesto) and Claude (Claudio) was everything they had hoped for. It had been a dozen years since they had seen each other, an interlude that evaporated through hugs, kisses, laughter, and tears. Daddy had returned.

When Emilio was older and frail and had to step down as the *pater familias* in the family, it was Eddie, not his older brother, who was unofficially anointed as the family leader. This man was certainly not the Fast Eddie whom everyone had known in his formative years and during his first marriage. Eddie assumed the mantle of leader as readily as he had in fighting in Vietnam, in becoming sales manager at work, and in making a family with Lucy and Audrey. He was proud of his sons, his wife and daughter, and himself. He had finally achieved the respect and appreciation he had always sought.

If Eddie's family is lucky, the transmission of the Morales genetic characteristics will be restricted to diplomacy, military acumen, leadership, and the love of family. Both Emilio and Eddie hope their early illicit business interests and those of patriarch grandfather, Ramon, are not in the cards for Ernesto and Claudio. So far, so good.

The Four Bs

Eddie's struggles stemmed from many things, but once again, we see that they began with his sense of being. In his case, he hid behind a persona of bravado as he took on the persona of Fast Eddie on the used-car lot. In Vietnam, he truly belonged for the first time, and even though many of his friends were killed or wounded, that sense of belonging was so sustaining that he found it difficult to leave the army behind. At home, all of the four Bs went missing until he finally hit bottom and began to claw his way back up. Thanks to the benevolence of his boss, Eddie was able to do just that.

Being

Eddie's old pattern of running away from stress or toward trouble ended. His life became stable and satisfying, and he was a responsible, caring dad. He came to grips with his past follies, fears, and frailties.

The mistakes he'd made in his earlier years were reminders of his weaknesses, but he was proud of having been a leader and protector of his men in Vietnam and now being a good family man. The fact that he had served his country with honor gave him cachet in the Morales family. Eddie liked what he saw in the metaphorical mirror of life—he had achieved a sense of being.

Belonging

As a child, Eddie felt he could never match up to his family's lore and expectations. He felt like an outsider and loser in high school. But in the cauldron of war in 'Nam and in his nest at home with Lucy and Audrey, he felt needed and respected. Leading the men in battle filled him with pride and responsibility, as did returning each evening from work to his haven, his wife and daughter. He renewed warm bonds with his sons, who palpably loved him. He rekindled his relationships with his parents and brother. Emilio (his "Colombian father") and Bernie Strickland (his "Jewish father") were proud of Eddie. After all the years of being a loner, Eddie had that sweet sense of belonging.

Believing

Eddie's family was irreligious, or secular, but they were immersed in the code of military honor, which he had derided as a young man. Eddie became proud of having been a soldier and leader. He had become a strong adherent of the values represented by the military codes of honor, courage, loyalty to comrades, belief in one's self, and, surprisingly, the importance of family. Like his grandfather, father, and brother, Eddie displayed his ribbons and medals on the walls of his home. Even when he was demonstrating at the White House, Eddie felt he was making a personal statement of these fundamental values. He was honoring fathers and mothers who had served and given their lives. This was his strong and abiding code of values to live by. Eddie did indeed achieve a sense of believing.

Benevolence

Eddie proved himself as a compassionate leader in Vietnam. His sons, Ernesto and Claudio, continued the family tradition of serving their country. Ernesto joined the marines, was in Kuwait during the first Gulf War, and returned as a decorated officer. Claudio graduated from college with a degree in political science and went into a career in the diplomatic corps, as his grandfather, Emilio, had done.

Eddie had contributed to the paths of his sons and was helping raise his daughter, Audrey, who was now a student in college. Lucy felt lucky to be married to him. Eddie represented veterans' groups in improving their benefits after years of service. A mature and caring Eddie, whose presence helped many others, supplanted the Fast Eddie who had been "running for his life," as he put it. Eddie attained a sense of benevolence.

Resilience

Fast Eddie did not live an examined life. He was always too busy hustling, literally and figuratively. After multiple self-inflicted setbacks and losses, including drugs and alcohol, greed, exploitation, two failed marriages, job disappointments, his stint in the National Guard, and family rejection, Eddie was called up to fight in a war. He had resented the military lore in his family; he was apolitical, used the National Guard as soft recreation, and knew nothing about Vietnam; and he had no intention of ever serving in the US Army.

How ironic that the pain and horrors of his two years in Vietnam served to bring out attributes in Eddie that even he had never known he possessed. He learned that he could be responsible, organized, dedicated, fulfilled, a leader, protective of others, and compassionate. No one would have used any of these words to describe Eddie as an adolescent and young adult. The war also inflicted an enormous physical and emotional toll on Eddie, who returned to the United States a broken, debilitated man.

Yet we know that Eddie turned his life around. This man, whose brother called him a bum before the war, is now gainfully employed as a good auto salesman with a modest income; is happily married to a lovely, caring teacher; and is the caring adopted father of a teenager. He doesn't drink or smoke, he plays tennis or works out regularly, and he lives comfortably in a modest home. Against all odds, Eddie has proven himself to be resilient.

Emotional Footprint

Young Eddie avoided responsibilities, exploited customers, was an unreliable husband and father, and engaged in illicit activities—not a pretty picture. One can attribute his failings to his grandfather and father's models of behaviors, his ADHD, his lack of confidence, and his low self-esteem. But the buck does stop there: adults must take responsibility for their actions and not blame failures on genetic inheritance, poor parenting, or unfortunate experiences.

Was the older Eddie a different incarnation? That same man with all those flaws went on to be a guardian of his platoon in the storm of war. After horrific injuries and arduous recuperation, he was a depleted individual who built himself into modest success and respectability. He fell in love and had a fulfilling family, reconciled with his sons, and was seen as the father figure for nieces, nephews, and other extended family. That same man left a positive emotional footprint.

Postscript

Flora forgave Eddie for his destructive behaviors in their marriage. She'd become an adherent to a New Age healing community and had cast aside her anger and adopted forgiveness. She accepted her role in their escapades and knew she was complicit. Without her brains and Fast Eddie's energy, their business would have foundered.

9

Nora Jenkins and Howard Gladstone

The Observer

You see a woman in her midforties in an aisle seat next to a man she's obviously in love with. She's dressed nicely, and she's got enviable poise as she stands up to put a heavy tote on the rack. She laughs at something the man says. Her smile is warm and kind. You remember seeing the couple when they boarded the train awhile back and noting that the man looked as if he were at least twenty years older than she was. You wondered if she was a typical trophy wife.

You think more about both of them. What is their story? You've looked into the faces of the people around you and tried to figure out what made each individual person tick, and even if you're wrong in your guesses, which you know you probably are, it's been an exercise that conveniently kept your mind off your own worries and troubles.

You are now three stops from the city. Your estimated time of arrival is only fifteen or twenty minutes away. You feel a knot in your stomach. You know it's not from hunger pangs, even though you didn't eat much of a breakfast. No, it's not hunger—it's nerves. The woman with the older man laughs again. Somehow, her voice is soothing, like cool balm on a nasty burn.

The Riders

Nora's Story

Nora Jenkins grew up in an atmosphere that she remembers as gray: the walls of the small apartment in which she lived with her parents and brother were a patchwork of faded gray wallpaper and peeling paint, the row of apartment buildings in the family's working-class neighborhood were made of drab concrete, and the weather was often overcast. To go along with this dull environment, the mood in Nora's home was dour and dark.

In spite of these surroundings, Nora was a cheerful child. She was bright and warm, and when home alone, she was happy being in her private thoughts, playing or reading, satisfying an active curiosity.

The Jenkins family lived on the top floor of an austere six-story apartment house near the airport. The surroundings didn't bother Nora, since she had never known anything else, but the airplane roars jarred her. From an early age, she knew that she wanted to "live somewhere quiet," she said, referring to her parents' frequent squabbling and especially to the shuddering roars of planes taking off and landing. This din started at the crack of dawn and continued all day and well into the night. The sounds would get so loud that all conversation had to cease unless the speakers yelled, which they often did. The airplane noise and vibrations would often prompt her parents to mutter resentment at their lot in life.

Her mother, Mabel, and father, Arthur, were unhappy with the hand they'd been dealt, and they were angry with the God who had let them down despite their churchgoing and praying. They had emigrated from England in the hope of a much better life than the one they had led in grimy, working-class Manchester.

Arthur worked long hours as a maintenance worker for one of the small factories that had sprouted around the airport. By a quirk of fate, Mabel had a job in that same factory, but she was a secretary to the general manager. Arthur resented that his wife earned more money than he did, as well as her airs, since Mabel emphasized her executive status to Arthur. She criticized him and blamed him for their dull surroundings and life.

As a young child, Nora loved fairy tales and dreamed she'd someday live in a beautiful home that would be serene and quiet. She would marry her handsome Prince Charming and be swept away to a life of happily ever after.

She kept her good cheer even when things at home were unpleasant, her pleasant disposition not to be denied by others' gloominess. Her teachers called her Little Nora Sunshine because of her effervescence and enthusiasm.

She was an above-average student, was fairly attractive, and had a social ease with people. She loved both private conversations and public speaking, a pleasure that continued throughout her life. Nora was a popular teenager, and she didn't smoke, drink, or indulge in drugs or sex.

Even as an adolescent, Nora had a firm belief that things would work out for her, that she would realize her dreams. Unlike her parents, Nora had no quarrel with God, and while she didn't believe in a Supreme Being, she had a spiritual bent, attributing her good fortune to her karma.

In college, Nora studied media and journalism as her majors. She at first wanted to be a journalist and writer, but she soon realized that her skills in that area were not good enough. However, she learned quickly that when she was speaking in public or on camera in the college studios, she was relaxed, and the listeners or viewers were captivated. Her performances were good, but it was the combination of her appearance, voice, and engagement with her audience that won people over. Nora was naturally appealing and telegenic. A professor said, "The camera just seems to like you."

Nora often anchored college performances and television shows, and by the time she was only a couple of years out of school, she was hosting a daytime television talk show. New opportunities and experiences opened up, and the interesting people she was meeting swept her away, but she never lost her humility.

She had a few close girlfriends whom she enjoyed seeing from time to time, but she was so busy now that she liked being alone at home. She turned down most date requests, though when she did spend as few evenings with men, there was no spark. Her professional ambitions were her priority, and her youthful dream of a Prince Charming had disappeared.

Nora was amused by some of the ambitious men she met, finding some immature, others pathetic, and many inept, and she handled any tension with sensitivity and aplomb. She showed interest in them but gave them the message that she didn't share their romantic goals.

Nora blossomed into a self-assured and fulfilled woman. She enjoyed her professional life, and while she considered seeking a more national spotlight, she also began thinking of the meaning of her life. What else was there that she wanted? The benefits of remaining in her home city were apparent. She had a better relationship with her parents, who enjoyed the local celebrity status of their daughter, and she helped them financially as well. She was close to her younger brother, Caleb, who was now in graduate school, getting his MBA.

On her daily TV show, Nora interviewed Donna Landry, a media celebrity who had written a new self-help book based on her experiences in Scientology. Nora was searching for something more in her life, and she accepted Donna's invitation to an evening at their headquarters, in part because she was impressed with Donna's positive attitude about everything. She read as much as she could about Scientology and its curious mixture of science fiction, religion, zealotry, and pop psychology. After a couple of visits, the positive vibes and commitment of the people there impressed Nora.

She began spending a few hours a week there. Most of the members of Scientology were young adults and unattached. They were clean cut and didn't appear to be involved in any destructive behaviors. She liked their optimism and apparent willingness to discuss all kinds of issues.

At times, she felt uncomfortable with their proselytizing, and their self-assuredness was at times off-putting. After a while, she began to find them self-righteous and arrogant, but she kept spending time with them because they seemed to share her interests in personal growth. She had neither seen nor experienced the elusive feeling of inner peace and spirituality that they espoused.

The True Believer

A true believer in any fundamentalist doctrine is absolutely certain of the validity of his or her belief. These people are often self-righteous and even zealous, feeling that they always, as Bob Dylan wrote in 1967, "have God on their side."

When I studied members of religious cults, I found that their average stay as members was limited. The vast majority of even the most fervent are out in less than two years. The upheavals in their families, however, can be dramatic and painful; the period when the member is wholly committed to the group's leader and ideology often wreaks havoc on parents.

The early zealous feelings of true believers are typified by a state of bliss, with worship of the leader, parroting of tenets, renunciation of past beliefs and affiliations, and unshakable certainty about their faith. Within months of joining, however, these sentiments usually give way to doubts, self-questioning, and home-sickness, which are soon supplanted by a desire to leave the group, sometimes with antagonistic reactions.

Despite the widely different traditions and beliefs among these groups, their members usually follow this remarkably similar path. Former believers have healing work to do afterward, but usually there is little or no permanent harm. However, there have been tragic outcomes. The effects of radical, absolutist leaders on mesmerized followers are worse when the groups are charismatic and have militant goals and behaviors. Their members are convinced their causes are vital and justify any means to accomplish their ends.

But before we decry all intense belief systems as cults, we must remember our accepted religions were looked upon as cults in ancient times.

Nora's original youthful goals were nonspiritual—her nice, quiet home and mythical Prince Charming. Her beautiful and soundproof apartment overlooking the water brought her great pleasure, but she no longer sought a man who would rescue her. "I still wanted to fall in love, but I just wanted a decent human being," she said. She knew he wouldn't be shallow, narcissistic, or filthy rich.

Nora was reconsidering what was truly important to her. She was grateful for the blessings life had bestowed yet was embarrassed at times by her good fortune. She had recently moved more into news broadcasting, which opened her eyes to the world, to the deprivation and suffering that existed at home and abroad. Her goals were changing. Instead of materialism, she wanted spirituality; instead of a Prince Charming, she wanted a substantial, decent man; and instead of pushing herself to stardom, she was interested in working for the benefit of others less privileged.

Nora's father, Arthur, died suddenly, succumbing to a massive heart attack while sitting in his car at a stoplight. Caleb rushed home from his finance job on Wall Street, and Nora managed the funeral arrangements. She gave emotional support to her mother, Mabel, who was a mess. The loss of her lifelong partner, whom she had disparaged over the years, devastated her. Mabel missed Arthur's calming presence, which had given her comfort.

Mabel came to depend on Nora, who visited her regularly and began taking her to social functions. She helped her out financially and served as her mother's confidante. Nora enjoyed getting close to Mabel and came to depend on her mother's maturity and counsel. Mabel was proud of both of her children's accomplishments and especially appreciated that they were strong supports during the period of mourning.

Her two successful grown children needed their mother as well. She would advise them if they asked, but Mabel was wise enough not to offer advice gratuitously, especially on touchy subjects. However, when asked for an opinion, she did not mince words. They appreciated their mother much more now than they had when they were children.

Mabel advised Nora that she should quit Scientology. She had noticed Nora's discomfort whenever she discussed her experiences there. Donna, the woman who had originally pushed her to join and had raved about the church's power for growth and healing, had long since left. Nora was becoming increasingly uncomfortable with the corporate atmosphere and high-powered marketing. She found the atmosphere stifling, smothering any contrary perceptions. Nora disliked their self-righteousness and their intolerance toward nonbelievers. She heard hostility to others and a kind of groupthink that chilled her. She questioned the worship of L. Ron Hubbard—the deceased, controversial science-fiction writer—as a kind of earthly deity.

When Nora raised the possibility of leaving the church, the leaders and other members at first made an appeal to her, ostensibly based on their intense caring for her. They pointed out the psychological and spiritual essence of Scientology. As she became more adamant

Quest for Spiritual Enlightenment

In her quest for spirituality, Nora was searching for a state of enlightenment and inner peace that had eluded her. Every time she thought she'd found happiness and a sense of being she could accept, the sentiment vanished like mist on a warm summer morning. A cynic might say, "Why on earth wasn't she happy? She's successful and rich! Who wouldn't feel blessed and spiritually connected with a great job and no financial worries?" But wealth and success do not equate with spirituality. Many wealthy materialists do not wonder about things metaphysical, and there are spiritually satisfied individuals who are living frugally.

Spirituality is not easy to define. People discuss words like enlightened, mystical, and sacred as if we all understand them as meaning the same thing. To Nora, spirituality meant a state of inner fulfillment, self-knowledge, and serenity. Nora's quest was at least as authentic and compelling as yours or mine.

For every path to satori, or inner peace and enlightenment, one can find a teacher or a master to take him or her there, so caveat emptor.

Many thousands of people have attained a state of spiritual awakening, and millions more are searching for that holy grail. There is an innate human need to grasp some meaning to life's wonders and travails. Whether through meditation or chanting, art or music, distance running or writing or through myriad other possible ways, those who have truly achieved an advanced state of consciousness are transported from the preoccupations and demands of everyday life to a state of inner peace and compassion above the fray of life. There is wonder about getting there, but there is no wonder about why we are on that quest.

about leaving, they showed impatience and anger, including what she perceived as veiled threats. When she told this to Mabel, her mother blurted out, "Everyone knows it's a cult!" Nora was not going to get into a theological argument with her mother, but she decided that she was never going back.

Nora was in a strange space after leaving Scientology—she was relieved to be free of their expectations and demands, yet she felt at loose ends, uninspired. Her work was going well, and her social life was busy, yet she felt lonely and unfulfilled and still felt no sense of spirituality.

Howard's Story

Howard Gladstone was a man-about-town, known to be a hard-driving businessman and a self-made multimillionaire (with investments in real estate, development, the stock market, airport duty-free shops, and a financial trust company). Articles about him abounded in newspaper business and society pages. He was handsome, wealthy, and ambitious as well as narcissistic and arrogant. He'd been married three times and had fathered three grown children, who avoided him.

Howard was intelligent and well read, though he was a pretentious intellectual wannabe. He spoke with carefully chosen polysyllabic words and measured cadences to give the impression of intellectual weight. In fact, he'd never graduated from college, from which he dropped out, he said, "to make some real money." He accomplished this with ease, but his envy of those with university degrees and professional careers grated on him for many years.

His immigrant Jewish father, Manny, was a Holocaust survivor whose family had been killed in concentration camps. A self-taught and knowledgeable man, he became a tailor in order to support his family in a small town. Manny was modest, warm, and soft-spoken. "Manny is such a sweet man," people often said with emphasis, meaning he was the opposite of his son. Manny wanted to give his family a good life but barely made ends meet. Howard stated that he was not going to make Manny's big mistake: he was going to be rich.

Manny wanted Howard to graduate and become a successful physician, and he was bitterly disappointed when his son dropped out of college. Years later, in spite of Howard's wealth, he knew he didn't have his father's genuine respect, which he craved. *"A charpeh un a shandeh!"* (Yiddish for "A tragedy and a shame!") his father scolded when Howard cut his education short.

Over the years, Howard kept the secret of his lack of a college education hidden, even from his own children. He tried to befriend intellectuals, artists, and musicians, hoping they'd accept him in their circles. His need to be respected as an intellectual caused him to relentlessly pressure his children to excel scholastically. He craved money and respect but never received the latter.

When Howard left the mother of his children (his second wife), he faced hostility from all of them, further fueled because it was clear he had fallen for a young, vivacious French beauty known in social circles simply as Madeleine. She loved the life of luxury, which was ironic, given that she was originally from a poor rural village in France. She had married a much older, wealthy man who had died of a massive coronary, leaving her with a great deal of money. He had also left her a surly, troubled adolescent son, Serge (from his first marriage), and US citizenship, which he had somehow arranged. After a whirlwind romance, Madeleine became Howard's third wife.

This marriage of beautiful people lasted for only four tumultuous years. Stories circulated about wild parties in their palatial home, physical battles, and affairs and separations, not to mention arrests and psychiatric hospitalizations of Serge. As some had predicted, their turbulent marriage ended abruptly and tragically.

On a Monday morning, their housekeeper returned from a weekend off to find the naked Madeleine, white and cold, lying dead on the marble floor of her upstairs boudoir. She had succumbed to an overdose of a lethal cocktail of prescribed medications, including tranquillizers, antidepressants, sleeping pills, and painkillers, which she had swallowed at least two days earlier. Howard was in Europe on business with a woman and flew home immediately. Madeleine had received no calls in at least two days from her husband, son, stepchildren, or friends, a telling comment on Madeleine's demise.

The autopsy report stated that her death was due to an accidental overdose, which is sometimes is a valid description of what occurred but is often a code for suicide, used to protect the reputation of the deceased and the family.

The cocky Howard visibly crumbled. For years, he had dismissed criticism from his family, his few friends, and others as malicious envy, but now he felt he deserved the animosity. He felt complicit in Madeleine's death—suicide or not—and ruminated about letting down his father, hurting his wives, and ruining his children's lives. He felt he was a destructive force in many lives, and he remembered and exaggerated his misdeeds.

His suffering had all the earmarks of clinical depression: sadness, lack of pleasure in any activities, self-criticism and self-loathing, fatigue, insomnia, withdrawal, and some thoughts of ending his own life. It might have been an ideal time for Howard to see a psychiatrist, but he ignored that advice out of hand: "*They* are going to help *me?*" That was how he felt, as if he were above the fray of the common person. Of course, he wasn't.

Howard had a love–hate relationship with doctors. He'd addressed his father's disappointment in him for not becoming a physician by his ownership of a prestigious art deco building that housed physicians' suites. He was thus in close contact with many doctors and often in conflict with them, deriding their poor business sense and their lack of intellectual depth. Most of all, he resented their status in society, which he coveted more than anything.

As bad as he was feeling, Howard had no intention of going to see a so-called shrink, viewing that as a cop-out. He'd seen too many people, including his wives and children, in psychotherapy or on a slew of useless medications. Always a doer, he knew he had to do *something*. He hated that he was wallowing in self-pity and self-hate and that he was spinning, making no forward moves. He had always detested this when he saw it in others.

Howard's parents had raised him in a nondevout Jewish home, where the food laws of kashruth (kosher laws) were not followed, blessings were not part of domestic rituals, and his parents only went to *shule* (synagogue) on the High Holidays or for weddings and bar mitzvahs. But Manny and his wife made sure that Howard learned Hebrew and Yiddish in school; they had a *Pesach* seder (Passover meal) with matzo (unleavened bread) and latkes (potato pancakes) and had a menorah (candelabra) on Chanukah (the Festival of Lights). This was the totality of Howard's exposure to his religion. Manny was a proud Jew, strongly supportive of Israel and suspicious of any hint of anti-Semitism from any source, but he had forsaken religion. Manny became an atheist after losing his family in the Holocaust. "No God would have allowed that to happen," he'd often say, and that statement left a lasting impression on Howard.

But in in his hour of need, Howard turned to a religious source—and not just any religious source. He sought the brilliant Rabbi Bernard Felstein, an outspoken rabbi who wrote regular iconoclastic and provocative newspaper columns, magazine articles, and books on varied subjects. His columns were literate and entertaining, but his opinions were often inflammatory. Some in the Jewish community adored Rabbi Felstein, but many more disliked him. At the age of seventy-seven, he still held annual High Holiday services in a rented Unitarian church. He was an eloquent speaker, and his sermons, like his writings, never failed to antagonize some of his yearly congregants.

Rabbi Felstein readily agreed to meet with Howard because he wanted to be of spiritual guidance, and he was curious, given Howard's reputation. These two men were similar in that they had each achieved success at some price of public criticism. They met in a booth at a local deli, and they hit it off.

Rabbi Felstein tried to reframe some of Howard's self-recriminations, and after almost two hours of listening and discussion, he suddenly came up with a suggestion that jolted Howard: "You know what would be good for you, Howard? Why don't you go to Israel and work on a kibbutz?" Kibbutzim (collective farms), socialist models of community and labor, began in the 1930s and later became highly successful industrial and intellectual powerhouses. The rabbi and the ultracapitalist discussed this idea, and Howard was captivated; he decided on the spot to take on this radical departure.

He took off from work, calling his departure "a sabbatical," giving it a spin of acceptability and even respect, though few were impressed, and many laughed. Although he could afford this self-funded hiatus, he would never have left his business interests in the past, fearing that he would lose a fortune. But he knew that he had to get away—in fact, his very existence depended on it.

For the next two years, Howard worked on a kibbutz in the Negev desert in the south of Israel. He worked as a laborer in the fields, a dishwasher and floor cleaner in the communal kitchen, an assembly-line worker in the kibbutz plastics factory, and an English teacher in the school, and months later, his business expertise was utilized in the kibbutz enterprises.

Howard had never been happier. The kibbutz was not a socialist utopia. The system had more equitable distribution of wealth and common group goals than other social systems, but they had their share of human pettiness and frailties, difficult people, competition, and conflict, as in most human communities.

He also saw more commitment, communal caring, idealism, and satisfaction in work without personal profit than he had ever seen at home. Howard had taken a quantum leap downward from his life of affluence. On the kibbutz, he lived in a one-bedroom apartment with few amenities and shared many facilities. There were some activities, movies, and concerts, but there was no thriving social scene. However, there were many meaningful conversations with good friends, and he felt fulfilled. His depression lifted, he felt energized and healthy, and he enjoyed being in a warm group with great values and goals.

In the middle of his second year there, he began thinking of returning home. He considered starting life afresh there—making amends, rekindling the relationships with his children, and meeting two new grandchildren. He knew he still enjoyed making money, but the possibility of a new way of living and doing business excited him. His kibbutz mates tried to convince him to stay, but it was soon clear that Howard was determined to leave. However, he was committed to his newfound sense of empowerment and communal involvement.

Six months later, Howard was back home. His attempts to reconnect with his children were tenuous at first, but he was determined to keep trying. He was again overseeing his businesses, but his zeal for self-aggrandizement had disappeared. When his name began to reappear in the papers, it was because he was giving philanthropic gifts to health, educational, and cultural institutions. Cynics derided him, assuming that he was using these gifts as tax dodges or that they were a sham.

Howard fully expected this criticism and felt it was part of his penance for contributing to Madeleine's death, hurting others, and being a greedy jerk. The fifty-five-year-old college dropout was completely serious about changing his values and behavior and was committed to making a positive difference. But when he publicly stated that he wanted to contribute to future generations of citizens, he was mistrusted.

Love at First Sight

On a cold winter day, Nora Jenkins was to emcee a charity function on behalf of Children's Hospital, and she wasn't pleased. Not only were the streets impassable, but she also had recently learned that the honoree at the function was to be Howard Gladstone, who had just given CH a major donation. Nora had heard of his reputation as flamboyant and self-seeking, and she regretted accepting this gig. When she caught a glimpse of him sitting alone in a corner of the ballroom, his presence offended her, but he did look somewhat forlorn. *An act,* she thought.

Nora steeled herself for a self-promoting speech, but if anything, Howard was modest about the financial gift he had made for a research wing named to honor his father (the Manual Gladstone Medical

Research Building). In his brief speech, he said he had given the bequest to honor his dad and contribute to society. He alluded to mistakes he'd made, talked about working on a kibbutz, and outlined what he had learned about "the responsibility we all have to each other."

Howard's speech moved Nora. She'd heard about his faults and excesses, with embellishments by her mother, but he had exuded humility, the opposite of the arrogance she had expected. When he approached Nora after the ceremonies, she was somewhat uneasy, but he was polite and respectful. She found him to be attractive and felt a spark between them, which embarrassed and unnerved her.

Howard asked her if she would like to join him for coffee at a nearby café, and she was surprised at how quickly she accepted. They were both nervous at first, and Nora frankly admitted to Howard her misgivings and even her negative expectations of him. She found Howard interesting, intelligent, and worldly as well as surprisingly warm and self-critical. They sat for a couple of hours, both entranced yet wary. Nora remembered Mabel's warnings, and Howard, in turn, was already having a déjà vu ("Here I go again") experience. He was smitten by Nora and was terrified that he would rush headlong into romance and then inevitably destroy it and her.

It was getting late, and the next day was an early workday. They nervously exchanged phone numbers and agreed they should meet again soon. They exchanged stiff, tentative hugs and parted, both feeling uneasy and excited.

By the time Nora got home, an insecure-sounding voice mail from Howard awaited her, in which he sounded hesitant, even frightened. This man whom Mabel described as an egotistical scoundrel sounded to Nora like a lost little boy. He told her, "I had a wonderful time, but I don't trust myself." His anxiety and trepidation were completely understandable. He was smitten by her and didn't want to hurt her. While he had changed, he was still not fully trusting of himself and questioned whether he could finally have a healthy intimate relationship.

Nora called him back, and they agreed to meet for lunch the next day. They walked in a park on the weekend, and they met the following Tuesday in a bistro. Still, caution prevailed, but they kissed quickly on parting. The following Friday afternoon, their conversation was more personal, and their kiss was lingering. It was clear to Nora and Howard that in spite of their apprehensions, they were falling in love.

Nora had become convinced that this special feeling she had read and heard about in so many poems and love songs would never be hers. She had long dismissed her childish Prince Charming expectation, but here she was. For all her avowed need for spirituality and meaning, she had fallen in love with someone who was infamous for being materialistic and shallow. She had told herself that her love would be a man of substance, anything but an arrogant entrepreneur.

She knew that she would look like a fool to others, but she also knew—hoped—they were wrong. "I knew one thing: he made my heart sing," she said, referring to the old rock song "Wild Thing."

When she told Mabel how she felt about Howard, the reaction was predictable. Mabel was appalled. Nora protested, saying, "There is something so sweet about Howard."

"Have you lost your marbles?" Mabel asked. She heaped scorn on Howard, describing him as an "old reprobate" and "a dirty old man."

Offended by her mother's tirade, she told Mabel to knock it off and said she knew what she was doing; she was a mature, independent woman and could protect herself. "Howard Gladstone is a wonderful man," she blurted out, "and I love him."

Nora was convinced that through the prism of love, she'd seen the true Howard Gladstone, and she was not going to let her mother's fierce opposition deter her. At first, Mabel wouldn't hear of meeting Howard, but she finally relented under Nora's pressure. She was beside herself with nervousness, dreading the encounter, but after a couple of hours together, Howard's warmth and apparent honesty won her over. Most important was Nora's palpable happiness.

Their marriage was a modest and private event, held in the garden of their home and attended by Nora's mother and brother and Howard's three grown children with their spouses and children. Nora did not convert to Judaism, but she read books written for those who were marrying from out of the faith. Still searching for a personal spiritual awakening, she was taken with Judaism's traditions of communality and caring and with what she'd read about the traditions of Jewish spirituality.

Howard's confidant, Rabbi Bernard Felstein, and Nora's Presbyterian minister (for Mabel) conducted the wedding ceremony. Rabbi Felstein followed the Hebrew script and liturgy, and he included the traditional chuppah (canopy above the betrothed) and the shattering of the wine glass. His personal speech brought them both to tears, and the ceremony and exchange of vows included romantic poetry from the biblical Song of Songs, Nora's favorite love songs, and music from other traditions. Manny Goldstone, a widower in his early eighties and in failing health, was proudly at the head table at the reception, and he gave a moving speech, saying to his sixty-one-year-old son, "I am so proud of you, Howie. I love you." Howard and Nora both cried, as did many of the guests.

Nora and Howard have now been married for over ten years, and contrary to many predictions, Howard has not wavered from the values he converted to some thirteen years ago. They have a son, Bernard, named after the late Rabbi Felstein, whom they are raising in the manner of their wedding ceremony—with Jewish traditions mixed with ecumenical, humanistic, and spiritual influences, in keeping with Nora's quest for her spiritual awakening. They belong to a unique old Jewish synagogue downtown, which had been abandoned and then restored by the members. The heterogeneous congregation is much like the one Rabbi Felstein led years earlier, consisting of family members, gays and lesbians, disenchanted traditionalists, iconoclasts, secular and religious Jews, agnostics, and atheists. While Nora and Howard are not regular attenders, they feel they are part of this close community, led by their spiritual leader, Rabbi Lynn Silver, who has a PhD in sociology and is a single mom.

Howard, at seventy-three, is increasingly balding, paunchy, and somewhat slower afoot, but he enjoys his life and family and has been working less. He is toying with retiring in order to devote himself to his family and charitable causes. He gives considerable thought to the specific recipients and nature of his gifts, all of which carry a message of encouragement and hope to the beneficiaries in the fields of health, education, and the arts.

His sons have reconciled with their dad and have joined his businesses, but he insisted that they first spend a few months each on the same kibbutz that helped him turn his own life around. The city's denizens now respect Howard Gladstone as a generous and creative philanthropist.

Nora has made her young son her top priority, but she still finds time to do a few television specials and public appearances. She is grateful for her life. Her personality has not changed much since she was living in the drab apartment house near the airport—she is still optimistic, cheerful, modest, and introspective, and she still hates noise. She continues her quest for a spiritual experience and existence but feels she is much closer to achieving that goal.

The Four Bs

Nora and Howard both experienced significant changes in their lives as they matured and found their unique places in the world. Their first positive steps forward involved refining their own sense of being, and that, in turn, led to all of the good things that followed, including a firm belief in themselves and in humanity, a sense of belonging to each other and to the wider community, and a desire to give back in a way that truly led to a intangible legacy of good.

Being

Howard Gladstone changed dramatically, some would say beyond the realm of possibility. People can indeed accomplish meaningful and transcendent change if they are strongly motivated and show authentic dedication, humility, and restitution to those whom they have hurt in the past. Nora accomplished her sense of being through her journey into Scientology and her subsequent rejection of some of its teachings, which led her indirectly to Howard and her acceptance of his love.

Belonging

Nora and Howard's sense of belonging changed over time. At first, Nora felt secure in her career. She belonged with her colleagues in broadcasting. She was at home in her world, but that life eventually left her with a feeling that there had to be something more—and there was. Howard found his need to belong playing out in the context of business, through his dedication to working long hours to make as much money as possible. Both of them as individuals sought belonging in the bedrock of careers, and both ultimately found that they needed more. In the end, they belonged to each other and their families.

Believing

It's interesting to see how believing also changed for Nora and Howard. They initially believed only in themselves—their own unique talents that made them successful in their careers. As we've seen, careers weren't enough. Nora moved into the realm of Scientology, hoping to find a connection to a community and to herself that would satisfy the spiritual emptiness she felt, but she ultimately discovered her beliefs rested with a melding of Judaism and spirituality after she met Howard.

Howard didn't find his connection to believing until he traveled to Israel. A recurrent theme in this book is that nobody does it alone, especially in achieving examples of believing, as we have seen time and again. In In Howard's dramatic turnaround after he hit an emotional rock bottom, it was first Rabbi Bernard Felstein and later the kibbutzniks (members) who helped him face and overcome his demons. However, this would not have happened if Howard hadn't already realized that he was on a path to self-destruction. He was already strongly self-motivated to save himself. Believing reinforces itself, because there is no doubt that Nora would have been repelled and would have had nothing to do with the previous incarnation of Howard.

Benevolence

In a sense, Nora's most important act of benevolence was her acceptance of Howard's love. In accepting his love, she helped open up his world. Indeed, her acceptance reinforced Howard's determination to continue his path of philanthropy and his desire to reconcile with his sons. Thus, the benevolence was linked in their case. Howard's generosity would have probably continued because he was on the road to great change in his life even before he met Nora, but her influence allowed him to extend his generosity to his family in ways he had never done in the past. Often, benevolence ties directly into the kind of emotional footprint a person leaves as a legacy.

Resilience

Nora was inherently resilient as a little girl growing up in a working-class neighborhood comprised of tenements, factories, and warehouses sprinkled like dirty clumps of snow around a busy airport, the din of aircraft coming and going so ubiquitous that she was numb to it. Her parents were largely unhappy in their marriage, and conflicts within the home occurred frequently. Yet Nora remained cheerful most of the time, bouncing back every time despair threatened to knock her flat. She used her talent for resiliency to forge a career in television. Broadcasting is not an easy path to follow. You have to fail before you can succeed, and that was the essence of Nora. She had a sense of herself, a belief in her abilities, and a generous soul that helped her feel as if she belonged. Nora was also resilient after she made the decision to leave Scientology. Her experience did not turn her off religion. It actually led her to find a compromise of beliefs that now make her happy.

Howard's resiliency also traces back to his youth, though at the time, it was born of negativity. He could have given up at an early age, but he was determined to make something of himself, regardless of his lack of education. He persevered and climbed his way up in the world of business. Entrepreneurs fail. They all do! So did Howard, but he bounced back every time and parleyed his failures into stunning financial success. Sadly, his resilience did not initially influence him in a positive manner. In fact, he lost his humanity.

When Madeleine committed suicide, Howard hit bottom. You might say that his wife's tragic death led to the impetus behind his reconnection with humanity and himself. His exploration of his religious faith and eventual foray to the kibbutz in Israel led to a resilience of a most positive nature. He discovered for the first time that he had an abiding love of helping others, and that discovery changed his life, allowing him to meet and fall in love with Nora. The combination of the four Bs can be powerful in life, and Nora and Howard discovered just that.

Emotional Footprint

As with most of our passengers and in many of our own lives, Howard's life is yet another example to us that few humans are as pure as the driven snow. His emotional footprint will be strangely contradictory, contrasting, and even conflicted.

His earlier existence prior to the tragedies that befell him and before his forced sabbatical escape to find himself represented unseemly behavior and detrimental effects on many different people. He himself would now agree that he acted abominably in those days of greed and arrogance. He would also agree that he was the epitome of narcissism in his personal and professional relationships. Most people who knew him at that time vilified him.

Yet it was this same individual who—after months of escape, hard manual and psychological work, learning and repentance, and an epiphany-like realization—seemingly transformed into a radically different, benevolent, compassionate, selfless, generous person.

Is this transformation even within the realm of possibility? The answer is yes, as we see when we discuss these kinds of personal revelations and redemptions.

There will be some family, friends, and associates whose equilibrium was truly shaken by the negative vibes given off by the younger Howard. To them, his emotional footprint was unequivocally and irretrievably a negative one. But to other family, friends, and associates and especially Nora and their son, Howard will always be the epitome of decency, leaving a positive emotional footprint.

Nora's emotional footprint was consistently positive. She is one of those rare individuals who seldom creates negativity while going through life. When she accepted Howard's love in spite of protestations from her mother and friends, she solidified her positive emotional footprint, and she continues to do so with her family and in the wider community at large through her involvement with philanthropic endeavors.

10

Michael Kounigis

The Observer

T he engineer announces the imminent arrival of the train, using a public-address system that garbles his voice, making it almost unintelligible. You join the other passengers as they all stand and retrieve their belongings from the overhead rack. Coats, handbags, briefcases, wheeled carry-on luggage, and other items descend from the heights to the seats adjacent to each lone passenger or couple.

You catch sight of a man pulling a laptop out of a briefcase; he's been sitting there all along, but you only now notice his interesting appearance: a deep olive complexion and thick, wavy black hair offset by deep, penetrating blue eyes.

He doesn't see you, but you're the one doing the noticing on this trip into the city. You think this gentleman is content, but as with most other people, you sense that he has a past he's had to come to terms with.

The train slows, and the rhythmic *clack-clack-clack* eases. The passengers all stand, grabbing the overhead rack for support. They've been intriguing, as most people are if you look inside their minds and souls to learn their stories. In fact, there is no such thing as a common story or a common person. You realize how unique each individual is; all are worth something more than a statistic of employment, divorce, trauma, or economic turmoil. You smile as you disembark from the train. Several trains have arrived at close to the same time, so the platform is crowded. You don't mind, as you're enjoying being carried along by the energetic crowd.

The Rider

The gloomy old Holy Trinity Orphanage sat behind a fence at the top of a hardscrabble hill, in contrast to the manicured lawns surrounding the ornate parent church down below. The atmosphere inside the orphanage was austere, reminiscent of *Oliver Twist*, until the arrival, in 1946, of the baby Michael, which seemed to enliven the mood there. Everyone, from the nuns in their black habits to the kitchen staff in their starched white uniforms, was taken with his engaging personality and striking appearance: a cherubic face, dark skin under a mop of wavy pitch-black hair, and deep, penetrating blue eyes.

As soon as Ethel Kounigis saw Michael, she wanted to adopt him on the spot. She and her husband, Max, were of Greek Orthodox origin but had turned to the Catholic diocese for adoption purposes. Father Sean Connelly, the unctuous priest at Trinity deemed few children there to be good enough for the well-to-do families in his parish, whom he said "deserved only the best." But he enabled this adoption quickly, perhaps because of a large donation from Ethel's wealthy father.

Max and Ethel had all the material comforts, but they were an unhappy couple in suspended animation, waiting for something good to happen. Max bragged that he was an executive in his father's successful development company, but he did almost no real work there, which Ethel resented. She was missing two things she craved: love and children. They had been married for thirteen years, and she had given up on having either. Ethel desperately wanted a baby to bring some meaning into her life and save her marriage. This was quite a burden thrust on little Michael's shoulders.

Michael couldn't compensate for his parents' emotional neediness, and he couldn't save them from themselves. There was little affection between Max and Ethel, and they squabbled like children. Max paid little attention to Michael, and Ethel was overly indulgent, smothering him with affection, compensating for Max's disinterest in either of them.

As early as Michael could remember, he felt uncomfortable in the family, as if he didn't belong. His tall, thin appearance was so unlike his heavyset, dark-eyed father; his bronze skin looked out of place next to his mother's ivory pallor; and his deep blue eyes seemed strange there.

Max refused to tell Michael about his adoption, and Ethel reluctantly agreed. Michael discovered this secret—with a vengeance—when he was eleven years old. In a fit of rage, his father snarled, "You think you're too good for me? You're scum! We adopted you from the orphanage because nobody wanted you!" This terrifying outburst deeply wounded Michael, as Max had intended. It also served to whet his curiosity about his "real parents," words Michael thereafter used as daggers, adding to Ethel's sadness and Max's enmity.

Michael was bright and learned to manipulate his parents' conflict to his own advantage, siding with whomever would benefit him. His need for self- protection and some degree of control made him feel better, perhaps safer, which became a kind of M.O. over the next few years.

In high school, Michael had a few friends who drank beer or smoked a few joints on the weekends, but he faked sips or drags. His need for control over himself and his environment was too important for him to risk. He didn't work hard in school, which concerned his teachers, who knew he could do better. He attended his classes and crammed before exams yet graduated with a respectable 3.7 GPA. He ended up going to a state college, which he had previously disdained.

Max was relieved when Michael left for college, and he even bought him a car and paid for his tuition and living expenses. The looming empty nest saddened Ethel, who dreaded the return of the cold atmosphere at home.

Michael found his college freshman year difficult; the many strangers in the large dorm made him feel uncomfortable. He was experiencing insomnia, muscle pains, a racing pulse, and headaches, and he went to see a college counselor, who told him these were signs of anxiety. In addition, his introductory psychology course covered early infant-maternal bonding, which reawakened his thoughts about his adoption, how different he looked from his adoptive parents, and, most of all, questions about his biological roots.

He learned about adolescent identity, which further raised issues in him about his biological parents and who he was. He became preoccupied with finding out about his biological parents and perhaps even meeting them. He conjured up images about them and their reasons for putting him in an orphanage. Was Max right? Was he scum that nobody wanted?

Michael found the field of psychology fascinating, and for the first time, his studies engrossed him. But his wondering about where and to whom he belonged became an obsession. He was willing to put his personal life on hold until he found answers to these questions burning inside him.

Michael graduated with honors in a ceremony attended by a beaming Ethel and even a proud Max. Michael was delighted they were there and relieved they were together. Cal Berkeley accepted him on full scholarship for doctoral studies in clinical psychology.

Despite the improved relationship with Max and Ethel, Michael was on a mission to find his biological roots. His emotions fluctuated widely; he felt both excitement and trepidation.

Michael contacted the Catholic diocese office holding the records of the Holy Trinity Orphanage. (The orphanage had been shut down a few years earlier because Father Connelly and another priest were indicted for sexually abusing a number of boys there.) Michael felt gratitude toward Ethel and Max for having rescued him from that fate. Mrs. Gwendolyn O'Connor, the office manager of the diocese office, put him at ease, saying that many adoptee searchers were nervous about the searching process.

She explained that the adoption records would be examined but that the biological parents always retained the right of refusal. Therefore, even if Michael wanted to meet them, the biological parents could refuse. Mrs. O'Connor cautioned Michael not to get his hopes up too high that all would go as he had hoped or fantasized.

Adopted Children: Who Am I?

When an adopted child is first informed that he or she is adopted, it can be difficult, but for Max to tell Michael in so brutal a manner that his biological parents rejected him was abject cruelty. The child's sense of trust and security are thrown into upheaval when learning of the adoption. Even in the best of circumstances, adopted children wonder about their roots. In attempting to achieve a sense of identity, all adolescents search for answers to the question "Who am I?" but this search is magnified in the case of adopted children.

Over the last few decades, as society explored genetic and cultural identity, adopted children began to search for their biological roots. Simultaneously, family law progressed, and adoption agencies modified their arcane processes and facilitated searches by children for their biological parents. Face-to-face meetings between them nowadays do occur, with the proviso that there is agreement of both the searching child at an age of majority and of the biological parents.

Gnawing questions and fantasies about biological and social origins are on the minds of many (not all) adopted children. This is especially so when adopted children are living in unhappy situations and wonder if their lives would have been better if their biological parents had not given them up or given up on them, which is a dreaded but not a rare thought. These fleeting thoughts can become obsessions.

Fantasies abound. Adoptees may ask themselves, "Why did they give me up? Were my biological parents rich or poor, urban or rural, normal or crazy, attractive or homely, musical or athletic? Were they married? Did they get to know me? Did they love me? Was I bad? Or ugly? Why don't I resemble my new family? The core question is "Who am I really?" Practical questions about medical histories and risk factors also drive many efforts to identify biological parents.

Adoptive parents face some challenges as well. Many inquire, "Do you know the real parents?" The questioner means the biological parents, but the inference that the adoptive parents are lesser or interim replacements can be confusing to adopted children and potentially hurtful to the parents.

Loving experiences over many years can be wonderful salves. Most adoptees have fulfilling lives and make positive contributions to society.

Michael knew something was wrong when she said, "There's been a problem finding your records." He'd been told the records were easily obtainable. He feared his biological parents didn't want to see him, but Mrs. O'Connor reassured him.

She hemmed and hawed; he cajoled and begged. The missing preorphanage records suddenly materialized.

The records were in boring prose, but the revelations were dramatic. The fertilized egg that had become Michael had been the result of an ignominious event. His biological mother was of a mixed Caucasian and African American heritage and was a long-term patient at a state psychiatric facility, with the diagnosis of "mental retardation and chronic psychosis." She had wandered off the premises into the countryside and been accosted and raped by an inebriated college student who had just left a nearby fraternity beer fest. The records described him as tall, pale-skinned, blue-eyed, and an "arrogant drunk."

The police returned Michael's biological mother to the hospital after the assault. The rapist was the scion of a prominent family, and his father arranged to squelch any publicity. The police investigation suddenly evaporated, and not a word appeared in the local press about the assault, the pregnancy, the victim, or the perpetrator. There was no news, no scandal; it was as if nothing untoward had ever happened. Such was the cultural climate at the time.

When the institution director realized that the patient was pregnant, he made arrangements to have the infant, named Michael, placed in the Holy Trinity Orphanage shortly after his mother gave birth.

Twenty-year-old Michael Kounigis had finally discovered his roots, and his unseemly origins stunned him. Any dreams of a glamorous background were shattered. He finally grasped his unique appearance. He was dejected and angry with himself for his magical fantasies. He thought, *Be careful what you wish for.* He'd wanted the truth, and he'd gotten it: Michael was the product of a sordid rape.

The ugly word *miscegenation* is an emotionally loaded word that is, thankfully, no longer in use. People once used it as a term filled with prejudice, racism, and oppression, referring to the then-unlawful and immoral mixing of races. It reflected unambiguous denigration and hate. It was into this cultural climate of endemic racism that Michael was born, and this environment enabled the white, wealthy, and wily father of the rapist to trample on laws, due process, human rights, people's feelings, and any semblance of decency. Racism was thriving at that time in America, so the shameful scandal had to be prevented at all costs. And it was.

Michael now understood why his father disliked him: he knew all the dirty details and thought Michael was damaged goods. Michael decided not to share these findings with his parents. For the first time, he missed them, even feeling some new homesickness.

It was 1967, "the Summer of Love," and Michael was a graduate student in psychology at Berkeley. After discovering his pedigree, he gave up his quest to know more about his origins. The discovery of his sordid beginnings was a rude awakening. His quest had begun on the heels of his father's nasty outburst, and he feared his dad was right: nobody wanted him. He felt powerless, he'd lost control of his environment, and his composure was upended.

He was angry with himself and couldn't see a way out of this morass. He was avoiding friends, shirking work, and feeling sorry for himself. The Free Speech Movement (FSM) at Berkeley, Students for a Democratic Society (SDS), the Southern Christian Leadership Conference, and the Black Panthers were all prominent then at Berkeley, but he couldn't bring himself to get involved. People his age were dancing with flowers in their hair, smoking up, making love, or demonstrating against the war, and he was feeling miserable. Here he was, studying to be a psychologist, yet he felt paralyzed with melancholy and ashamed of being pathetic.

The San Francisco Bay Area was the epicenter of the late sixties, and it soon impinged itself on Michael's senses. The smells of grass, incense, and patchouli oil; the sounds of evocative music; and colorful dresses and flowers were everywhere, and many were involved in the roiling political and cultural forces. Michael got caught up in the heady atmosphere of Haight-Ashbury and Golden Gate Park, where chemicals, music, and politics intermixed in a fervent atmosphere reminiscent of a perpetual street in the Age of Aquarius, which Michael began to enjoy.

There were marches and demonstrations, protest songs, and calls for social justice, which also moved Michael and actually improved his mood. He was soon swept up in these causes, gradually becoming an activist on campus and in the community and taking part in antiwar demonstrations in San Francisco, Los Angeles, and New York.

Michael was feeling better, his energy level was higher, his sleep and appetite improved, and he was more gregarious.

Michael graduated with a PhD in clinical psychology in 1969. He invited Ethel and Max to attend his graduation ceremonies. Both of them cried sad tears of painful memories and joyful tears of pride.

Michael was working, demonstrating, and enjoying himself. Now a bona fide clinical psychologist, he noticed that what had brought him out of his depression was his involvement in the world outside himself.

Feeling Blue, Being Depressed

We all experience feelings of sadness (being down, having the blues) at some points in our lives, but the severity and the frequency varies. Some are seldom afflicted by the doldrums, while others are often beset by black clouds. But nobody is completely immune to some personal experiences with sadness. Some individuals are predominantly dour and sad, but these are unusual. Famous and creative people in all walks of life have spoken about these dark spells (e.g., Churchill, Lincoln, Beethoven, and Mark Twain).

You are likely familiar with the blues, the popular form of music expressing feelings of longing and loneliness. The blues originated in the Deep South, but the music and words resonate throughout the world. Whether describing a broken heart or being down and out, blues singers, such as Muddy Waters and BB King, gave evocative voice to these feelings.

People can sometimes get through these periods of despair on their own. Friends or family supports, creative fulfillment (e.g., music, art), hobbies, exercise, religion, and just the tincture of time itself all help. Most people have the perseverance to hang in until the clouds lift, as they usually will.

The causes vary. The death of a loved one, serious personal setbacks, or genetic vulnerabilities, such as neurochemical imbalances, can cause or contribute to the experience of intense sadness. Some people self-medicate with alcohol or illicit street drugs, which might work as a quick fix but invariably end up as exercises in futility or self-destruction.

Serious depression can be so emotionally debilitating that one can't simply wait out the despair. There can be a sense of urgency, especially when there are thoughts or plans of suicide. In severe depression, prescribed antidepressants and psychotherapy can be vital and effective treatments.

The incidence of depression has been shown to diminish in wartime or natural disasters, and it also drops among people who are caught up in ideological causes. Sometimes a people's moods can improve significantly when they are engaged outside themselves in meaningful acts of generosity and caring. External challenges that focus our energies beyond our own anxieties can lift our mood.

Michael finally told his parents about his painful quest to discover his roots, and he was astounded to learn that he had been totally wrong: he had attributed his father's rejection of him to his lowly origins, but his parents had been totally unaware of his preadoption history.

Things at home settled down after many years of strife. Ethel told Michael she loved and missed him, and Max expressed his regret for having been "a rotten father," as he put it. He admitted to Michael that he'd always felt like a failure in all aspects of his life.

When he told his conservative Republican parents about his antiwar activities, he expected stern criticism. Instead, he heard, "Please be careful, Michael; we love you." He was moved and embarrassed again, blown away by life's complexities.

Michael was sharing an apartment in San Francisco with two young men also involved in the social and political scene. One was an African American MBA student, and the other was a gay social worker. The three made an avant-garde statement in those years.

One Saturday morning, they heard raps on the door. When Michael opened the door, two men dressed in dark suits flashed FBI ID cards with their names and photos. Evidently, he had been photographed a few times at Anti-war demonstrations, and they advised him to "keep his nose clean." They left quickly, and Michael was shaken. His friends were certain the visitors were delivering a message from J. Edgar Hoover because Michael's draft deferments had run their course, but he wasn't worried about being called up, because the war was winding down.

Two months later, he received his US Army draft notice. He didn't want to fight in a war he'd been decrying. He'd seen young men burn their draft cards, others had declared "conscientious objector" status, and some went into hiding. The vast majority reported for duty, and Michael was in a quandary.

The assassinations of Bobby Kennedy and Martin Luther King Jr. pushed his decision. He called his parents and told them he was going to Canada, knowing he'd be classified as a draft dodger, a felon. Max and Ethel urged him to be careful and wondered if he needed help or money. They said they would visit him in Toronto.

Michael had no difficulty crossing the US/Canadian border in Buffalo, New York. He was prepared for the worst, but the guards asked few questions, just the routine "Business or personal?" and his estimated length of stay. He headed to Toronto, where the "underground railroad" had given him some contact names, such as Mary Douglas.

Mary had left the United States after the Korean War and McCarthyism of the early fifties. She was a white-haired, heavy-set middle-aged woman who exuded warmth while uttering strong antiwar sentiments. Mary was the heart of the draft-dodger (DD) community and the owner of a New Age shop called Mother Mary's (a name taken from the Beatles' "Let It Be"), which was located downtown, near the University of Toronto, where many in the DD community lived.

Mary's store sold clothing, snacks, and groceries as well as incense, oils, pipes, clips, posters, beads, hookahs, and books. It was also action central, serving as a hangout, communication center, and information clearinghouse. Many of the draft dodgers came through there when they first arrived. It was estimated that upward of twenty thousand draft dodgers lived in Canada in 1971.

Mary was impressed with Michael's presentation, and she offered him a job as resident supervisor of a three-story house she owned, which was an urban commune where about twenty young tenants resided. Draft dodgers, deserters, students, buskers, and drug users made up the community. Getting this group to live in some semblance of order and cooperation was difficult. ("Herding cats was easy compared to stoned hippies," Michael said.) He introduced some basic rules of civility and cleanliness, began collecting rent, and assigned chores and communal responsibilities. A few of the "stray cats" were angry, and he had to ask them to leave.

Mary was taken with his interpersonal and organizational skills and urged him to use his talents and PhD in a professional job. Through Mary, he met people in government and academia who offered to help him. He applied for citizenship and was given an interim work visa. As a legal resident, he received a clinical faculty appointment at the university and a job as a psychologist at Student Health Services.

Michael thrived while at the university and in a small private practice. He made friends and enjoyed the urban scene. He dated occasionally but was wary of commitment because of his early history.

Jennifer Marpole was from a fundamentalist Christian family in a rural town about one hundred miles west of Toronto, where she'd recently moved when offered a position as vice principal of a small high school. She was introduced to Michael at a dinner given by one of her friends. They hit it off, bantering about the relative merits of Canadian football and health care versus the American brand of both. Jennie's family was not particularly fond of Americans, but she found Michael different from the typical American they disliked. Michael was smitten by this pretty, gentle, warm, and witty young woman, with whom he was totally relaxed. Within a few months, they were in love.

Michael couldn't remember a time in his life that was so fulfilling; he had a woman he loved and a profession he enjoyed. However, Michael admitted to close friends that he was missing the Bay Area, and he even considered returning there. This angered many of his friends, who seemed as annoyed as if he were offending them personally. Some accused him of betraying their trust and values and even of being ungrateful to Canada. Meanwhile, his California friends were encouraging him to come back home.

When the United States, in 1977, granted amnesty to expatriate draft dodgers, Michael and Jennifer had a dilemma. They enjoyed their lives in Toronto—they had friends and were thriving in their professions. Canada was a more sedate culture, and they liked the universal health-care program, but Michael missed the energy and the ideals (if not the reality) of the States. He hadn't crossed the border for almost a decade, for fear of arrest, and here was an opportunity for him to clear his record and travel back home. Jennifer's family was appalled that they'd even consider moving to that country.

Michael and Jennifer married at her parents' home in a traditional Christian wedding attended by half the local townsfolk. Michael's friends from California and Toronto were there, as were Max and Ethel.

Michael went back to the States in 1978 to make his amnesty status official, but he and Jennifer remained in Toronto until they each had a job offer and Jennifer had her green card. Their plan was to start a family in Canada, in part because medical services were free. They played at sex and worked at procreation but to no avail. In spite of normal sperm counts, hormonal levels, and ova produced, Jennifer did not become pregnant. They tried a series of medications and in vitro fertilization procedures, but nothing worked.

After repeated failures, Michael and Jennifer were at their wits' end; they'd had their fill of medical procedures and disappointments. They were tense, and they wondered if they should just forget about having children. Michael found himself in a similar dilemma to the one Max and Ethel had faced some thirty years earlier, which had led them to adopt him. When Jennifer brought up adoption, Michael's heart pounded; he felt dizzy and sweated. His own adoption and his early years in a dysfunctional family were vivid in his mind. He was certain he could never adopt a child.

To Have or Not Have a Child

Most adults would like to have children, but as marriage rates are falling and birth rates are dropping (in developed countries), many are opting not to have children. These individuals aren't driven by an overwhelming urge to raise children and carry on their families' lineages. For some, the vision of children is as an ominous intrusion into their lives, diminishing personal freedoms and increasing drudgery and debts. Others make the decision on moral or sociopolitical ground, thinking that they won't contribute to overpopulation. There are financial considerations and age and health issues. It takes some courage to choose not to have children, considering that others might criticize those who have done so as being selfish.

Yet many women who have trouble conceiving can become despairing and desperate to have a child and can spend inordinate amounts of time and money in this quest. It pains them to hear about one-night stands culminating in unwanted pregnancies, while they can't conceive no matter what they do. Reproductive science has recently offered new techniques, such as in vitro fertilization, surrogate sperm or ova donors, and even surrogates to bear the fetus. These options are now available to help the natural process of creating a child, and there will no doubt be more breakthroughs, perhaps involving cloning or stem cells (presenting new dilemmas).

Many couples adopt homeless children from all over the world with wonderful results for the adopted children and their new parents.

They moved to the San Francisco Bay Area in 1981 and settled in a modest home in a family-friendly area. Michael opened a psychotherapy practice, and Jennifer planned to open a tutoring academy for children and adolescents. Her top priority was still to raise a family. "If only," she would say with a sigh.

In the local supermarket, Michael bumped into Nancy Sheridan, a social worker he knew, accompanied by her cute seven-year-old Chinese daughter. Michael assumed that she was married to a Chinese man, but she told him that they had adopted Mei-Ling in China five years earlier and that she and her husband were returning to China to adopt their second little girl. Michael told her of his situation, and she offered to give Jennifer and him information that would be helpful if they were interested in adoption.

When Michael returned home, he told Jennifer about his chance meeting with Nancy and Mei-Ling. Jennifer was interested but was even more taken with Michael's enthusiasm. They agreed to meet with Nancy the next week.

A few weeks later, they met with the Chinese-American director of an international adoption agency established to facilitate American adoptions from China (and to make money). Over the following months, they submitted more personal and official documents about themselves than they had known existed. Finally, the agency informed them that they would assign them a child after a special bureau in Beijing analyzed the data and selected their child according to an ancient Chinese method. Then came many months of waiting, wondering, and worrying.

After a long year, Michael and Jennifer received a black-and-white computer printout of their daughter-to-be, with whom they immediately fell in love. Eighteen adoptive parents from across the country would meet in Guangzhou in eight weeks before dispersing throughout China to receive their daughters from various orphanages.

Michael and Jennifer took eight-month-old Hannah from the crowded, humid, and hot orphanage just two days after they arrived in China. They were told that their daughter had been found in her first day of life, wrapped in a blanket in the anteroom of a post office. (This was not unusual, given China's one-child policy, which made having a second child a serious criminal offense. Young mothers in that predicament often gave their babies up for adoption or sold them.)

The daughters (no healthy boys were available for adoption) were handed over in an emotional ceremony. The fuzzy photograph they'd seen had not done Hannah justice. She was beyond beautiful, and the other parents dubbed her the Dalai Hannah. For the first twelve hours with Michael and Jennifer, Hannah was barely responsive. "Her muscles were flabby, and her head was floppy," Michael said. She would not sit up and stared blankly, but a few hours later, in the middle of the night, she seemed to "come to life." For Michael, the experience was a liberation from the shackles of his own adoption. He felt transformed, recalling later that he'd had his first-ever spiritual experience.

Michael and Jennifer gathered again with all the other parents and babies in Guangzhou for three weeks of feeding, changing, worrying, exulting, and bonding, as all new parents do. When they were finally flying home to America, they sang, "And baby makes three," from "My Blue Heaven."

Eight years later, Michael, Jennifer, and Hannah lived in a comfortable redwood home in the Oakland Hills. Hannah was exquisite and deeply attached to her parents. Her simple words *Mommy* and *Daddy* were magic salves to them.

Hannah did well in school, and she had friends and enjoyed piano and dance lessons. Her parents told her of her adoption when she was five years old, and she was full of questions about her biological parents, as she still is. She bonded with her adoptive mother and father in a profound manner that belied dire predictions from a few naysaying experts. Some had warned about children growing up with an inability to love and emotionally attach. Michael and Jennifer joined other parents in a foundation to improve the conditions and care in Chinese orphanages. When Hannah was seven, Jennifer became pregnant the old-fashioned way with Hannah's brother, Carl.

Hannah, at sixteen, is happy and well adjusted, full of teenage exuberance. Michael and Jennifer are grateful for their family and their lives.

The Four Bs

Feelings of abandonment often come when a person finds out he or she was adopted. Most ask, "Why did my parents give me up? Was there something wrong with me?" These are natural questions, and the answers vary. The bottom line is that the revelation disrupts the person's sense of being, at least to a certain extent, regardless of whether the adoptive home was a happy one. Michael felt he had to find out about his past. He couldn't come to a fully realized sense of being without having the answers he desired. When he discovered the truth, the truth hurt, but the pain set him free and enabled him to move on with his own life.

He was also able to find a sense of belonging in Canada, where he fell in love and aspired to have a family of his own. The quest that began amid confusion and persistent self-doubt ended with his full acceptance of his adoptive parents and with his ultimate success in his professional and family lives. Sometimes answers to important questions matter more than we think.

Being

Michael, in his middle adulthood, has a sense of self-acceptance. This didn't come easily to him: his beginnings were bizarre, his early childhood was troubled, and turbulence and self-doubt marked his adolescence and early adulthood. It was a difficult voyage at times, as we observed.

In spite of all these challenges, Michael recognizes how far he's come and appreciates the dramatic changes in his parents, his marriage, he and his wife's move, and his transformation after Hannah arrived. He is fulfilled, grounded, and realistic, with an authentic sense of being.

Belonging

For more than two decades, Michael felt uncomfortable in his family, among classmates, and with himself. In order to protect himself from anxiety, he had to maintain a semblance of control when he felt out of place and alienated.

However, circumstances changed. Michael had a series of experiences that served to reinforce his self-image and strengthen him for life's setbacks: his family revelations, his fulfillment and activism in graduate school, his reunion with his parents, his social and professional success in

Canada, his return to the Bay Area, good friends, a fulfilling career, and his wife and children. Michael had personally enhancing experiences with different groups of people who respected and appreciated him, as he did them.

Michael is now an integral part of the lives of those with whom he lives, works, and plays. He is comfortable and authentic in all his relationships and has clearly achieved a sense of belonging.

Believing

Michael was not a firm believer in God. His adoption from the Catholic orphanage had no spiritual effect, his Catholic mother and Greek Orthodox father were members of their respective religions in name only, and he received no religious teaching, either by education or by example.

When he later became involved in political and social causes, these commitments were salves and catalysts for his positive energy. Fairness, respect, and equality came naturally to Michael's sense of right and wrong and to his view of justice, and these values guided him. The more involved he became, the healthier and more fulfilled he felt.

When he met Hannah, he had a spiritual experience—an other-worldly awareness that has stayed with him. He now wonders whether there are things like synchronicity or providence or fate. He never pursued materialism for its own sake, and he's had a core value system that emphasizes fairness, respect, and compassion for others. He wishes to pass this sense of believing on to his children.

Benevolence

After college, Michael was committed to improving the lives of others in difficult circumstances, including youths protesting social issues, indigent students, and orphaned Chinese girls. One need not agree with his political stances to recognize that his is a generous and generative spirit. His commitment to caring also manifests itself in his feelings for his family, friends, and patients and in his involvement in improvements in society. He exemplifies a sense of benevolence.

Resilience

Michael's start in life was a rough one: he was born in a state hospital after a drunken lout raped his psychotic biological mother, and he was placed in an austere orphanage and then adopted by a distressed couple, including an adoptive father who disliked the young boy and essentially told him as much while informing Michael that nobody wanted him.

Many years later, that same "unwanted" child has grown into a happily married man with his own children (one adopted) and a career as a clinical psychologist.

What happened in the between? What contributed to Michael's resilience? There were many positive factors: Michael's intelligence, appearance, and, especially, inner fortitude; his discovery of his sordid biological origins; his realization that his father never knew of that history; his parents' healing and father's acceptance of him; his college success and friends; his passionate involvement in social and political causes; his new life in Canada, new friends, and career; and his marriage to the love of his life.

Emotional Footprint

Michael has proven himself to be a resilient soul, a productive member of society, a wonderful husband and father, and a responsible citizen. A kind and empathetic soul, he's had a positive effect on many people over the course of his lifetime, and he continues to do so. That this was not always so should remind us that the die is not cast with finality by our earlier personalities. Humans can and do change, as we have seen in our passengers and in your own lives. I have no doubt that Michael will leave this world a positive emotional footprint.

11

Reflections on the Journey

As I said at the outset, life is never static. In addition to death and taxes, one can count on a third inevitability: *Change.* Unpredictable and unexpected events can and do occur. Sometimes these are positive and enhancing in nature, and at other times, they can be unsettling or painful. How we respond to both types of changes throughout our lives will largely determine whether we get the most out of our lives. The passengers we met on our metaphorical train suffered, cried, laughed, hoped, struggled, loved, despised, gave, took, faltered, rallied, and led their lives as best as they could. They represent the complexity of the human condition, with all of its graces and imperfections.

We can now look back at those stories within the context of the four Bs and the role of resilience in our personal journeys. We can also see the importance of coming to terms with how we treat and affect others in shaping our emotional footprints. We have learned that we have critical choices to make throughout our lives.

The lives of our train passengers—and certainly our own—should cause us to take an additional reflective look at some of the more prominent facets of the human condition in general. We will examine those bigger-picture issues that played into our stories of the train passengers.

Who exactly are we? Why are we here? What is the essence of love, hope, and forgiveness? Are our fates predetermined by our genomes or by the mysterious heavens, or are we merely subject to the capriciousness of random chance? To what extent can we author the stories of our lives?

Let's take a closer look at some common core issues that permeate all our lives' journeys.

Identity

Adolescents ask themselves questions like "Who am I?" and "Where am I going?" and "How will I get there?" This concept of identity, taught in college psychology courses, was developed by Dr. Erik Erikson, who felt that developing a core identity was *the* major developmental challenge for adolescents, and that these questions should be resolved before embarking on the adult journey.

Adolescence is a period of transformative changes occurring within a short span of years. Biologically, they include growth spurts, hormonal surges, brain changes, and sexual urges. Socially, relationships and romance, education and career issues, and autonomy and independence from parents characterize this period. Psychologically, abstract and philosophical thinking develop.

Many expect the worst from adolescents: Shakespeare's comment in *A Winter's Tale* captured this notion: "I would that there were no age between ten and three-and-twenty, or that youth would sleep out the rest, for there is nothing in the between except getting wenches with child, stealing and fighting."

The truth is that identity resolution is not solely the domain of adolescents, and one never completely accomplishes it during his or her adolescence. The same questions (e.g., "Who am I?") asked in adolescence are revisited throughout our lives. Our answers can relate only to that moment in time, but the answers change over a lifetime, depending on one's health, relationships, and personal satisfaction.

Jane Whyllie (in her thirties) confronted the challenges of these questions when her *la dolce vita* lifestyle hurt her, and when her husband, Sam, died. William Nguyen questioned his worth as a family man when he was in the refugee camp (in his thirties), when his mother was murdered, and when his business was on its last legs (in his late forties). Neville DaCosta asked these questions when his lover abandoned him, when his two ex-wives and children rejected him, and when many people ostracized him (in his fifties). Jose Alvarez questioned his identity when he was imprisoned and lost the support of his parents and Rev. Alice (in his twenties) and later when his wife deserted him (in his forties).

We ask ourselves these same existential questions throughout our lives, especially at milestones or during crisis situations, and in our dreams and unconscious thoughts. Identity is a lifelong quest, an important beacon to help set our personal goals, make decisions, and evaluate how we are doing.

Work

For the vast majority of adults, our sense of well-being and a good part of our identity stem largely from our work. Work is integral to who we are, no matter what we do for a living. Whether we do routine jobs or are high-powered CEO's, whether we are, actors, authors, accountants, or acrobats, our roles and our relationships to our jobs shape how we feel about ourselves.

Whatever work we choose, one of the most painful experiences that can befall an individual arises from prolonged unemployment. Apart from possible financial devastation, there is often profound psychological damage done to that person. One loses a sense of self-worth and dignity, and feels demeaned and disparaged in the eyes of others as well as themselves.

Yet on Sunday evenings, many of us moan, "Ugh, we have to go to work tomorrow." We disparage Monday-morning blues. We cherish our weekends and celebrate Fridays (TGIF is now a *mantra*). This is so especially if the work is seen as drudgery or causes high stress levels. But even those who enjoy their jobs might occasionally think, "There must be a better way to earn a living."

Work plays an important role in our psychological and social lives. We're educated or trained for jobs or professions and encouraged to pursue our career dreams. There are workaholics who are have little interest in other aspects of their lives; their opposites are slackers who do anything to avoid work. But the majority of us work responsibly and want to work, despite occasional assertions to the contrary. Even with sufficient money, most people have a need to work in order to enhance their mental, physical, and social well-being. We all like to feel useful, and work or service of any type contributes to our self-esteem.

Being unemployed often carries a stigma of personal weakness. Layoffs or lack of jobs cause terrible burdens for wage earners and their dependents and add insult to injury. The loss of face brings feelings of shame and humiliation and leads to psychological and physical problems.

Our passengers often used their work to help them deal with the travails of their personal lives. Ken found his psychological center and self-esteem through acting, Eddie Morales realized his strengths in the midst of a war zone, Jose Alvarez grew as a psychotherapist, and Patricia Arbitson blossomed as a lawyer. Productive work was an effective coping strategy for personal stress in their lives.

Nowadays we can be gainfully employed from our teens or twenties until our late sixties or often older. Our physical and emotional health and our relationships and sociability strengthen when we are working. For the vast majority of us, work enhances our well-being.

Loneliness and Loss

It is rare that one goes through life without experiencing loneliness and loss. Loneliness most often occurs after the death of a loved one, or a separation. We feel sad, an empty void described as "the presence of a deep void." Anguish can envelop us; we cry, we grieve and mourn, which are normal reactions. But we know that time and caring people are remarkably effective healers.

Sometimes sadness and withdrawal evolve into clinical depression, which might need professional help. This is the exception, not the rule, and if such depression occurs, psychotherapies and medication are often helpful.

When a lover or spouse leaves, we suffer the proverbial broken heart, an emotionally anguishing and even physical wound. If the lost lover is alive, his or her presence keeps hope burning, preventing closure. The death of a beloved spouse, parent, or child is an especially devastating form of loss and cause of loneliness. Agony follows, and grieving and mourning ensue, and then one heals.

There are highly publicized expected stages of grief, described as shock, denial, protest, and despair, followed by accommodation and resolution. But these do not occur in a cookbook fashion, as we all grieve in different ways. I've been taken aback by criticisms of those who are "not mourning correctly." Some invoke those stages and make comments like "Why is he still down?" or "Why doesn't she cry?" or "Why is he dating so soon?"— as if there were one correct way to grieve (*their* way). The stages of grieving and mourning are not "programmed" in a single timetable or pattern. Especially in tragic circumstances, we need to cherish and respect our differences.

There are sources of help which can provide healing energy when we are experiencing a painful loss. A survivor can ask himself or herself, "What would [the deceased] want me to feel and do?" This can be a strong revelation and an impetus. Also. It has been shown that when the griever can be of help to others in similar situations, this can be a critical to healing. Finally, love of family and friends are crucial, as we saw when the Nguyen family lost Grandmother Hahn. In the absence of "natural" supports, most communities have peer support groups whose members have suffered similar losses contribute communal healing to each other.

Loss and loneliness are inevitabilities of life., and grieving is a poignant but necessary, and "healthy" human ritual. Our relationships and the passage of time, combined with inner mourning, provide healing and ultimate relief. We are remarkably resilient in these circumstances.

The Random Factor

"Man tracht un Gott lacht" (Ger.). Man plans and God laughs. The random nature of events has perplexed, challenged, and sometimes irritated us since the dawn of humanity. We strive for reason and order in our lives, and chaos makes us feel uncomfortable and even angry. Change and unexpected events will occur in everyone's life: implausible coincidences and twists of fate occur, and unforeseen roadblocks and detours appear out of the blue, as do new routes and opportunities. These are all parts of our meaningful journeys. Stuff happens...

We've known disappointments and indignities as well as pleasure and serenity. We've been brimming with confidence, and we've had self-doubts. As the saying goes, "Life giveth and taketh." We live in some uncertainty and ambiguity, which we deal with in a variety of ways. Some think they're immune to bad fate ("I have good karma"), but a sense of invulnerability ("It can't happen to me") is foolhardy. Others take a pessimistic approach, *expecting* the sky to fall and having perpetual clouds over their heads.

Religious people might feel reassured by a benevolent Supreme Being who will shepherd them, accepting whatever fate brings. Believers often weather the storms of personal disasters better than others. Patricia Arbitson, Jose Alvarez, Alice (Ken's wife), and Neville DaCosta were buoyed by their belief in God. On the other hand, some religious folks interpret tragedies as punishments for misdeeds.

The majority of us learn to compartmentalize, avoiding constant vigilance by walling off dangers in a safe compartment in our minds so that they don't interfere with our everyday lives.

We also try to prevent problems. We childproof our homes, eat healthy foods, and avoid dangerous situations, but we realize we can't stave off Mother Nature's disasters, prevent all accidents, or always keep our loved ones safe. Tragedies are a sad but natural part of the ebb and flow of life, like wildfires in overgrown dry forests.

"Ride the waves," we're advised, but we are emotional beings. When unwelcome physical or emotional pain occurs, we're prone to be sad and shed tears. But we need to remember that time, help, and people will eventually make things better. After the initial shock and feelings of helplessness, we regroup, gather our thoughts, and use our strengths, resources and relationships to recover.

When we experience success or serenity, we enjoy the glow. However, just as loss is never an ultimate defeat, success is never an ultimate triumph. The present situation is a mere snapshot in our exciting journeys and doesn't reflect the way things were or how they will be in the future. In periods of calm, we need to cherish what we have, because blips on our radar screens will occur. How we courageously face setbacks, graciously accept successes, and cherish good fortunes are good indications of our inner resources and wisdom.

Transient changes will appear on the road of life, but rest assured that the pathway will most often return to a state of stability. As Rudyard Kipling put it, "If you can meet with triumph and disaster, and treat those two *imposters* just the same, you are a better man than most."

Hope

"Hope springs eternal in the human breast," Alexander Pope's dictum, is as profound as it is poetic. Hope is unique to our species; it enables us to envision a better future and encourages us that things will improve. By its very nature optimistic, hope prods us to work toward goals of overcoming or achieving. It might have religious overtones for believers, but hope is secular and universal.

According to the ancient Greeks, without hope, there is despair. Hope is a personal beacon, a light we move to during periods of darkness. Its strength is in its capacity to encourage and galvanize us, to enhance our mood and creative thinking. Hope is one of our greatest motivators, providing a sense of purpose and aspirations even in difficult times. Even when there are few possibilities of fruition, humans persist in hoping.

Hope contributed to the resilience shown by many of the train passengers, such as Jose Alvarez when he was languishing in prison; William Nguyen during war and when his business was going under; Eduardo Morales, Jane Whyllie, and Neville DaCosta when they suffered rejection by those around them; and Ken when he was in an abusive home environment.

Hope can be ineffective when it is based on faulty assumptions, or false hopes. Waiting for an impossible situation to resolve can be demoralizing and self-defeating (vividly captured in Samuel Beckett's play *Waiting for Godot*). True hope is expressed by eloquence and artistry on behalf of humanity, as in Martin Luther King's "I Have a

Dream" speech, Picasso's remarkable painting *Guernica*, and Beethoven's "Ode to Joy."

We light our internal candles of hope when we're in the midst of tough situations. There have been times when you felt your problems were insurmountable, yet your fervent hope that things could turn around ultimately saved the day.

Epiphanies

Hope can spawn epiphanies—flashes of insight that can lead to positive changes in people's lives. Your mind is open to new possibilities, and sometimes leaps of thought or intuition lead to exciting new paths.

People who have gone through a wide array of experiences, such as profound religious visions or moving group experiences, have reported epiphanies. People who are truly, madly, deeply in love sometimes feel this way. Epiphanies might appear during prolonged meditation or in psychotherapy in a sudden crystallization of understanding. Some experience this sensation while surrounded by nature or in the midst of an artistic endeavor.

Life-altering revelations can also occur after one survives a traumatic accident or a cataclysm of nature, like an earthquake, tsunami, or fire, or after recovery from a suicide attempt. Finally, some users of psychedelics, such as LSD, mescaline, or peyote, have had these experiences as well. Any of these experiences can evoke a new state of being and different beliefs.

Many of our train passengers experienced new insights into themselves and made major changes. Jane Whyllie gave up her wanton ways and became a nurturing mother and wife. Neville DaCosta gave up alcohol and destructive behavior and became an accomplished artist and mentor. Jose Alvarez left the gang life and ended up as a father and effective clinician. Howard Gladstone changed from a greedy narcissist into a generous, caring man.

People you know might have had transformations from the way they were years earlier, when you thought you knew them. These can be radical yet authentic and long-lasting makeovers in personalities.

There are critical points when intense experiences can change our lives, but they don't occur out of the blue; they are the result of thoughts and feelings that were roiling in minds and hearts over years.

Epiphanies and dramatic changes can occur even in the later stages of people's lives. Cantankerous individuals might become kind and generous, prejudiced people might become tolerant of others, and feuding individuals might become empathic and caring toward each other.

Epiphanies and revelations can help and heal individuals who feel stuck in emotional ruts of stifling boredom, or are beset by self pity, or anger. Our human wells needn't be poisoned in perpetuity. We can embrace new perceptions and values, and become authentic and caring in a new way.

Dr. Harry Stack Sullivan coined the term "corrective emotional experiences" to describe the emotional changes that can occur in people who are in psychotherapy. However, I am referring to similar and much more common and salient experiences. Events and relationships that occur in life can contribute to life-changing perceptions and resolutions that dramatically improve people's lives. (Our passengers' stories are filled with myriad examples of these inspirational changes—for instance, Jane Whyllie, Eduardo Morales, Jose Alvarez, Patricia Arbitson, Neville DaCosta, and Howard Gladstone).

Corrective experiences encompass our deepest thoughts, feelings, and behaviors. We are capable of inspiring changes in our perceptions, personalities, and values—in the very essence of our being.

Love

Through the ages the theme of love, both lost and found, has filled volumes of poetry and prose, and music and art. Whether in evocative paintings, in opera and rock ballads, and even iconic buildings like the Taj Mahal, artists have long felt inspired by the joys and sometimes the despair of love.

We've been romantically in love, with ardor and passion. We've all experienced other kinds of love: Love between longtime-married spouses; parental and grandparent–grandchild love; sibling love; and bonds with friends, close colleagues, teachers, and mentors.

We first learn our ability to love in infancy and childhood by bonding to our closest intimates (our mothers or committed caretakers). Nurturance of infants, babies, and toddlers is crucial in developing the ability to form love bonds. All the senses are involved in teaching babies and kids to feel, receive, and give love: Familiar faces, sounds of voices, tastes and aromas of bodies, holding and kissing.

When we're in love, our worries seem to melt away. The poem "How Do I Love Thee?" by Elizabeth Barrett Browning conveys that intensity, as do Irving Berlin's lyrics "I hear singing, and there's no one there, I smell blossoms, and the trees are bare, All day long, I seem to walk on air, I wonder why..." Feelings of love stimulate neuronal activity in parts of the brain, which light up on brain scans. The song "You Light Up My Life" was prescient!

Love is bittersweet, but not without pain: When love mysteriously ebbs from our beloved, we feel lost and forsaken, as if our hearts have been wrenched from our bodies. A broken heart feels like unbearable agony that will never end. We seek relief from pain, yearn for the return of lost love, and long for our soul mate.

Our need for intimacy is neither affection nor fantasy; it is palpable and real. There is magic in the early blush of romance, and most people hope for a lifelong partnership of commitment, caring, and companionship.

But passionate romance is no guarantee of a good marriage or long-term relationship. Conversely, there are successful prearranged marriages and others based on practical considerations. (An Indian friend told me, "We don't marry the woman we love; we love the woman we marry.")

Our bonds of affection and intimacy are like our lifeblood, our emotional equivalent to oxygen and nourishment, and of equal importance. From our first breaths in infancy as we are coaxed from our mothers' wombs until our last gasps of life before we die, we need love.

Without the nourishment of love, we might atrophy and shrivel, desiccate and harden. Without love, children do not develop as well intellectually, emotionally, or socially, and adults are more prone to loneliness and depression. A life bereft of love diminishes our soulful essence and, some would say, is barely worth living.

Happiness

Americans have a unique relationship with happiness. This is the only country in which happiness is enshrined in its Declaration of Independence, where the "pursuit of happiness" is included with life and liberty as "unalienable rights."

Happiness is thus ingrained in children's consciousness as an over-riding goal. Everyone wants to be happy, right? We are encouraged to "keep smiling" and "whistle a happy tune," and there are myriad how-to-be-happy books on the market. There is social pressure to always "put on a happy face," or there must be something wrong.

But what is happiness? Perpetual elation? People from different cultures sometimes see this as an American conceit, a sign of adolescent immaturity. Mahatma Gandhi and the Dalai Lama wrote about happiness as a worthy state of feeling but not as an emotional nirvana.

Satisfaction and contentment are the key words; they encompass acceptance, gratitude, and appreciation, all of which are reflected in actual biological changes. Our levels of immune factors and biochemicals, such as dopamine, endorphins, and oxytocin, are enhanced, with related changes seen in brain-imaging studies.

Constant euphoria can be worrisome: This kind of elated mood is seen in those with hypomania, a serious psychiatric disorder, or in a cocaine-induced high. The driven ecstasy associated with psychosis or the fleeting highs induced by sex, drugs, and rock and roll are decidedly not the same as a sustained feeling of satisfaction and being at peace with one's self.

People who are satisfied tend to have more generous and benevolent views of life. They are more tolerant and empathetic, and affect others positively (a phenomenon known as "social contagion"). Those at ease make others feel better and attract others who want to share that experience. They heighten their sense of belonging in themselves and in those around them.

People experience satisfaction when they have meaning in their own lives and when they are generous to others. The cliché that "money can't buy happiness" is actually borne out by research: The superrich are not more content.

Contented people have no illusions that life will always be easy sailing. They recognize there will be upheavals and can accept setbacks and joys with more equanimity. This is the natural flow of life, and neither is a permanent fixture or a predictor of the future. Satisfied souls appreciate the small pleasures—the hot bath when cold and tired, the sandwich when famished, a touch when lonely, a smile when feeling down, and, of course, the smell of flowers just about anytime.

Friendship

Close friends enhance our lives. They provide understanding and caring; they stimulate and support us, serve as confidants, and provide companionship. We rely on them for honest feedback and warranted criticism, they appreciate our strengths and accept our frailties. Friends are meaningful treasures to br cherished.

The foundations for friendship are laid down in early childhood. Young children learn how to socialize, interact, share, disagree peacefully, and get close to someone else. Communicating well and accommodating others' feelings help children make and keep friendships throughout their lives.

When we get down or depressed, we might think we're not likable and we tend to withdraw, but it's at these times when we most need the support of others. Life without friends can feel empty and lonely, as you might have felt at some point, and as we saw in the lives of some of our train passengers, such as Jane Wyllie, Eddie Morales, Kennie Stursberg, and Patricia Arbitson.

Dr. George Vaillant of Harvard studied a large number of men over the course of their lives. Their paths, like our passengers' and our own, took unexpected twists and turns, but those who had close friends with whom they shared pleasures and pains fared much better than those who were less social or more isolated. Close friendships enhanced their emotional and physical well-being.

Friends exchange care, celebration, and solace, and have to be cultivated and nurtured in order to thrive. I've gained immeasurably from close friends who've been part of my life since childhood, and I hope I have given them as much in return.

The Internet enables people to keep in touch with old friends via social sites, such as Facebook, Twitter, Google+, and LinkedIn. However, there is an inherent artificiality to online virtual friendships. They can, at times, be anything but authentic, and are often means of *not* engaging meaningfully. In the guise of generating friendships, the Internet can serve to keep people apart. Online chatter can't replace bonds between close friends.

As Barbra Streisand famously sang, "People who need people are the luckiest people in the world." We are social beings, and most of us want and need close friends in our lives. This doesn't mean that these relationships run smoothly all the time, but having ultimate trust in those you can count on to share joyful events or support when the going gets rough are to be cherished. Likewise, your friends should be able to rely upon you, whether they are celebrating or despairing.

In later life, fortunate individuals might participate in their friends' children's or grandchildren's milestones, and they might be there for each other in times of pleasure and sorrow. Some mourn the losses of dear old friends almost as losses of parts of themselves.

Steven Sondheim wrote about old friends, "Here's to us, who's like us?" The knowledge that we have intimate attachments and are not alone helps us feel grounded and secure. Good friendships are some of the best stuff of life.

Resilience, Continued

We all love stories of comebacks—individuals who "got back on the horse," whose personal courage turned their lives around. The old song lyrics "Pick yourself up, dust yourself off, and start all over again" appeal to human nature.

These stories and lyrics reinforce the belief that we are all able to rebound from life's setbacks entirely on our own. But the truth is that individual comebacks most often need the help of at least one crucial person who plays a key role in that recovery.

In studying people who turned their lives around after near ruin, I found that nobody does it alone. I can't emphasize this enough. Even in the United States, where individual responsibility is revered, if one looks at those who went from the depths of degradation to the pinnacles of success, one finds crucial contributions of at least one meaningful other.

I use the term "the arm" as a metaphor to represent reaching out by an individual to someone in need. The bestowal of the arm can take the form of listening, advising, teaching, supporting, or even confronting and staging an active intervention. That arm, involving words, feelings, and actions, can make a critical impression on a vulnerable person. You have helped others and you may have seen the positive effects of your contribution, but sometimes we are unaware of our influence in others' lives. True benevolence (see The Four B's) doesn't require tangible returns; it intrinsically rewards on its own.

You might remember a few choice words of wisdom someone uttered to you, sometimes even inadvertently, that have stayed with you all your life as a kind of touchstone. Those words might have come from anyone, a friend or neighbor, teacher or physician, shopkeeper or employer, camp counselor or policeman. Sometimes memorable 'magic' words are uttered in a close relationship, but they are often said by a passing acquaintance, yet never to be forgotten.

People in difficulties want to hear from us, get advice or find hope. We extend our arms to our children, and in our relationships with students, people at work and in our everyday lives. As social beings, we need one another as members of communities: No man is an island, even in America. We all need a sense of belonging to feel whole and fulfilled. Anyone who insists that he has no need for other humans is in a way denying his own humanity. It can be done, but at a tremendous cost to one's essence as a human being.

In comeback stories, crucial helpers can be serendipitous or purposeful. Family, friends, teachers, or mentors, anyone with meaningful contact with a hurt person, can be of pivotal help. We call these helpful acts of support, counsel, or inspiration 'corrective emotional experiences'.

Manchild in the Promised Land, is an extraordinary autobiography, describes Claude Brown's difficult life as an antisocial African American youth in Harlem, a life that is turned around in jail by a compassionate, elderly Jewish librarian.

This is similar to the experience of Jose Alvarez with the Rev. Alice. Patricia Arbitson had her grandmother, Sonya; Nora was there for Howard Gladstone; Ken Stursberg had his wife, Alice; Jane Whyllie had her husband, Sam, and, when he died, her psychiatrist; and Neville Da Costa was a savior to his grandson, who, in turn, saved Neville.

If a helping relationship is to be effective, however, the person in need has to grasp the arm offered. There are sad examples of despairing or self-destructive people who fail to grasp or angrily reject the benevolent outstretched arm. If the person in need of assistance doesn't grasp the arm, he will have lost an opportunity, but still might learn from his or her mistake. New opportunities and other extended arms might well occur down the road.

Extending that arm, whether it is physical or emotional, is a win-win situation, positive for both helper and recipient. We all can be that special person who enhances the life of someone else. By taking advantage of the opportunities to be helpful to others, we are actually helping ourselves.

Forgiveness

The major world religions, imperfect as they are, speak of forgiveness as a salient human goal. The ability to forgive is as much a part of the human condition as love and hate, and it gets to the heart of how friendships last or wither. We all feel wronged in some way at some points in our lives, but it's how we respond to these trespasses that really matters.

There are often good personal reasons to turn the other cheek instead of lashing out when someone wrongs you. Without forgiveness, bitterness can infect the individual with revenge, which takes a greater toll on the angry individual than the target of his anger. This darkness can take over and banish love, serenity, satisfaction, pleasure, and security from our lives and can replace these elements with discontentment, loathing, and vengeance. These negative broodings can permeate everything and engender a negative emotional footprint.

Those who hurt others should surely suffer consequences for their transgressions, but are there ever circumstances that enable us to forgive? Some of our train passengers acted badly at times and were severely criticized. Neville DaCosta, Jose Alvarez, Jane Whyllie, Eddie Morales, and Howard Gladstone hurt themselves and others and were vilified, even by their own families and friends.

When self-destructive individuals turn their lives around, people are dubious and cynical at first, but they're willing to forgive and show generosity of spirit if, over considerable time, there are genuine displays of accountability, contrition, restitution, and benevolence by the transgressors. They have to show contrition, that they recognize their destructive behaviors were their own responsibilities, that they are aware that they harmed themselves and others, and they have to make restitution to those they hurt and dedicate themselves to making personal changes.

Ultimately, the transgressors have to convince themselves and others about the authenticity of their resolutions and contrition. This is arduous work, as it should be. Temptations abound, and the process goes on forever. Alexander Pope said, "To err is human, to forgive is divine" but one needn't be religious to forgive. Forgiveness is indeed human—but only when it is deserved.

Gratitude

Gratitude is a critical part of personal satisfaction. Individuals who are grateful for even modest aspects of their lives, such as health, food, and relationships, feel more satisfied than those who forever want more of everything. Those who appreciate each day and the beauty in nature tend to have a grounded sense of being and show more benevolence toward others. Conversely, those who feel entitled or are frustrated by their lives tend to be negative and resentful. Nora Jensen's parents, Ken Stursberg's mother, and Michael Kounigis's father railed about the unfairness in their lives, and they left negative emotional footprints that adversely impacted the people close to them.

Constantly bemoaning one's fate is counter-productive, and the negativity repels others. One might cynically feel that those with health and wealth are of course more positive than those less fortunate. It is true that people in the midst of physical or emotional pain don't exactly count their blessings. But studies have clearly shown that riches do not buy a sense of satisfaction, gratitude or fulfillment. Those wealthy individuals who strut like peacocks (need I name them?) because of their material acquisitions are offensive to us, but this is often a defensive posture that belies the true nature of their unhappiness and insecurity. These people are annoying, but they show the true worth of what is really important.

Being grateful for what we have even in times of setbacks and struggle helps us overcome and heal more quickly. Studies show that among people who are equivalent in health and social class, those who are grateful are more optimistic get more emotional support from others, and more readily overcome their problems.

Of course, saying, "Just be grateful," sounds inane, like the Monty Python song "Always Look on the Bright Side of Life," which demonstrated forced self-happiness in the midst of losing one's limbs. The truth is that gratitude enables us to better withstand setbacks and mobilize our resilience. Those who do better in crises and in their day-to-day lives tend to be grateful for the mundane as well as the magical

Studies show that optimists live longer and healthier lives than pessimists, and our predominant attitude toward life is much more crucial than our wealth or status. As long as basic necessities of life can be provided (e.g., food, shelter, health, opportunities for children), a positive attitude plays a major role in personal and social well-being. If one is fortunate enough to have health, love, gratitude, satisfaction, and an authentic sense of self, relationships and values, then he (she) can enjoy a most fulfilling and generous life. In other words, The Four B's and a positive Emotional Footprint..

Aging and Wisdom

When we are young, the world appears to be full of limitless possibilities. We find love for the first time. We have dreams.

As we mature, the world becomes far more familiar, and we learn that limits exist, loves are lost, and successes can occur if we accept failure as part of the path. Life becomes more complicated, and we also learn that while we have choices in our individual lives, we accept that the random ups and downs will always be with us, and that some things are beyond control. Change, that most reliable facet of life, is always with us.

Getting old is as integral to our existence as our youthful, starry-eyed view of the world when we first started our journeys through life. Those of a certain age have the benefit of experience in the varied joys and sorrows that life brings. Sadly, our culture doesn't put much stock in the wisdom that comes with age, but that is changing, especially as the eighty million baby boomers continue to hit retirement age. More of us are going to have to come to grips with our own inevitable mortality and seek the wisdom to positively respond to life's changes.

As we age, we develop insights into others and ourselves, with a new calmness and worldliness, and we often embark on new challenges. We have seen these transformations in the stories of our train passengers. Jane Whyllie's transition from her family's outcast to its mainstay; Jose Alvarez's transformation from destructiveness as a gang member to social constructiveness as a therapist; and Howard Gladstone's conversion from a greedy narcissist to a social activist are examples.

There are frequent departures from long-standing patterns in roles and relationships. Older people have moved from rejection to appreciation, from social outcasts to confidants. They've learned from achievements and successes and from mistakes and failures. They've become wiser, more generous, and generative, eager to share their wisdom with younger generations.

The multiple demands of young adulthood have dissipated, they have raised the children, work demands have reduced, and the pressures of "making it" have proven illusory. No longer harboring illusions of wealth and power, perfection and glory, they are often more grounded and more accepting of their own and others' limitations. Appreciation, contentment, and respect for others are more often hallmarks of older people.

The elderly have illnesses and limitations, but there are new realities in terms of life expectancies, health advances, and improved cognitive abilities. They continue to evolve psychologically and socially and yes, still wrestle with their identity-related existential questions like, "Who am I?" and "Where am I going?".

Even in older decades, active learning makes new neuronal connections, so many elderly are pursuing interests, work, or hobbies even in their eighth and ninth decades. Older people often better see the forest for the trees.

The wisdom of elders is important for themselves and their communities. Many countries perceive older individuals as elder sages to whom people go for guidance, and grandparents are greatly respected. In our own culture, young adults dictate the dominant themes, and society sometimes sees being older as a hindrance or a shame.

To be relegated to anonymity is an affront, and also a terrible loss to society, but as I mentioned earlier, the appreciation of elder wisdom might be entering our awareness. People are recognizing the vitality of older people as a valuable national resource, important to them and society. In a *New York Times* column entitled "The Geezers' Crusade," David Brooks urged seniors to share their energy and wisdom and called for them to lead a "generativity" revolution, emphasizing selflessness and communal caring. Volunteers in their seventh decade and beyond are offering expertise and energies in the Peace Corps, NGOs, and other agencies.

This is a win-win situation: Older people are making meaningful contributions of knowledge and spirit to their communities while deriving personal fulfillment and pleasure. There is now an annual Purpose Prize for older folks whose contributions have made a significant social impact. They know they belong to the larger community, and they believe in extending the hand of generosity to others.

The combination of the presence of able-bodied, motivated, and wise older people and the needs crying out all over the world for their contributions offers us a unique opportunity. We need the wisdom of our older citizens as a major impetus for education and social improvement. David Brooks ended his essay with these sage words: "The elderly: they are our *future*."

12

Beginning Your Journey

We have immersed ourselves in the stories of the ten strangers we observed on our metaphorical train, learning about how these characters faced adversity and loss in their lives and how they dealt with love and success. We saw that life is never a smooth and linear trajectory, and that there are unexpected events and upheavals, some enhancing and others challenging. We've also seen that even despair can give way to joy, just as rejuvenating love can follow loss and sorrow.

Thriving, as opposed to merely surviving, entails a sense of your own state of being and a belief in yourself and in the basic goodness of humanity. It takes a realization that all our lives are filled with drama and color, like a dramatic and dynamic tapestry made up of shimmering, brilliant colors alternating with unsettling, darker tones. We need to appreciate and cherish our time here and those who are close to us. Whenever we take the time to ask about the path or tapestry of someone's life, we inevitably learn that it has been much more textured and richly colored than we would ever have guessed. We all are enhanced by engaging in simple and singular acts of extending our hands of caring and generosity to those whom we encounter on our life journeys. The common bonds we share make us integral parts of the family of humankind.

The Four Bs are signposts we use for evaluating the worth of our lives. They help us appreciate the fullness of our journeys to enhanced fulfillment and inner peace. Being (the personal), Belonging (the social), Believing (the spiritual), and Benevolence (the altruistic) augment each other and are most effective in concert with each other. One without the others will not lead to ultimate personal enhancement, but together, they enable us to create a Positive Emotional Footprint.

We are constantly confronted with choices that challenge or excite us, and we must trust ourselves to make the right decisions for our loved ones, our communities, and ourselves. We must surely also be able to trust others.

Just as storms disturb idyllic climates, torrents turn streams into floods, and wildfires destroy lush forests, fate can occasionally deal our odysseys painful blows, and tragedies can upend our lives. How we traverse these periods of loss with courage and patience, planning and hope is a measure of how grounded we are in our communities, our guiding principles and values, and ourselves. Similarly, when good fortune smiles on us, our appreciation and generosity of spirit dictate our lives.

Our life trajectories are unique, yet we share many feelings and experiences. The four Bs and our own resilience are of immense help to us on our individual odysseys. In the end, however, we are the masters of our intangible legacies, the emotional footprints we leave behind.

As our lifelong journeys proceed, we should try to cherish each step forward. At times, it is hard slogging and we are trudging heavily, while at others, we will be skipping along. We need to be grateful for each day, and when we encounter others on similar excursions, we can help them as well as ourselves by sharing our humanity with them. We can revitalize our journeys along the way with the inner strength and wisdom we have acquired.

Life is a meaningful journey—an odyssey, really. It is a quest for stimulation, love, security, serenity, wisdom, and an awareness of our infinitesimal yet vitally important place in the cosmos. The Four Bs: Being, Belonging, Believing, and Benevolence, together with our Resilience, enable us to achieve our noble goals, and create Our Positive Emotional Footprint.

13

An Important Choice

We have crucial decisions to make about our attitudes and behaviors, and the stakes are high. We know that we humans are capable of inspiring creativity and acts of benevolence and that respect, tolerance, and caring engender the same attitudes and behaviors in return.

If we continue to express incivility and display the nastier sides of humanity, we threaten the quality of our lives and perhaps even our ultimate existence.

We have the wherewithal—and, at times, the animus—to eradicate our species. The same human intelligence and creativity that have bestowed on us awe-inspiring advances in the sciences and the arts have also been able to develop increasingly brutal weapons of mass destruction.

If we became sufficiently concerned about this issue, we could concentrate on improving our patterns of communication and behavior. We humans could establish a positive emotional footprint as an overriding and universal mission, a legacy to future generations.

Just as we are trying to reduce our carbon footprint, we could devote our remarkable intellect to diminishing our negative emotional footprint and increasing our positive emotional footprint.

Calculations of social and emotional emissions are imprecise, but what if by our acts of decency and by the kindness and respect we show in our daily lives, we add positive energy to the atmosphere and reduce the emotional toxins in our environment as we increase the quantum of goodness in the social ether?

Words are powerful, and they can be soothing or seething. A society that is benevolent ennobles all its members and enables affiliation and creativity, just as one filled with rancor diminishes everyone and increases conflict and danger.

We humans may be reaching a pivotal moment. Our options are simple but seminal: We have the capacity to enhance our social and psychological environment to the benefit us all, or we can poison the social atmosphere, reduce our quality of life, and endanger our species.

We can choose to give in to our baser urges and compromise the quality of our lives, leaving a *Negative* Emotional Footprint, or we can choose to use civility, cooperation, and community to enhance our lives, establishing a lasting *Positive* Emotional Footprint.

We *Extra*-ordinary people have an important choice to make.

Index

Recommended Readings

Allison, Jay, and Gediman, Dan. *This I Believe II: Personal Philosophies of Remarkable Men and Women*. New York, NY: Henry Holt and Company, 2008.

Brown, Claude. *Manchild in the Promised Land*. New York, NY: Touchstone Books, Simon and Schuster, 1967.

Collins, Francis S. *The Language of God: A Scientist Presents Evidence for Belief*. New York, NY: The Free Press, 2006.

Dalai Lama. *Beyond Religion: Ethics for a Whole World*. New York, NY: Houghton Mifflin Harcourt, 2011.

Dalai Lama. *The Little Book of Inner Peace*. Charlottesville, VA: Hampton Roads Publishing, 2009.

Devorkin, David, and Smith, Robert. *Hubble: Imaging Space and Time*. Washington, DC: National Geographic Society, 2008.

Frank, Jerome. *Persuasion and Healing*. Baltimore, MD: Johns Hopkins University Press, 1993.

Frankl, Viktor. *Man's Search for Meaning*. Boston, MA: Beacon Press, 1992.

Gardner, Howard. *Extraordinary Minds: Portraits of Individuals and an Examination of Our Own Extraordinariness*. New York, NY: Basic Books, 1997.

Hawking, Stephen. *The Grand Design*. New York, NY: Random House, 2012.

Hechinger, Fred M. *Fateful Choices: Healthy Youth for the 21ˢᵗ Century*. New York, NY: Carnegie Corporation, 1992.

Hitchens, Christopher. *God Is Not Great: How Religion Poisons Everything*. New York, NY: Grand Central Publishing, 2007.

Keegan, Caitlin. *Shakespeare's Love Sonnets*. San Francisco, CA: Chronicle Books, 2011.

Levine, Saul (with Wood Ion, Heather). *Against Terrible Odds: Lessons in Resilience from Children*. Menlo Park, CA: Bush Publishing, 2004.

Levine, Saul. *Phoenix from the Ashes: Rebuilding Shattered Lives*, Toronto: Key-Porter Books, 1993.

Levine, Saul. *Radical Departures: Desperate Detours to Growing Up*. New York, NY: Harcourt Brace Jovanovich, 1984.

Nobel Foundation. *Words of Peace*. New York, NY: Newmarket Press, 1990.

NPR. *Listening Is an Act of Love*. Oral histories. NPR StoryCorps, 2007.

Rosenthal, Robert, and Jacobson, Lenore. *Pygmalion in the Classroom*. New York, NY: Irvington, 1998.

Rutter, Michael, and Rutter, Marjorie. *Challenge and Continuity across the Life Span*. New York, NY: Basic Books, 1998.

Smith, Christian, and Davidson, Hilary. *The Paradox of Generosity: Giving We Receive, Grasping We Lose*. London, U.K.: Oxford University Press, 2014

Sheehy, Gail. *Passages: Predictable Crises of Adult Life*. New York, NY: EP Dutton, 1976.

Vaillant, George E. *Triumphs of Experience*. Boston, MA: Harvard University Press, 2012.

Yalom, Irvin. *Love's Executioner, and Other Stories of Psychotherapy*. New York, NY: Basic Books, 1989.

Yalom, Irvin. *Momma and the Meaning of Life: Tales of Psychotherapy*. New York, NY: Basic Books, 1999.

About the Author

Saul Levine, MD, is professor emeritus in psychiatry at the University of California at San Diego, where he taught for many years. He retired as professor of clinical psychiatry and head of the department of psychiatry at Rady Children's Hospital in San Diego. Prior to these positions, he was professor of psychiatry and head of the department of psychiatry at Sunnybrook Health Science Centre at the University of Toronto. He continues to teach at the medical school, has a private psychotherapy practice with patients of all ages, and serves as an expert witness and mediator in family and civil disputes. He is also a leader of a pioneering preschool program for thousands of indigent children in Ethiopia.

Levine is also an author, having published five previous books for general readers in the area of psychology, geared toward helping people deal with their problems in effective ways that lead toward personal fulfillment and happiness. He has published widely in magazines, newspapers, and scholarly journals, and he hosted a popular television show on how to best cope with life's ups and downs for more than a decade while he was a resident of Toronto, Canada. He is married, has three married sons and a teenage daughter, and is the proud grandfather of seven grandchildren.

Printed in the United States
By Bookmasters